POLICE CHIEF 101

ABOUT THE AUTHOR

Gerald W. Garner, a veteran of forty years in law enforcement, has served as chief of police in a city of less than 10,000 people and one in which the population approached 100,000. Prior to accepting the role of law enforcement chief executive, he worked as a law enforcement officer in the states of Texas, Kansas and Colorado. He retired from the nationally-renowned Lakewood, Colorado Police Department at the rank of division chief following a career of 30 years at the agency. While there he served as a patrol officer, supervisor, detective sergeant, academy director, lieutenant, internal affairs manager, public information officer, watch commander and captain.

Garner holds a Master's Degree in Administration of Justice and is a graduate of the Senior Management Institute for Police conducted by the Police Executive Research Forum. He has written six books and over 200 articles on law enforcement and leadership topics. His text on police supervision is currently in its fourth edition. He also has instructed for various law enforcement academies in addition to the International Association of Chiefs of Police and the FBI National Academy at Quantico, Virginia. Garner has advised various committees and professional groups at both the state and federal levels and has been a member of the board of advisors for two law enforcement publications.

POLICE CHIEF 101

Practical Advice for the Law Enforcement Leader

By

GERALD W. GARNER

Chief of Police
Greeley Police Department
Greeley, Colorado

CHARLES C THOMAS • PUBLISHER, LTD.
Springfield • Illinois • U.S.A.

Published and Distributed Throughout the World by

CHARLES C THOMAS • PUBLISHER, LTD.
2600 South First Street
Springfield, Illinois 62794-9265

ISBN 978-0-398-07937-6 (hard)
ISBN 978-0-398-07938-3 (paper)

Library of Congress Catalog Card Number: 2010003638

With THOMAS BOOKS *careful attention is given to all details of manufacturing and design. It is the Publisher's desire to present books that are satisfactory as to their physical qualities and artistic possibilities and appropriate for their particular use.* THOMAS BOOKS *will be true to those laws of quality that assure a good name and good will.*

Printed in the United States of America
MM-R-3

Library of Congress Cataloging in Publication Data

Garner, Gerald W.
Police chief 101 : practical advice for the law enforcement leader / by Gerald W. Garner.
p. cm.
Includes index.
ISBN 978-0-398-07937-6 (hard)–ISBN 978-0-398-07938-3 (pbk.)
1. Police chiefs. 2. Police–Supervision of. I. Title. II. Police chief one hundred and one. III. Title: Police chief one hundred one.

HV8012.G37 2010
363.2068'4–dc22 2010003638

To Kathy

PREFACE

There is not a job in the world like being the police chief. The chief must be part personnel manager, part politician, and wholly a role model for the people he leads. While being many things to many people, first and foremost the chief must never forget what it is like to be a cop. As any veteran chief will attest, the highs of the job can be truly exhilarating; the lows deep enough to send the unwary into deep depression.

This book will serve the new, veteran or wannabe chief equally well. Authored by a police chief with 40 years of law enforcement experience, it provides practical, common sense advice for doing the multitude of jobs the chief faces with effectiveness and efficiency. It furnishes sound advice intended to help the chief retain his physical, emotional and ethical health while leading a professional law enforcement agency. This volume accomplishes all of this at a time when too many appear to have lost their moral compass, or their ability to be effective as leaders.

While written especially for the CEOs of small- to medium-sized law enforcement agencies, the book will prove very useful to the leader of any law enforcement organization as well as those in the top ranks who aspire to head the agency one day. Its advice is just as relevant for the state police superintendent or county sheriff as it is for the chief of police in a city of 90,000. The author is well aware that the challenges faced by all of these professionals are similar. He also recognizes that the solutions to their problems are often similar, as well.

The author calls upon the experiences of many veteran law enforcement leaders in identifying common problems and offering practical solutions. This experience-based knowledge often comes from lessons learned the hard way by real people facing real tests and challenges. The author's intent is that readers can benefit from the trials of others in order to avoid previous mistakes and build on the body of knowledge that constitutes professional law enforcement leadership.

Chapter One offers the new or relatively new chief advice on taking control of his new department and putting his agenda in place. Even long-term chiefs can take advantage of the chapter's points to ascertain that they have done everything necessary to establish control and direction of their agency. Chapters Two and Three provide solid advice for leading a great law enforcement organization and emphasize the extreme importance of role modeling the behavior that the leader expects of his people. The "little things" that a successful leader does are featured as prominently as the major accomplishments of the effective CEO.

Chapter Four sets out the requirements for a productive relationship with the chief's top staff. It also delves into what is required to bolster a weak staff and further strengthen a solid one. Chapter Five and Six explore the multifaceted relationship a chief has with his employees. They delve into what is needed to keep those relations as positive as possible through good times and bad. They also cover thoroughly the law enforcement chief executive's responsibilities to his people.

Chapter Seven provides the chief with some guidelines for managing his relations with the various factions that make up the community, while the following chapter discusses one of the toughest mandates of all: getting along with the boss. One veteran law enforcement leader put it succinctly. "It's all about how you accomplish your personal and organizational goals without getting fired." The experiences–good and bad–of a lot of law enforcement leaders have been tapped for this key chapter.

Chapter Nine explores discipline in its various facts and emphasizes the chief's role in this vital process. Sound advice is proffered to help the police boss make the really tough calls when much is on the line. Next, Chapter Ten contains help for deciding on a course of action when things go wrong, as inevitably they will. The death of a police officer, officer-involved shootings, major misconduct within the department and "bad press" are among the organizational disasters discussed here. Organizational recovery from each must be the chief's ultimate goal, and the book presents sound advice for accomplishing just that.

Few chiefs have long survived by maintaining a hostile relationship with the news media. Chapter Eleven is targeted on helping the law enforcement leader maintain a good working relationship with the ladies and gentlemen of the press without giving away his soul or damaging his organization in the process. The chapter contains time-proven techniques for helping the chief keep his department's best foot forward in the eyes of the media. But it also tells him how to respond effectively when the news is not so positive.

The importance of personal ethics in the chief's personal and professional life is the focus of Chapter Twelve. The necessity of a periodic, ethical self-exam is noted. The chapter offers a simple conclusion: the chief must never abandon his personal integrity for political expediency or even job survival. Meanwhile, Chapter Thirteen summarizes the real-world experiences of successful law enforcement bosses in navigating the political minefields of the job. This discussion makes it obvious that while the chief should not be a shameless politician, neither can he be unknowledgeable about the power of politics.

The chief will find potentially life-saving advice in Chapter Fourteen. This section of the book offers common sense guidelines for staying emotionally, mentally and physically healthy in what could otherwise be a killing job. Finally, Chapter Fifteen attempts to help the chief decide for himself when it is time to leave the position and perhaps the profession. It also reminds him that there is life–and the potential for a very good life–after being the boss.

A couple of final notes: the text regularly refers to the chief in the male gender. This is for ease of reading only, as women have long since proven themselves equal to their male counterparts as effective leaders. Also, on occasion the reader will encounter repetition of points made previously in the text. This is not accidental; some key principles apply in more than one area of discussion and merit the emphasis of repetition. They are that important.

In the final analysis, the world does not have nearly enough truly effective law enforcement leaders. This book is targeted on vastly increasing the number. With that goal set, it is time to get on with its fulfillment.

G.W.G.

CONTENTS

POLICE CHIEF 101

Chapter 1

WHEN YOU'RE THE NEW CHIEF

Even if he or she had been a law enforcement chief executive before, most experienced chiefs will acknowledge the day they took the reins of their department was not one they will soon forget. For the novice chief taking on his first CEO position, the memories are even more intense years down the road. The truth is that there is not another job on earth exactly like leading a law enforcement agency in the twenty-first century. The demands are great, the challenges and frustrations are many. Yet for the man or woman who went into law enforcement "to help people," the opportunities to do just that are legion.

Every law enforcement "Big Boss" was once a rookie chief and has experienced at least some of the doubts and concerns that you, the new chief, are feeling today. At one time or another, most doubted that they had made the right choice. Most were unsure at some point if they really could do the job, or still wanted to. The good news for you is that most of these good people found that they did indeed want to lead the personnel behind them. They did so successfully, each in his or her way.

It is true that every law enforcement leader, like every human being, is just a little different from everyone else and from every other leader. It is a good thing that leadership allows for differences in style and personality. There is not one and only one way to do the job correctly.

The budding police chief does not have to be a clone of anyone else. At the same time, however, experience has taught that there are personal traits and practices that help one leader to be stronger or more effective than another. There are things which can be taught and learned that will make *you* a better law enforcement chief executive. Those things are what this book is about. Assembled from the experiences of a great many leaders over a great many years, this common sense advice will serve to make the attentive reader better at doing his difficult job.

Although targeted on the new or wannabe chief at a medium-sized police agency, the volume's advice will prove helpful to you if you are a veteran chief or upper management law enforcement leader in a big city or small town. Effective leadership skills work as well in a rural sheriff's office as they do in a big, metropolitan police department.

The truth is that law enforcement can never have too many very effective leaders. It is time to get on with the task of creating more.

DO YOUR HOMEWORK BEFORE YOU START

As a law enforcement manager you already know how to do research. As an investigator you likewise know how to gather information from diverse sources. You will need to utilize those skills as the newly-appointed leader of a law enforcement organization.

No doubt you assembled a lot of data in preparing to compete for the chief's position. You already should know a great deal about the perceived strengths and weaknesses of the organization, at least as seen through the eyes of the reporters, editorial writers, bloggers and letter authors whose views you have examined via the local media. Perhaps you have talked to members of the department and residents of the community as an important part of your information-gathering efforts. If you have not done so already, now would be a good time to organize and review what you have learned from these sources. In examining what you have recorded, watch for consistent themes that may tell you work is needed in specific areas: leadership, policies and procedures, integrity and so on.

Now that you are officially the new chief, you will be able to gain even more information from sources you likely did not reach when you were a contestant for the job. The list of people you might talk with is practically endless, but there are a number of people you certainly will want to contact. If your appointing authority has no objection, it would be helpful to sit down with each of your council or board members and get their insights on the department's strengths and weaknesses. You are there to listen to them talk. This is not the time to make big pronouncements or promises. Stay alert for any consistent, major issues that the speakers bring up. Do not be surprised if their opinions of what is important vary widely. If anyone has an ax to grind with the department or its former leader, the complaint is likely to surface at this time. Listen carefully and do not be too quick to respond. Realize that you may be getting incomplete or even inaccurate information in the mix of opinions.

Take your leadership staff's opinions on the organization, its problems, its strong points and its weak areas. Have your staff put their views in writing. Not only will you gain insight on how well they grasp what is going on in the agency, you will see how well they communicate with the written word.

You will want to collect the opinions of your mid-managers and supervisors, both cops and civilians, early in your tenure. Sit down with the leaders of any unions or other employee associations in the agency. Again, you are there to listen and take notes, not argue or make promises. You are still in the information-gathering stage; the formulation of action plans and responses can come a bit later.

Your fellow department heads also may be able to help you by sharing their observations on your organization and your boss. Law enforcement officials such as the district attorney and the sheriff should be able to provide their own insights on your agency and its reputation in the community. Other community leaders should be willing to contribute their observations, as well.

Take sufficient notes about what you learn. There is a lot of information out there, but realize that you are only human and will have neither the time nor the energy to get it all. Do the best you can. Know that this is a very busy time for you and your many other responsibilities will preclude you from listening to every soul in the community who has something to say.

Don't forget that you can learn a lot from your agency's own documents, too. Look at the most important sections of your department's rules, policies and procedures. You are seeking to educate yourself, but you also are looking for weak spots that need shored up immediately. Ethics, evidence handling, officer safety and use of force guidelines top the list of subjects that merit your close scrutiny.

Doing your homework now could save you a lot of frustration later. It will enable you to make good decisions as you begin to put your stamp on your organization.

KNOW WHY YOU WERE CHOSEN

An important part of the homework to be done by a newly-appointed chief is finding out why he was chosen over the competition. In some cases, the reason may be relatively obvious. Hopefully, you have been keeping up with the jurisdiction's news media in the months preceding the selection process. If not, review past stories on the department now. You should know, for instance, if there has been bad press about corruption, lack of leadership or poor customer service in the department. You should know if the last chief is departing because of a scandal or other personal ethics lapse. You should know if the vacancy was created by an evidence-handling or minority relations disaster. Whatever the case, it will be your job to demonstrate quickly that you know how to fix the problem and will do so as rapidly as possible.

There is another way of confirming why you were hired and what you are expected to accomplish: ask. It is perfectly acceptable to ask the appointing authority once the job offer has been made precisely why you were selected over the other candidates. Whether you have been selected by a mayor, council or board, city or town manager, you need to be clear on what it is you are expected to accomplish. Ask.

If things are going relatively smoothly and the employees, citizens and local officials appear reasonably content, the new guy or gal may be expected to keep the current course without rocking the boat too much. If things have not been going well, you are very likely expected to implement a course change in quick order. Whatever the case, you need to know what is expected so that you don't fire off in the wrong direction or commence fixing something that is not seen to be broken. Observing, listening carefully and asking some direct questions of the right people could save you time and grief while allowing you to focus your energy in the right areas.

SIZE UP THE DEPARTMENT AND ITS CHALLENGES

It is doubtful that there is such a thing as a flawless police department, even though a few perpetually dissatisfied cops may wander through their careers looking for one. As the new Big Boss, you will have to evaluate your "business" (for that's what it is) as quickly and thoroughly as possible. Any serious or dangerous problems you discover should be addressed right away. That category of issues could include officer safety lapses, illegal or unethical conduct and the improper handling of drugs and money.

You should have plenty of help in the evaluation process from the people you already have been talking to within the community, local government and the department itself. Generally, the more often you hear the same concern mentioned, the more likely it is that a real problem exists. After a while you should be able to pick up on certain themes that dominate your interviewees' concerns. You probably won't be able to deal with all of them simultaneously, so unless you have a truly exceptional memory you should make notes for reference later. Closer examination may convince you that some of the "issues" will not need addressed at all. Prioritize what you hear and divide the concerns into those that can wait and the ones that must be dealt with immediately.

While your early days on the job will keep you very busy observing and evaluating, remember this is a process that should continue throughout your tenure as the agency's leader. Circumstances change in an organization, as do the concerns and attitudes of its members. New and unexpected challenges will arise. You cannot afford to be surprised too often. Keep your eyes and ears open. Continue to ask questions. And never take your organization or your position as its leader for granted.

ASSESS YOUR STAFF

If you have risen through the ranks of the department, you already should have a pretty good grasp of the character and capabilities of the top staff. Make use of what you know in tailoring the immediate future of the organization and their place in it. If you are coming in from the outside as the new chief, your task of assessing the existing staff will be more difficult but no less critical.

You already may have some information on your staff gathered from your conversations with others in the community. Some of it may even be accurate. Remain mindful that much of what you have heard will be at least somewhat colored by the bias of the speaker. Your best information will come from your own, direct observations.

In addition to your interactions with your top managers in your command staff meetings, sit down individually with each and get his or her views on the organization and its issues. Some new chiefs have required their top staffers to put their evaluation of the agency in writing, thereby giving the boss an opportunity to evaluate his new staff's writing skills. This approach will work for you, too. After reviewing their written work you can then meet with each one to discuss his or her observations. The next, logical step is to ask your staff members for their recommendations on what needs to be done to make the department better.

As part of your early evaluation of your top people you also will want to watch their interactions with other members of the organization, particularly their subordinates. One chief was surprised to learn after a year as the department's leader that the troops were upset about the perceived rudeness of one of his staff members. The man never displayed this behavior in front of his boss, but apparently acted quite differently towards the employees who reported to him. Once more, you should not accept as the gospel everything that you hear. After some time, however, you likely will pick up on certain schools of employee opinion, positive and negative, concerning your staff members.

Your next obligation is to bring what you have learned to the attention of your staff member when it appears there is substance to the opinions and change is required. A few misguided bosses tend to believe that people problems will go away on their own if left alone. This is generally not the case. Especially when your top staff members display a need to do something differently, the sooner the need is brought to their attention the better it will be for everyone.

You appreciate directness and honesty with a minimum of beating around the bush. Your staff members deserve the same consideration. An efficient and effective law enforcement organization requires no less.

MEET THE EMPLOYEES

Most of your employees are curious to meet the new chief and find out what his or her appointment means for them. The need is even bigger if you are a stranger to the department. It is your responsibility to introduce yourself to your people as quickly as possible.

The get-to-know-you task obviously will be a lot easier in a small department where you can learn everyone's name within your first days on the job. Bigger departments will require more introductory work on your part. The investment of time and effort is necessary and worth it for the long haul.

Whether you do it by visiting roll call briefings or some other way, meet with your people. If you are new in town, tell them a little about your background. (One chief sent a copy of his resume' to the union and posted another copy on the lunchroom bulletin board.) Do not neglect to get in front of your civilian employees in the same time period. Putting them off until later will signal they are not important to you.

This first meeting is not the time to get into an in-depth discussion of your philosophy and opinions on the origins of the universe. You can fill in the details of where you plan to take the department and how you plan to do it later. Right now everybody simply needs to see you and learn for themselves that you do not have horns or a tail. Tell them in nonspecific terms what is important to you. Putting crooks in jail, demonstrating personal integrity and providing great customer service are good, for starters.

Even if you know that the department has a number of warts that need to be excised, this is not the time to spotlight them. If the department truly is a seriously troubled one, chances are that most of the employees already realize that. You do not need to rub their noses in it. It *is,* however, acceptable to tell your people that you know there is work to do and things are going to get much better. In other words, you can give your employees something to look forward to without tearing them down in the process.

The new chief should never introduce himself to his people by saying or implying that the organization they all belong to is a bad one. That is a cardinal rule you disobey at your peril.

Remember to commend your people for who they are and what they do. They are part of a cause. Let them know that you like police people. And let them know you are very happy to be employed where you are.

BE SURE YOU'RE ON THE SAME WAVELENGTH WITH YOUR BOSS

It is important to know what your staff and employees are thinking. It is even more important to understand what the person or persons who hire and fire you have on their minds. Finding out your boss's views on the community, the governmental organization and your department and people is vital for the new chief who must get a quick sense of the lay of the land. Especially when you are new on the job you will want to take every opportunity to talk with your supervisor. In reality, you are there to do more listening than blabbing.

It is alright, of course, to converse with your boss in your office or his. But you probably can learn even more over lunch or coffee, or even in the car getting there. The more relaxed atmosphere may enable you both to find out more about what the other is really like. Keep your ears open for what your supervisor has to say about his ideas on what a police organization and its leader should be doing. Also listen for indications of where he or she believes a weakness exists in the organization. You will be expected to fix it. If it doesn't require repair, your boss will need to know that, too, and your evidence for believing as you do.

If you detect that you and your boss have widely divergent views on the community's law enforcement issues and how the job of policing is to be done, you have work ahead of you. He may be right. If not, it will be up to you eventually to dispossess him of mistaken notions. That is part of your collateral task of educating your supervisor about what a law enforcement agency and its leader really do.

Talking with your supervisor as often as possible in the early days of your relationship also will help you gauge how much he or she really knows about police work. Many city and town managers and mayors will concede that they do not know a great deal about policing. That's why they hired you–to make their police issues go away so they can concentrate on other things. One veteran city manager was quite honest about what he expected of his police chief. He wanted his telephone not to ring with "police problems." He expected the chief to take care of those issues so that he could concentrate on what he enjoyed: economic development.

Another manager teased his chief by telling him that he knew all about police work because he watched *Law and Order* on television. Yet another manager was an avid *CSI* fan. If that truly is how your boss gets his knowledge of policing (it generally won't be!) you at least need to know.

An experienced police chief put it thusly: "Know what your boss is thinking. Know it before he does, if possible. You can save yourself a lot of grief that way."

MEET THE PLAYERS IN THE COMMUNITY

Your research as the chief wannabe should have told you who the leaders of the community are, at least the ones who operate on the surface. Your boss, your fellow city department heads and your top staffers should be able to tell who some of the others are. Meet them as you can at official functions or over a cup of coffee. Your goal is to let them see that you are a likeable, "normal" human being (you *are,* aren't you?) who is down to earth and can be trusted. Remember that you are not asking for things or trying to curry favor. You just want to meet them and measure them for size and quality, just as they are measuring you.

Be pleasant at these meetings, but do not come across as subservient or ingratiating. You must convey that you are an ethical, intelligent leader who is going to make their lives better as the result of your leading the police department instead of someone else.

Seek these individuals' opinions of the police department and the job it is doing. Make actual or mental notes of what you learn. If these people actually are leaders in the community, their views will influence others. Once you determine that their expressed concerns are legitimate, how you respond to these issues will influence what these folks (and possibly many others) will think and say about you and your organization. Work hard to remember these peoples' names and go out of your way to speak at least briefly to them at affairs and events. This act of courtesy by itself can buy you support.

Realize, however, that getting on a first-name basis with some of the movers and shakers in the community may occasionally lead to a request for a "favor" from you. If the request is proper and one that any citizen could make, your reasonable course of action is to try to assure that it is accomplished in the name of excellent customer service. If your judgment tells you that the request is ethically out of line, it will be your task to let your acquaintance know in a courteous manner that you cannot do it, and why (department rules and that sort of thing, you know).

Your objective is not to leave the individual thinking he did something evil by asking. You may, however, need to explain that granting the request ultimately could embarrass the both of you. Most public figures will comprehend that logic. If the person making the request is an ethical as well as a courteous human being, he will not make a fuss over the issue. If he does, you have learned something vital about his character. Put the incident behind you and move on.

ESTABLISH A CHECKLIST AND A TIME FRAME

Your new job will feel overwhelming if you do not bring some order to all the things you have to do. One means for doing that is literally to make a list of things that must be done within the first few days, the first week, the first month, and so on. Cross things off the list as you get them done. That by itself will give you a sense of accomplishment.

Resist the temptation to work 18-hour days in trying to get everything done right away. You'll only succeed in exhausting yourself and getting sick, thereby setting your timetable askew and generating even more stress for yourself. Prioritize instead and accept that some tasks will have to wait until later.

Some of the well-intentioned advice you will get from other police chiefs will tell you that your early days as the new chief will feel overwhelming. That may be true, but you cannot be overwhelmed unless you permit it to happen. Make your list, check it twice and work your way through it on your own schedule. Realize that events may alter the schedule for some tasks. Take comfort in knowing that you control the time frame, in most cases.

ESTABLISH YOUR AGENDA AND COMMUNICATE IT

The political leadership, the community and your own people want to know where you are going to take the police department. Particularly if there have been well-publicized problems within the agency, many people want to know as soon as possible what the new chief plans to do about them. Your own employees may well be the most anxious of all to learn the plans you have–and their part in them.

On the other hand, if things have been going well and the now-departed chief was well-liked within both the department and the community, people will want to know that you are not going to turn things topsy-turvy. Especially your own people will feel threatened if they sense you are going to tear down a home they feel comfortable in.

If you and your boss feel that there are major issues that need dealt with as soon as possible, promptly announce your intent to address the problems. Publicize your goals. The detailed plans for accomplishing these objectives can wait a while, but your intent must be made clear right away. Spread the word both inside and outside the organization.

Do not make the mistake of criticizing your own people in front of the world. Just identify your objectives for all who want to listen. Then, start taking visible steps to accomplish them. As they say in officer safety class: "Do it now!"

If things are going pretty well and there are no real issues in front of your employees or the public, just let people know that you are observing, listening to people and gathering information. Let everybody know that you have inherited a very good police department and will be looking at how it can be tweaked to be even better. Let them know as well that the employees will be helping with the self-examination and adjustment effort. Meanwhile, deliver *justified* praise for your sworn and civilian employees every chance you get.

MEET THE PRESS (ADVERTISE YOURSELF)

One of your best tools for letting the public and your own employees know who you are and what you plan to do is the news media. Early in your tenure you will want to meet the media representatives you will deal with most often as the chief. This group should include the print media as well as the electronic journalism crowd. You need to meet the editors, publishers, police reporters, photojournalists and media outlet owners. The idea is not to try and ingratiate yourself but rather let everyone meet you and determine for themselves that you are a personable human being who doesn't slobber on himself too often.

These early meetings with the media are not the time for you to go into great detail about your plans. That will come later. You should give your media contacts a general idea of your ideas for the agency. Your major goals can be announced at this point. If your audience's members like what they are learning about you and your general plans they will be ready to start showing you some support. These observers will include some of your own employees.

It is also alright to talk a bit about your background and credentials. While you do not want to go on and on about yourself, the basics of your career can be mentioned. Your goal is to let everyone know that their police agency is in the hands of an experienced, competent leader who will take care of it–and them.

Do not overlook the Internet for its value for introducing yourself to a lot of people. Put a letter from the new chief on the department's web site immediately. Let the site's viewers know who you are and what you stand for: integrity, customer service, a safe community. Invite comment from the public and answer the messages that you receive. This is another means for finding out what the public thinks of your department and the concerns that may be out there. Even though you are presently embarked on an effort to advertise yourself and your goals, you still need to listen and learn at least as much as you talk.

DEAL QUICKLY WITH MAJOR ISSUES

Consider yourself fortunate if you have walked into a police agency that does not have problems and the employees appear content. More likely you will assume control of a department that has issues to be addressed, even if their origin is tied largely to not having a chief executive for a while. More serious issues will, of course, require more immediate and drastic responses.

The list of "serious issues" can, of course, be practically without end. If there is even a whiff of corruption in the air, that perception will have to be addressed as a priority. Whether you utilize internal resources or call on the help of an outside law enforcement agency, the allegations must be investigated immediately. Leaving cancer cells at large in the body of the organization will sicken and eventually destroy it. You will find your leadership career destroyed along with it, so act quickly and decisively to remove bad cops, regardless of their rank or seniority.

If information-gathering has told you that members of your agency engage in illegal, unethical or unsafe practices, these, too, demand your immediate intervention. Changes in policy and procedure can be implemented to help address these kinds of problems. But an executive order from the top will be the quickest means for fixing major mistakes in how the department conducts operations. Once you know that you have the straight facts, do not hesitate to order change. Then, follow-up to be sure it takes place as ordered. You may need to enforce sanctions against those who allowed grossly improper practices to find a home in your agency. The emphasis must be on fixing the problem promptly.

Some new chiefs have discovered that their departments had been engaging in improper activities not out of ill intent but simply from a lack of knowledge. Sometimes police agencies have followed poor practices because "we've always done it that way." Regardless of the reason for the missteps, the new chief (that's *you!*) is bound legally and morally not to allow them to continue.

Big problems requiring immediate correction can be as varied as the environments that have created them. One chief discovered that his unarmed civilian employees had long been permitted to transport felons to a regional jail half an hour away. He halted the practice immediately, much to the chagrin of the employees who enjoyed the duty. (Not all of the changes you must make will make your people happy.) Another new chief learned that his predecessor had denied his officers access to the less-lethal tools they needed to do their jobs safely. A third new CEO found that his department regularly locked juvenile offenders in cells with adult prisoners, even though prohibited by statute from doing so. Yet another new boss determined that his town denied overtime to police personnel who were guaranteed O.T. pay under federal labor regulations. In each case, the new chief executive abruptly encountered the need to act quickly and decisively to right a wrong. In each instance he did so. You must be prepared to do the same from your first day on the job.

From your beginning moments at the helm of your department you become liable for the shortcomings of your agency, even though you had nothing to do with creating them. The quicker you can set things right the better it will be for you and your peace of mind. More important, it is the right thing to do.

OTHERWISE, DON'T MOVE TOO QUICKLY ON MAJOR CHANGES

A new chief who finds himself at the head of a department without any major issues (at the moment) has just received a gift from Heaven. If he's smart, he will enjoy the relative peace, for it is unlikely to last indefinitely.

A senior chief of police had this advice for the new CEO finding himself in such an enviable if temporary position: "Don't muck it up by changing things around just to say you've changed something. If it is working well, leave it alone."

You can take your time in gathering data for the eventual changes you will want to make at a smoothly functioning agency. If you rush on the minor stuff you could miss something that would have affected your decision-making had you known about it. You want to avoid, if possible, going back to undo a decision you made as a result of incomplete or inaccurate information. Do it if you must in order to fix a mistake. But avoiding the rush that leads to making a mistake in the first place should be the preferred course of action. Take your time and do it right.

EXAMINE THE HIGH-RISK AREAS

While it is no secret that there are lots of things that can get you and your department in trouble, certain areas stand out as the deepest reservoirs of potential disaster. Your "high danger" regions include at least the following:

- Use of lethal and less-lethal force
- Vehicle pursuits
- Evidence handling
- Unethical or unlawful conduct by police employees.

Your own locale may present some additional, unique challenges. But the Big Four you certainly should examine very carefully. What are the department's policies regarding both lethal and less-lethal force? Are they in compliance with pertinent statutes? Are they actually enforced by supervisors and managers?

How about high-speed pursuits? You've likely got a problem if your agency goes to either extreme of banning all pursuits or permitting them for virtually any offense. What you want, of course, is a common sense chase policy that permits the pursuit of dangerous offenders but prohibits high-speed chases of minor criminals and traffic violators.

More than one or two chiefs have lost their jobs due to poor evidence-handling procedures in which they had no personal involvement. Have you examined your new department's evidence-handling guidelines and then checked to see if they are being followed? Do so if you have not. If you are new to the department, consider having an evidence audit done by an outside agency. Is everything there that should be? If things are missing, is it the result of accident, incompetence or criminal conduct? If you are the boss, you'd better have the answers to those questions.

If you discover a problem, fix it right away. Missing drugs have laid chiefs low, but so have evidence section staffs that have destroyed evidence that should have been preserved. Know what is going on in your evidence unit or plan on having a short career as the new chief.

Watch the handling of your agency's money, too. Cash taken in as evidence naturally should be carefully stored and periodically audited. But your department's other funds need attention, too. One law enforcement leader lost his position over a few bucks missing from the department's party and flower fund. Another chief resigned due to irregularities in the handling of his agency's confidential informant account.

You can help prevent your sudden and embarrassing departure from employment by seeing that procedures are in place governing the handling and auditing of the department's funds, especially cash. Assure that regular audits are done and done right. Also, be sure that more than one person is watching the department's various cash depositories, from petty cash funds to "going away" kitties. Be sure receipts for expenditures are obtained and good records are kept. Look into anything and everything that smells like a "questionable" expenditure.

Any unethical or improper conduct by your subordinates, especially your leadership staff, will have serious consequences for you unless detected and dealt with promptly and effectively. One new chief discovered that some of his supervisors regularly engaged in sexual harassment. Not surprisingly, until it was solved, fixing that problem became the chief's priority ahead of worrying about money, pursuits and use of force. Here was a problem that he *knew* existed. He was obligated to fix it as rapidly as feasible. Should you uncover such a situation, go after it right away.

As a chief of police, risk management is one of your most important responsibilities. Make clear to your leadership staff that risk management is their responsibility, too. By minimizing your risks and managing the organizational dangers that you and your people face you can help assure that you all enjoy more happy days than dark ones.

SCORE SOME SMALL, EARLY VICTORIES

As any winning coach will tell you, not every victory has to be for the title. Teams like winning; it gets to be a pleasant habit. Winning the easier ones can lead to wanting the big ones, too. Winning builds confidence. The same holds true for the members of a law enforcement organization and their boss.

Some very successful law enforcement CEOs have demonstrated their "can do" abilities to their employees by looking for something that truly needs fixing early in their tenure–and then promptly fixing it. A Canadian chief recalled that by asking around he learned that the troops were uniformly unhappy with a flap holster that covered their sidearm. The officers felt that it delayed their accessing the weapon and thereby made them less safe. The chief agreed that officer safety was negatively impacted and immediately ordered replacement of the holsters. The officers were elated. "From that moment on, I had them," the chief remembered.

Whether his assumption was correct or not, the fact remains that the new boss made a lot of friends by solving what his cops saw as a big problem. He was able to do it without spending a fortune.

Another new chief won over his uniformed cops by doing away with the widely-detested and sporadically-enforced rule that required patrol officers to wear their uniform hats every time they exited the police car. The fix was accomplished at no dollar cost whatsoever.

Yet another new CEO won over many of his sergeants by granting their long-expressed request to place "supervisor" decals on the sides of their marked cars. For little cost, a number of smiles were created.

At the same time, you must not seek a cheap victory by "fixing" something that your common sense tells you should not be changed because of safety, ethical, or other good reasons. You must never be so anxious for a quick and easy win that you "fix" something that did not need repaired.

That brings to mind yet another reminder for the brand new chief. You can expect to hear a lot of ideas and suggestions placed before you that were rejected during the prior administration. That is to be expected, as employees naturally will seek a friendlier ear for ideas that had been shot down in the past. If you're wise, you'll take it all in for consideration. Your staff should be able to enlighten you as to the history of most of these suggestions. Probably, many have been rejected for very sound reasons. But among the remainder may be a few that hold the promise of quick little victories for very little cost. They will be worth pursuing for the early results they will bring.

COMMUNICATE YOU'RE IN IT FOR THE LONG HAUL

As you already know, law enforcement officers are very practical people. Before they are willing to give you their support, they want to know that you are going to be around for awhile. If you are planning to make some significant changes, as many new chiefs are, you must line up support not only from your command staff but from some of your front-line officers and supervisors, too. (Realize that you are unlikely ever to get *all* of them.)

Particularly if some of your ideas for change appear controversial, your people need to know that you are going to be around for years to support their implementation before many of your employees will be willing to back you in public. Help them display their courage. Let people around you know that you intend to be there for the next ten years, or whatever time period you foresee. Just don't announce it as a period of months!

One new chief was told by a couple of his officers that they assumed he was just another in a long series of "drive-by" chiefs who were on their way to a bigger department. They were unwilling to show much loyalty to him as the "flavor of the month" until he convinced them he was actually sticking around. The chief let them know he had no plans to go anywhere, and he meant it. Slowly his officers came around.

Just as the good cops won't rally to your cause if they think you plan a short stay, neither will the problem children see a need to behave for a "temporary" chief executive. One cop from an agency known to change its top leader with great frequency put it this way: "The attitude of the bad ones, the lazy ones, is that 'we've outlasted the bright boys and reformers before; this one won't be any different.'"

The wise boss will want to show by words and deeds that he'll still be standing after any rotten wood in the department has been trimmed. Announcing a course that will take years to accomplish will help set the stage for department-wide improvements–and let any naysayers know that you will be around to finish the task.

Local leaders outside of the department also will want to know that you plan to stay. Especially your boss wants to feel comfortable that he will not have to repeat a time-consuming, expensive and emotional hiring process again soon. And, like your own personnel, the community's civic and political leaders do not want to waste their time and support on a short-term leader. Make it plain to everyone within earshot that your plans for the agency will take years to carry out. This may have the side benefit of reminding your several audiences that culture change will take time.

The chief who leads a successful department is often seen as treating his organization as if he was the owner of a profitable business. It is also true that many successful businesspersons work hard to leave the impression that, like the mountains, they will be around for a very long time. You as the new chief will do well to send the same message.

SUMMARY

It is true that the amount of work you will encounter during your first days and months on the job can feel overwhelming. Refuse to be overwhelmed. Organize, schedule and plan carefully what you have to do and when it must be done. You must continue on your quest to gather accurate information about your organization, your people, your boss, your community and the challenges you all face. Establish a timeline and start checking off your accomplishments. Win some early victories and let people know it. Let everyone know that you will be around for quite awhile.

Now is the time to let everybody know that you are the new chief and that things are going to be just fine. Then you begin making that promise come true.

POINTS TO REMEMBER

- Do extensive research on your department and your community before you start to work.
- Find out what your boss is thinking and why you were chosen to lead the department.
- Determine early on the strengths and weaknesses of your top staff.
- Meet as many of your employees as possible early in your tenure.
- Learn who the movers and shakers are and start meeting them.
- Communicate your goals and agenda to your people and community.
- Make a checklist and establish a schedule to accomplish it.
- Meet the press early.
- Deal with major issues and major risks immediately.
- Identify irritating problems that you can solve quickly for your people.
- Let everyone know that you intend to be the chief for a long time.

- Let everybody know that your new department is a good one and that it will get even better.

Chapter 2

LEADING A GREAT ORGANIZATION

It is like nothing else you have ever experienced. Being at the head of your very own law enforcement organization can be a heady experience. It also can be a humbling and sobering one.

You, more than anyone else in the agency, are now responsible for the quality of public safety service delivered to the community. The level of professionalism, integrity and customer service to be found in the organization is your responsibility, too. When something goes right, you may get little of the credit. (If you're wise, you promptly will pass the kudos along to your people.) When something goes wrong, you almost certainly will get the blame. It's all part of being the leader of a highly-visible organization that generates a great deal of interest and opinion from a public that is fascinated with crime and crimebusters.

Now that you are the man or woman in charge, you no longer simply want to lead an organization. Unless you are unusual, you want to lead (and be recognized for leading) a *great* organization. The *best* organization. An agency recognized locally and well-beyond as an *outstanding* organization. Fortunately, leading such an organization of earnest professionals is within your grasp. Following are some pragmatic, common sense guidelines for getting it done.

BE PROUD OF YOUR PEOPLE AND ORGANIZATION AND SAY SO

Talking to anyone and everyone who will listen about how good your people are should become your fulltime occupation, almost to the point of obsession. Your department is not perfect, and you know that. Not all of your people are saints. In fact, a few may be downright naughty. Dealing with that is a separate task of yours. As far as the outside world is concerned, you are always proud of your agency, its employees and they job they do in contributing to a cause: providing service and protecting the innocent from harm.

Being the number one cheerleader for your people and department is something that you must accept if you are to be a successful chief of police. It is a cardinal rule of law enforcement leadership that you must not publicly criticize your department or its people.

You should own up to it when you or your people make mistakes. None of you is without flaw, and most of the watching public won't expect you to be. A few gripers will. Regardless, in order to maintain your credibility you absolutely must acknowledge an error when you are sure that an error has been made. Do not dwell on the mistake or publicly beat up yourself or your organization over it. Instead, acknowledge the mistake and march on.

Immediately resume talking about the positive. Simply put, your attitude should be one of "Yes, we made a mistake but we're a very good department as evidenced by. . . ." Fill in the blanks yourself. And don't forget to fix the mistake!

Brag on your people to individuals and in front of groups. Do it in a radio or television interview. Do it on the Internet or in a letter or guest column for the local newspaper. Just do it. Your employees will appreciate it more than you'll probably ever know. Never make-up stuff that isn't true. (There's that credibility thing again.) But do broadcast widely the good news that is.

IT WON'T HAPPEN OVERNIGHT

An industrious, energetic leader with lots of good ideas will want to see his agency transformed overnight. (That super-energized leader is *you.*) Your boss or bosses may want the same, with the exception that they want it done before midnight of your first day on the job.

Reality dictates that it is not going to happen that way. A big ship does not change course on a dime. Even a smaller one needs time and space to maneuver. Your police agency will require the same.

You and your boss both need to realize that, if the organization has blemishes, they probably did not appear overnight. They will not vanish overnight, either. Even the best ideas and intentions require time to take hold.

As noted already, there are indeed situations and issues that must be dealt with immediately. The better the existing organization, the fewer of them there should be. But the majority of the changes you will make will not have to be in place on Day One. Give yourself time to do it thoughtfully–and correctly. Now that you are on the inside and privy to additional insights and information, an apparently black and white issue may begin revealing hints of gray.

Do not frustrate yourself or damage your physical or emotional health by expecting your new "business" to reverse course overnight. It will not happen. You may need to tell your own boss that you have discovered that reality. Hopefully, he or she will get the point. If not, be more direct. Major change *will* take both time and effort, in some cases quite a lot of both.

CULTURE CHANGE TAKES YEARS

A new chief came into a department that had seen years of "absentee landlord" leadership by its previous CEO. The prior chief had retired on the job and pretty much left the organization to run itself. As a consequence, a "just get by and stay out of trouble" attitude prevailed throughout the agency, from top leadership through the cop on the street. Some moral lapses had led to incidents that embarrassed the agency, and the community's leaders demanded change.

The new chief told himself that he could have the agency turned around in six months, a year at most. Unfortunately, he told his boss the same. Within that first year the chief did make some positive, noticeable changes in the agency. The public, the employees and the chief's boss were generally pleased with the way things were going.

But the chief was not. He could see that he still had some rude employees, a few lazy managers and at least a couple of sub-par, first-line leaders. Some old attitudes were still in evidence. The chief was disappointed in missing his self-imposed deadline for a major culture change. He became depressed over his apparent lack of progress. Finally, he consulted with some more experienced law enforcement leaders.

The veteran chiefs told their disappointed colleague that his overnight culture change goals were admirable but unrealistic. They advised him, based on their own experiences, that major culture change in an organization might take eight to ten years to accomplish fully. They noted that attitudes were learned over a period of years and would take that long to be altered. They reminded him that, in some cases, the organization's culture would change only as some of the practitioners of the old way of doing things left the department.

The new chief's experienced cohorts reminded him of the need to continue doing exactly what he was already doing: identify the desired changes and maintain the pressure to see that the changes actually occurred. Then, they counseled, be patient and take pleasure in the tangible victories and signs of progress that happen along the way.

You can take the new chief's somewhat painful lesson to heart and avoid some hurt of your own. Go after the change you want. Recognize and reward those who help it happen. Praise and correct as merited. But keep to a reasonable timeline for major culture change. It will not all happen today, tomorrow or even next year. Given your capacity for patience, perseverance and leadership, it *will* happen over time.

REMOVE THOSE OPPOSING POSITIVE CHANGE

It sounds harsh, but it must be done if you are to have the great organization you are seeking. This rule applies to your command staff, the senior leaders of the organization. If they have made it obvious through their statements, action or inaction that they oppose what you are doing, leaving them in place will sabotage your efforts at achieving change. Don't do it.

Tell your top managers what you expect, and let any laggard know that he is not delivering. Give him a fair opportunity to get on board. Observe his performance carefully. If he is clearly obstructing what you want done, he will have to change immediately or vacate his leadership position. Your task will be easier if your top staff members are "at will" employees. If not, you may have to remove your problem people via the more time-consuming performance appraisal process. If your employer will cooperate, it may be possible to encourage your obstructionist into early retirement through a financial incentive included as part of a severance deal. Talk with your Human Resources director. Investigate the options available in your organization.

Mid-managers and first-line supervisors also must clearly understand what you expect and what their role is in making it happen. Give them the opportunity to comply with your directions and make clear what's in it for them: an organization to be proud of and the opportunity to advance their careers. Unreconstructed supervisors and managers are harder to remove than your direct reports, but the disciplinary process exists to deal with clearly insubordinate employees. With the assistance of your legal and HR people, use that disciplinary machinery if you must. Oftentimes, one or two examples of your willingness to discipline intentionally bad behavior are enough to get the message across to the offenders' peers.

Be aware that there are others in the organization that can have great influence in accomplishing positive culture change. Training officers have considerable impact on new employees. New employees are among the most important people for you to reach if you are seeking to mold a new, department-wide attitude and way of doing business. Personally explain to the trainers what it is you want to emphasize to their charges and why it is important. Then, monitor their performance and remove from that assignment anyone who is not carrying out your instructions. Personally talk with the rookies, too.

Change takes time and effort. It is worth it for the better police organization that will result. Be patient, keep repeating your message of positive change and stay the course. Deal directly and firmly with human impediments to progress, even if that means their place in the organization must change drastically.

BE RELENTLESS IN SEEKING YOUR GOALS

Refuse to be turned aside from what you know is the right course. Be prepared to overcome arguments or active opposition to your plans for making your organization better. Do not water down your goals because others do not see or feel them as clearly as you do. You're the boss; it is not unexpected that these things are more important to you than they are to anyone else.

Be reasonable, be patient, but do not let up on your quest to lead your department where you have envisioned it to go. Expect surprises and delays. But know that you can overcome them.

In the real world that chiefs of police inhabit, the drive for where you want to take your organization may have to pause while the "surprises" of police work are handled. One chief was determined to seek national accreditation for his department. He was forced to put his plans on hold when very tight budgets precluded his getting the funding he needed to complete the objective. He did not surrender his personal goal, however. He simply waited until financial times got better. Then he resumed his drive for the prize.

Almost certainly you will encounter people or events that will serve as obstructions on your path to achieving a coveted goal. Expect such impediments and refuse to be disillusioned by them. Don't lose your momentum, either. Vow to remain irresistible in pursuing your targets. Continue to thrust forward when the moment is right. You *will* get there if you persevere.

EXPECT SETBACKS AND ADVANCE PAST THEM

In the real world, nasty surprises occur. "Personnel issues" occupy the time that you intended to use to create a master plan for your department's future. A double-homicide steals the public's focus from the new crime prevention program you planned to launch. A public furor over stray cats replaces the discussion you wanted to have with your citizens about community policing.

Welcome to the world of the contemporary police chief. You may have carefully scripted precisely what you wanted to accomplish and when. The problem is that the rest of the community doesn't have a copy of the script. Your own employees may not, either. All of those interests have their own agendas, which sometimes will not match yours. If you are going to retain your sanity, you will have to include flexibility in your planning.

Your boss's list of "things to do in the police department" may not match your own "to do" checklist. His timetable for getting those things done may not suit you, either. If you have established with your supervisor the good communication you will require to be effective, you may find that he has some room for flexibility on what he wants done and when. You also may be able to demonstrate to him that some of his concerns do not need to be, and that by pursuing your own list of things to be done you also will address his worries. Good communication and persuasiveness on your part can overcome a lot of obstacles.

When you do encounter a roadblock that cannot be moved, realize that these things are inevitable and get past your disappointment. Do not get angry or frustrated, as both emotions only will waste precious energy. (Granted, it's much easier said than done.) Try to re-direct your focus to whatever the intervening problem to be solved happens to be. Then, resume the advance on your goals as soon as opportunity presents.

THE VALUE OF ROLE MODELING

You absolutely must be an excellent role model for your people in everything you do, on and off the job. You will encounter that advice repeatedly in this book. It is *that* important to your success and survival as a police chief.

Every leader, good or bad, sets the example for those he would have follow him. If the example is one of sloth, immorality, unethical behavior or just plain incompetence, he should not be surprised when he sees his underlings demonstrating the same behaviors. Most important, he will lose any moral authority he would otherwise have to demand that his people correct their own bad behavior if he engages in similar misconduct himself.

One rookie chief mentioned to his staff that he was amazed by the number of officers carrying on extra-marital affairs in his new department. They promptly advised him of a likely contributing factor: his predecessor had done the same, and made no secret of what he was doing. The former chief also had not exactly overworked himself, a trait the new boss detected in his troopers. The new guy clearly had some positive role-modeling work ahead of him.

There is nothing that you will do as chief of police that is more important than setting an example of what you expect your people to emulate. That starts with your top staff. Setting a positive example for (first) your employees and (second) your community must be evident in everything you do from officer safety to personal morals, driving habits to alcohol consumption.

If you cannot remember when you last practiced with your weapon or where you might have left it, you cannot very well expect your people to value firearms proficiency. If you regularly "forget" to wear your seat belt, you lose the right to squawk when your patrol officers do the same. If you virtually never wear your sidearm, you will be hard-pressed to bark at your plainclothes cops for doing the same. And if you drive your vehicle like a bat out of Hell, do not be surprised if you are accused of following a double standard when you discipline one of your officers for a driving disaster.

You are highly visible, inside and outside the department, in most everything you do. If your yard looks like a pigpen, the neighbors will report that fact to the community. Ditto if you scream at your kids or spouse. And if you so much as show your nose in public after having had too much to drink, you can expect your stumble to become citywide news in no time at all.

If your officers see you occasionally involved in police work (as they should,) your officer safety practices should be above reproach. Your people will not expect you to be a super cop, but they *will* expect you to know what you are doing. They will expect you not to look or sound like a buffoon when you represent them in public. They probably won't expect you to look like a model for a men's fitness magazine, but you should not come across as a grossly out-of-condition slob, either.

It is a cardinal rule of being the chief that you must not embarrass your boss. It is equally vital that you do not embarrass your people. They *need* to be proud of their leader, as you need to be proud of them. Setting a positive example at all times in all things will help assure that your employees never have just cause to disown you.

DON'T ACCEPT "GOOD ENOUGH"

One new law enforcement CEO confessed that he found so many problems in his agency that he was elated when enough cops showed up sober to staff the shift. He was exaggerating, of course, but his perhaps poorly-chosen attempt at humor points up a reality of life for some new leaders: your new home may not live up to your hopes and expectations. In fact, it may not come even close to them.

As one of the hoods in the classic *American Graffiti* put it, "Rome wasn't burned in a night, you know." Neither was it re-built in that time frame. Leading your new agency to where you want it to be cannot be accomplished overnight. But that does not mean you should give up and settle for less–ever.

One first-time chief walked into a department where he quickly discovered the prevailing attitude was one of "it's good enough for us." That thinking was applied to equipment, facilities, and, most damaging of all, the quality of the people on the payroll. Worse, he discovered the same attitude prevalent throughout the town government. The whole town, it appeared, suffered from a major inferiority complex. He had his work cut out for him. To the man's eternal credit, he refused to accept such a defeatist attitude and eventually left the department and the town in much better shape than he found either.

This chief's experience can prove useful to you. Do not lower your expectations of your employees and your organization just because when all the closet doors have been opened you find you have more skeletons on your hands than you had anticipated. Most flaws can be repaired; many shortcomings can be corrected. It all takes time, but it is absolutely doable.

Refuse to lower yourself to the abilities, ethics, energy level or competency of a challenged organization. Its challenges may be why you are there in the first place. Instead, bring the organization and its members up to your level. This is especially true in what you expect of the department's supervisors and managers, including your top staff. Do not dumb down your expectations because your initial analysis tells you that these people do not necessarily share your outlook and desires. Realize that you have some work to do in getting them there. Praise and reward their efforts to meet these expectations.

Never lower your expectations out of disappointment or frustration. That's the first, stumbling step on the dark road to accepting "good enough." Refuse to go there. It's a road you never want to travel.

Always expect a lot of your people. In time, most of them will not disappoint you.

HAVE A GROUP OF PEERS FOR "SECOND OPINIONS"

If it is a problem for you today, it was probably part of a scenario faced by another leader at one time or another. You should maintain a directory of chiefs of police and other leaders whom you can call for advice when things get dicey. That does not mean you always will agree with them or follow their advice. But their views should provide additional food for thought as you seek a solution to your current dilemma.

During your career as police chief you doubtlessly will make the acquaintance of a lot of individuals who share your very unique responsibilities. You can learn something from all of them. Beyond those relationships you should maintain a much shorter list–there may be no more than half a dozen names on it–of peers you can turn to for advice on the really tough ones. At least some of them should be veteran law enforcement leaders whose character and reputation you admire. But it is also quite acceptable to include on your list a few colleagues whose experience levels or backgrounds mirror your own. In other words, it is OK to ask your friends for a second opinion, too. Just recognize that, in the end, no one is accountable for your decision-making but you.

Naturally, you should offer the same willingness to serve as a sounding board for your colleagues. No doubt, you have earned the respect of a number of your fellow law enforcement leaders. You owe them your honest opinions and advice when they ask for either. Information exchange among law enforcement's brightest is one way in which the profession gets better.

STAY IN TOUCH (MANAGEMENT BY WALKING AROUND)

The chief who remains hidden away in his office is asking for a surprise he almost certainly will not like. As chief, the fewer people you interact with each day, the greater the chances you will be overtaken by events that you did not see coming.

It is no secret that you have an imposing number of things to do. Your day is, without question, tightly scheduled. It is admittedly hard for you to fit in time to wander the halls of your department. Hard as it may be, you nonetheless must do it on a regular basis. To do your best, you *need* to know what is going on in those nooks and crannies of your organization.

You are not embarking on a walking tour to spy or find fault. Your actual purposes are twofold: to educate yourself about your organization and to meet the people who labor in it. As chief, because you have so many other things to do it is easy to get out of touch with the operational side of things. Getting too out of touch can result in your being unable to answer some of the questions you get asked, both inside and outside the organization. You thereby run the risk of appearing not to know what is going on in your own department. Learn how your organization works and which sections of it do what.

The second reason for wandering around is to acquaint or re-acquaint yourself with the people who work for you. Doing so lets them know that you care enough to get off your overstuffed chair and come to see who they are and what they are doing. Naturally, you want to wear your happy face instead of your scowling one (if you even have a scowling one) during your visits. You want your people to welcome your presence, not dread your arrival. Remind yourself again that you are there to catch someone doing something right, not execute a "gotcha" drill.

Relax and actually *meet* your people as opposed to inspecting them. You might be amazed at how much you can find out about them and their tasks through a little informal chit-chat. Recall that you are not there to grill them but to find out who they are and what they have to say.

If your agency has off-site operations it is especially vital that you visit them from time to time. Personnel who work away from the main body of employees sometimes feel that they are the forgotten stepchildren, anyway. It is important that the boss comes to *their* house on occasion. Events such as promotions and retirements offer good opportunities to do that, but you should show up when there's no reason to do so, too. Once more, you are there to learn things about your agency. Even more important, you are there to show your far-flung people that you really do have a face and a personality and care about *theirs.*

You also will want to show up on a call from time to time or spend a few hours riding with a street officer or supervisor. You are not present to get in the way or take over the call. You are there to lend a hand if it is needed and simply show your interest if it's not.

Occasionally going with your detectives on an operation or accompanying your narcs on a raid is a good idea, too. You are not there as a major participant. (You don't want your people to have to assign someone to protect you!) Once more, your purpose is to learn and demonstrate your sincere interest in what your people do. Here's a bonus: you are permitted to enjoy yourself in the process!

EVERYONE MUST KNOW THE MISSION AND GOALS

A veteran West Coast chief put it like this: "Police people may whine from time to time, but they're very good about doing what they're supposed to do if they *know* what they're supposed to do."

One chief made it a point to ask his new cops at random what it was they were supposed to be doing. Often their responses amazed him for their lack of specific goals. One patrolman told him that it was his job to drive around, take reports and write the occasional ticket. That was it. The chief was unable to elicit a clue that the officer had any further grasp of what his or the agency's grander purposes for being there might be. Clearly the organization's leadership had failed to communicate to the man the department's mission and goals.

One of your most important responsibilities as your organization's acknowledged leader is to determine what it is you want your employees to accomplish. "To protect and serve" sounds great but you'll need to be a lot more specific about how you and your organization intend to carry out those noble intentions.

With the input of your staff, establish half a dozen or fewer primary goals for the organization's members to accomplish. Then, use every means at your disposal to tell your people what those goals are. Memorandums, posters, e-mails, website postings and word of mouth all can be used to spread the message.

The mission that you all seek to accomplish is the broad, master plan to which each of your goals must contribute. It is the reason your department exists. It is a condition or outcome that all of your efforts are targeted on producing. A typical mission statement for a modern-day law enforcement agency might read: *Our mission is to improve the quality of life for the people of our community.*

Such a mission statement is simple, direct, and to the point. It should be understandable to virtually everyone inside and outside your organization. It recognizes that no one has a very good quality of life if he or she is afraid of becoming a victim. It emphasizes that the members of your organization are charged with improving life's quality for everyone.

You have seen corporate or governmental agency mission statements that drone on and on and incorporate all the latest warm and fuzzy buzzwords. (How does a cop leverage, empower and celebrate his citizen-customers, anyway?) They sound good, or so it seems. But carrying them out will be an entirely different story if no one really understands them in the first place. Keep it simple and the people inside your department will understand what you are all trying to do.

Your goals will describe how you are going to achieve a better quality of life for your citizens, the stated purpose of your mission statement here, or whatever it is you are trying to attain. Goals are the road map for reaching your desired destination. Sample goals for the "improved quality of life" mission might include the following:

GOAL ONE: Improve traffic safety.
GOAL TWO: Reduce gang-related crime.
GOAL THREE: Improve customer service.

You will want to measure whether or not you are reaching your goals. You are attempting to measure outcome, not just output. You can, however, use numbers in helping gauge your degree of success. For instance, the preceding three goals might be attached to the following performance measures:

GOAL ONE: Improve traffic safety.

PERFORMANCE MEASURE: Reduce the number of traffic accidents by 5% from the preceding year.

GOAL TWO: Reduce gang-related crime.

PERFORMANCE MEASURE: Reduce the number of offenses known committed by tracked gang members by 5% from the preceding year.

GOAL THREE: Improve customer service.

PERFORMANCE MEASURE: Increase the number of citizen commendations for police personnel by 10% over the preceding year.

Keep your performance measures realistic. One chief announced a target of a drastically-reduced police response time to Priority One calls without first asking his staff if it was a reasonable expectation, given the department's limited resources. It wasn't, and the agency got nowhere near reaching its promised target.

Make your goals tough enough to make your people stretch to reach them. Do not make them so difficult that you are doomed to fall short before the race begins.

Let your people know what you require them to accomplish. Remind them periodically. Keep your expectations high but reasonable. Measure how you all are doing. Review and update your agency's goals from year to year. Do not be afraid to expect a lot from yourself as well as your people. "Good" is not good enough. "Great" is what you are seeking.

NEVER CRITICIZE YOUR OWN DEPARTMENT IN PUBLIC

Every chief of police has days when he is thoroughly disappointed if not outright disgusted with his organization, himself or both. Realize that leaders in other professions go through the same agonies every now and again. The bad feelings *will* pass. Do not do or say anything that may be terribly damaging before they do.

It is important enough to say again: Do not criticize your organization or its members in a public forum. That is a cardinal rule for an ethical police leader. If your department or one or more of its members clearly messed up, it is acceptable and expected for you to acknowledge a mistake. But admitting it when you are wrong does not mean lambasting the entire agency or its people. Doing so will bring you the undying ill will of your people. Simply put, it will be a big log on the bonfire that accomplishes your destruction. You can admit mistakes without publicly criticizing either your people or your department.

Honesty and openness do not require publicly attacking the organization of which you are the leader. Certainly you must discuss with your staff your department's shortcomings and the strategy for fixing them. Likewise you must discuss some of these things with your boss if you are to retain integrity in the eyes of your supervisor. But that is where the discussion stays.

No one but a crazy person stands in front of his own house and hurls rocks at the windows. As head of the enterprise, you are stoning yourself when you publicly blast your organization. Don't do it. Ever.

CONSIDER AN EMPLOYEES' ADVISORY COUNCIL

To minimize nasty surprises and succeed in your plans for the department you must keep your thumb on the pulse of the organization. That translates into staying abreast of what is on the minds of your personnel, sworn and civilian.

If you have a union or unions, you should meet with the groups' elected officers on a regular basis, probably every month or two. Meetings should take place even when there are no burning issues so that you can get at least somewhat comfortable with each other. You likely will invite your command staff to these meetings, as well. You can call more frequent meetings (or respond to the union's call for one) if events and issues dictate.

Your organization likely includes employees who are not members of a union or association. It is important for you to stay up with their concerns, too. One way to stay connected with your non-union employees is via an Employees' Advisory Council made up of members elected by their peers from all elements of the department.

Depending upon the size and make-up of your organization, this employee group may range in size from half a dozen to a dozen people. Sit down with them at least quarterly to tell them what is going on in the department and what will happen next. (Caution: Be sure your staff already has this information; they should not hear it first from their subordinates.)

Listen to your employees' issues and concerns. Answer the questions you can on the spot. Promise to get back to them on topics that will require some research or decision-making with your staff. Then, be sure to keep your promise.

Employee groups that regularly meet with the chief are one more way in which you can stay in touch with your people while showing them you are a real, caring human being, after all. Do not overlook their value for staying in touch with the far-reaches of your 24/7 business.

MAINTAIN SURVEILLANCE OF THE PROBLEM PITS

It has already been noted that you must be certain that your agency's operations in several high-risk areas are well-run. These are the areas that, when neglected, have cost more than a few chiefs their positions. They often include use of force, internal affairs investigations, money and other evidence handling, and high-speed pursuits.

In addition, every jurisdiction has its own, particular sensitive areas based on past practices and local experience. In one department the issue may be sexual harassment because of what has happened in the past. At another it could be cops working a second job on company time because the practice was winked at during the previous administration.

It will be your task to find out what your own jurisdiction's past and present problem areas might be and how they got to be that way. This you can learn by talking with your boss, your staff, your employees and even members of the community. Your own observations and research may already have revealed some sore spots, also.

Find out what is going on now in these potential problem locations. If action is needed to address an ongoing issue, take it right away. You are now the one held responsible for fixing the problems you uncover. You cannot afford to go about it via half-measures. "Failed to deal with problems" has been the epitaph for more than one failed chief.

Once you have addressed a problem area, do not assume it will stay fixed just because you fixed it. Keep an eye on it in the future. People and organizations can suffer relapses. But realize that you cannot be everywhere or do everything all by yourself. Assign a trusted staff member to watch a specific problem area. Hold him or her accountable for what happens there in the future.

DON'T HOARD INFORMATION YOUR PEOPLE NEED

In your role as police chief you will attend a lot of meetings with your boss, fellow department heads, community leaders and others. You will be privy to a lot of information, some of it sensitive or confidential. If you are not careful, it will be easy to assume that just because you know something everyone else in your organization does, too. That is often not the case, simply because your people do not have the same access to information that you do.

First, be sure you are not sharing information that was accompanied by instructions to keep it to yourself. If it is not labeled "confidential," get it to those who need to have it in order to do their own jobs better. Your staff through the chain of command will often be the best means for disseminating the news. Be sure you have it right the first time. Recalling bad information to correct it can be as time-consuming as it is damaging to your reputation for reliability.

Some misguided souls, a few police executives among them, seem to believe that their own self-worth is bolstered by the information they have that is denied to others. If you are going to lead an effective organization, you cannot afford to be one of them.

SHARE THE ROAD MAP OF WHERE YOU'RE GOING

If they are going to support you, your people need (and deserve) to know where you plan to lead them. It is not an unreasonable request. You expect no less from your own boss.

Publicizing the goals of the department to employees and community alike is a great way to tell people where their police department is headed. Do it clearly and often. Like the members of any organization, police employees often have to hear a message repeatedly before it becomes a part of their consciousness. The same holds true for the citizens of your community. They also need to know what you plan to do for and with them.

Beyond your department's official and declared goals, tell your people what else you expect of them. Let them know what will get them rewarded and what will get them in trouble. There should be no surprises. The road map will vary from agency to agency, chief to chief, depending upon local issues and conditions.

If your agency has had a recent problem with integrity lapses, your map doubtlessly will emphasize the importance of ethical behavior. If the community has experienced a rash of fatal accidents because traffic enforcement has been allowed to lag, your people need to know that they'll be expected to unlimber their ticket books for lots of use. Let everyone know what is expected in clear and certain terms.

No matter how smart they may be, your people, including your top staff, cannot read your mind. Share the vision. Let them see where you are all going together. Then, you can ask for their help in determining how you all will get there. Spread out your map for everyone to see.

DON'T BE AFRAID TO BE DIFFERENT (INNOVATE!)

The human animal is often the most comfortable doing what has been done before. The new and unfamiliar can be uncomfortable, even scary. Little wonder, then, that cops and cop organizations can be resistant to change.

Law enforcement agencies, like other organizations, often get better by changing in spite of opposition from their own employees and leaders. You should not be guilty of fixing something that was not broken just so you can trumpet change. At the same time, you must not fear to change something just because the alteration may not work out exactly as expected. Like everyone else, you are allowed a few false starts and errors.

The best organizations do not shrink from innovation. Their leaders understand that not every new idea will work out as planned. You should keep that in mind when your people bring you ideas that may contain some risk but also promise the potential for positive change.

Trying out new ideas does not mean that you have to get crazy. Altering patrol deployment by putting all 100 of your uniformed cops afoot is probably not a good idea. Changing how often they patrol their areas of responsibility may be. Requiring them to get out of their cars and interact with their customers for a specific amount of time during their shift may be even more innovative, and potentially more effective.

However you plan to innovate, expect some grousing if not actual opposition when you do it. Remember, cops like the comfort of the familiar. Have the courage to stick by your guns until the change has had a fair chance to work. Make revisions or even reverse the change if solid evidence shows that you should. But resist the temptation to give up on innovation just because it makes someone (including yourself) uneasy.

BORROW AND LOAN GOOD IDEAS

It has been said that the last original idea was formulated a very long time ago. Whether that is true or not, you should not be shy about exchanging ideas and information that could help make your department or someone else's better.

Law enforcement's professional associations and their publications are good sources for policies and practices that are working well elsewhere. Their websites can offer the same. Visit them regularly and scan the professional journals for articles applicable to your local situation. Try to attend conferences put on by national and state chiefs associations whenever feasible. The information you gain from the informal interactions and networking may prove at least as helpful as the program agenda.

Rely on the International Association of Chiefs of Police and the Police Executive Research Forum for good information on new ways of doing things. If you can, participate in the affairs of these organizations. You should find that most of the individual members you interact with will be helpful in addressing your own concerns. At the same time, do not hesitate to share accounts of your victories. Precisely this sort of information exchange strengthens the entire profession.

NEVER STOP TRYING TO GET BETTER

From the day you take the job as head of your agency until the day you depart you should have a single, overriding, personal mission: make it better. Hopefully, that is why you accepted the position in the first place.

You have a large amount of work to do as the chief of police. The demands on your time are considerable. At times it may seem that everyone wants a piece of you for one thing or another. The temptation to relax your expectations just a little for yourself and your organization may arise, as much out of a desire for self-preservation as from any other cause.

Resist the temptation to slack off on your reasonable expectations. You did not make your agency what it is by taking it easy. Your goal remains giving your citizens–your customers–a better, more effective, more compassionate law enforcement agency than they had yesterday. The status quo should not be enough for you. That is the idea you must pass on to your employees and the community you all serve.

An organization that does not strive constantly to get better is in danger of becoming stagnant. From there it is only a short misstep to backsliding. If you show that you are ready to stop working for improvement, expect that attitude to be quickly contagious throughout the organization. No good will come from it.

It is your duty as an ethical law enforcement leader to work always to make things better. One of those key "things" is your own organization.

SUMMARY

As the leader of your law enforcement organization you are the one ultimately responsible for making it great–or not. The good examples you set and the positive role modeling you demonstrate will have a lot to do with whether or not your department reaches the status of being great.

You have a right to be proud of your people and your organization. You should show your pride, publicly and often. Moving your department to the degree of excellence you want will not happen overnight. It literally will take years. But it is up to you to start it on its journey. Realize that there may be people and events that will temporarily sidetrack you. It is up to you to overcome opposition and continue the journey relentlessly forward. When it comes to your organization, never accept "good enough."

Stay in touch with the members of your organization and let them know what you want from them. It is vital that they know where the organization is going and their role in getting it there. Expect occasional mistakes that will need repaired, but do not criticize your people or your organization in public.

As you strive to improve your department, do not be afraid to try new ideas. Listen to your people as a great source of those new ideas. Never remain stopped on your journey to lead a better and better department.

POINTS TO REMEMBER

- You as the leader are the single most important factor in determining if your department is a great one.
- Don't expect major culture change to happen quickly.
- Set goals to be accomplished agency-wide and disseminate them.
- Expect setbacks and seek to overcome them relentlessly.
- Engage in positive role modeling at all times.
- Have a group of peers you can consult for "second opinions."
- Stay in touch with your people and listen carefully to their ideas.
- You must promptly and effectively address problems, but do not criticize your own people or organization publicly.
- Keep a careful watch on your agency's operations and policies most likely to cause you serious problems.
- Be sure your people know where you intend to lead the organization and their role in getting it there.
- Never accept "good enough" for your department; keep trying to make it better.

Chapter 3

ON BEING THE WORLD'S GREATEST ROLE MODEL

Today's police employee is unlike those who have gone before. He or she is willing to give a lot. But these good people are not hesitant to let you know that they expect a lot in return.

One of the things that these police people of today expect is that you, their leader, will demonstrate what you expect of them. The antiquated attitude of "don't do as I do; do as I say do" will not work for these employees. They expect more of you, and properly so.

Put succinctly, it is your job as chief to demonstrate consistently the behavior you demand of the other members of the organization you lead. That's what being a leader is about. You set the bar; you provide the example. You are the one that your young officers should look to in determining the kind of cop they want to be.

Being a great role model all of the time does not allow you a lot of slack. You are virtually always "on." You are allowed precious little forgiveness for error. Fair or not, you were not drafted into your job. You accepted the challenge willingly. Serving as the best of all role models is not beyond your abilities. Here is how it is done.

TREAT IT LIKE YOUR PERSONAL BUSINESS–IT IS!

A new chief of police was accompanying his senior peer in touring the latter's new building. Suddenly the senior CEO changed direction sharply and headed across the hallway. His colleague watched in surprise as the head of a major law enforcement agency bent down and retrieved a chewing gum wrapper and stuffed it into his pants pocket, all without interrupting his running commentary accompanying the tour. The new chief was mightily impressed by his senior's role modeling of pride in caring for the new facility.

Questioned about his trash-collection duties, the chief acknowledged copying the action from his own observations of the manager of a mega-mall who was giving the chief a tour of the retail palace. He, too, changed direction abruptly to collect a piece of paper he spotted on the promenade floor. The lesson was not lost on the chief: treat your organization as a personally-owned enterprise. In very many ways, it is.

There is a lesson for you in all of this. If your "business" fails, so will you. That means that you as the CEO are responsible for demonstrating at all times the behavior you expect from your employees. It not only means demonstrably keeping the place clean, it also means displaying the courtesy, customer service, integrity and personal courage you expect of your people. You are the "business" owner and they are your employees. It is vital that you demonstrate for them the character and job performance you require.

Not unlike the CEO at the corner dry cleaning establishment or a Fortune 500 company, to the extent that you are able it is up to you to teach, reward, and correct your workers according to how well they carry out your demonstrated mandates. You can do none of this in fairness unless you first serve as a *positive* role model of what you expect.

REMEMBER THAT YOU ARE NEVER INVISIBLE

Whether you are walking the halls of your own department or enjoying companionship and a libation in a local restaurant, as chief of police you are highly visible to everyone around you. Many people know you by sight. As some law enforcement leaders have learned to their sorrow, you are often being observed even when you are unaware of it.

One veteran chief began the slide to a forced retirement after engaging in a loud domestic dispute in a local restaurant. Another returned from an out-of-state chiefs' conference and alighted from the airplane–drunk. A third shortened his leadership career when he threw a curbside fit over a traffic ticket he received 200 miles away from his jurisdiction. The law enforcement jungle grapevine went into action and the news of his tantrum beat him home.

If you are mowing the lawn and drinking to the point of becoming loud and tipsy, your neighbors likely will tell others. If you are habitually loitering at a watering hole to "de-stress," word will get around. And if you engage in behavior that even remotely resembles sexual misconduct, you have just created the "best" news of all for the rumor mill.

If you want to keep your moral authority to require that your people do the right thing, you cannot afford to set a poor example in *anything* that you do. People who either like you or who are indifferent are watching and listening. At least as important, the people who dislike you and wish you ill are observing, too. That group may well include some of your own employees whom you have disciplined or otherwise "offended," at least in their own minds. These folks sincerely want you out of a job. If you engage in stupid conduct you are playing into the hands of your enemies. Don't do it.

PASS THE VIDEO TEST

Sometimes police recruits are lectured about the importance of passing the video test. They are told, perhaps by the chief, that they should perform their duties as if a television camera was always pointed at them. They are reminded of their duty to act always in a manner that they would not hesitate to have broadcast to their loved ones.

As leader of the agency, you should apply the same standards of the video test to your own actions, on-duty and off. You certainly want to assume that your loved ones are watching the show. But you should assume that the inevitable characters who don't like you are in the audience, too. That realization may serve to strengthen even more your motivation always to do the right thing.

By the very nature of your position as a community leader, many people are interested in what you say and do. You always want to come across as the professional, ethical, just-plain-decent human being that you are. Racist, sexist jokes and comments must be banned from your behavior. You can neither tell them nor guffaw at their telling. The camera is on.

The same holds true for the salty language of an old-time sailor. You probably cannot be perfect, but do the very best you can. The camera has a microphone attached, and it is eternally activated, too. Even in your time away from the job and well outside your own jurisdiction, the world is full of cameras, both figuratively and literally. You want to be on the evening news only to acknowledge good work done by your people.

You quite reasonably expect your employees always to pass the video test. It is up to you to role model how that is to be done. Hold your managers accountable for doing the same. You all will enjoy TV a lot more.

BE ACTIVE IN YOUR COMMUNITY AND PROFESSION

Law enforcement leaders like you want their people to be active in the Scouts, PAL, Rotary or other people-helping community groups. Once more, if you are going to expect that of your people you must set the example yourself.

As a recognized community leader (and you are, like it or not) you are expected by your boss and the citizenry to be involved in the community that pays you. The good news is that you should have some leeway in what you choose to join. Most chiefs elect to join at least one civic club, such as the Optimists or Rotary. Feel free to join more if you have the desire, time and money, but realize that time is a precious commodity for you. It is unlikely that you will have enough of it to do everything you would like.

Remember your absolute obligation to maintain your good health, which means that you must nourish a life away from the job. It probably often feels like everyone wants some of your time, which is precisely why you must guard jealously the hours you wisely have reserved for yourself and your family.

Do not overload yourself by saying "yes" to every membership offer that comes down the road. Investigate to learn which ones may help you the most politically. This is one area where it is OK to be just a little bit selfish. Take into strong account which one(s) you think you'd actually enjoy, too. Be very courteous and apologetic in explaining your limited time to those offers you must turn down.

You also should participate in the organizations of your profession. Membership in a regional, state and national chiefs' organization is a good idea for the information and networking opportunities it will bring. Again, do not overdo it. Leave some time for *you.* Also, recognize the different expectations of different departments and communities. One may brag on the chief who is active in national or state law enforcement affairs that take him out of town often. Others may expect the chief to stay close and take care of local issues, major and minor.

It is important for you to know which set of expectations apply to you. Ask your boss for his or her views. Where possible, a good balance of "home and away" is what you are seeking. You want the home folks to see you on the job a lot. But you also do not want to be a total unknown at the state level and beyond when you need something from your peers.

DON'T DO THINGS YOU'D PUNISH YOUR PEOPLE FOR

The existence of "double standards" probably makes you mad. There is a very good chance that your employees, your boss and your community don't much like them, either.

One of the requirements for being a good role model is a demonstrated proclivity for fairness in all things. Those things most especially include the ones that involve you personally. As your organization's leader you cannot do things with impunity when your agency would punish other employees for those same acts or failures to act. It really is as simple as that.

One chief of police suspended himself without pay for a day because he failed to go to the firearms range for a required qualification. It is easy to dismiss his action against himself as a "stunt," but it is, in fact, what he would have done to one of his officers had they committed the same violation. The chief wanted to demonstrate that firearms skills were important. He also wanted to make it clear that no one was exempt from accountability. His actions were intended to make his points.

Another chief liked to brag about how often his own people had stopped him due to his lead-footed driving behavior. He never received a traffic ticket for his vehicular misconduct. But his people talked–a lot–about their boss's irresponsible driving. The talk eventually reached the community. In the end, the chief's reputation for both integrity and fairness suffered. He did not lose his job over his ill-advised conduct. He did lose the respect of some of his officers whom he continued to punish for their driving transgressions. It was not fair, and they knew it.

In a great organization the rules and expectations are the same whether your toes are wrapped around the bottom or top rung of the ladder. In a *truly* great organization the expectations of the person at the top are often *higher* than they are for anyone else. That is the kind of organization that *you* want to lead.

WHEN YOU'RE WRONG, SAY SO AND APOLOGIZE

Law enforcement officers are proud people. They have a right to be. But as a consequence, too many of those justly proud people find it very hard to admit to a mistake. Some find it even harder actually to apologize for the miscue, particularly to anyone outside their own organization.

Some attribute this closed mouth tendency to what might be called the "lawyer effect." Their own attorneys have long-cautioned cops (and just about everyone else) never to accept blame for anything, including an honest mistake. They theorize that doing so will give the legal opposition a weapon to wield like a sword. The trite and overused expression "never say you're sorry" probably was first uttered by somebody's legal mouthpiece.

In fairness, your attorney's job is to give you, the chief, legal advice that he or she believes will keep you and your employer out of trouble. You would be unwise not to listen to his or her advice and, on most occasions, follow it. But as any experienced chief can tell you, there will be times when the police boss will listen carefully to the legal input he is offered, thank his legal advisor for the guidance and then do what his heart and/or experience tell him to do, regardless of whether or not his decision is in line with his advisor's recommendation.

An apology is certainly in order if you know you have wronged one of your people through a decision you have made. The next step is to repair, if possible, the damage you have caused. It's always the right and honorable thing to do.

You owe the same to the citizen who has been wronged by your organization. Your loyal attorney may caution you not to talk to the parents of the child your officer accidentally struck with his patrol car. He'll tell you something about never accepting liability for an error that appears headed for a lawsuit or out-of-court settlement. Your best bet is to follow what your heart tells you. What is the *right* thing to do; the *moral* thing to do? You are not going to promise to "make things right" or offer a sack of money. You are not going to discuss legal fault or responsibility. You are simply going to express your sincere condolences to people who are hurting and extend wishes for a better day tomorrow.

DON'T FORGET HOW TO BE A PEACE OFFICER

As chief, unless you head a small agency you probably will experience little hands-on police work. In spite of your best intentions, you likely will find yourself behind a desk much more often than you will experience the thrill of the chase after a bad guy.

Nevertheless, you cannot forget what it is like to be a law enforcement officer. Wear your uniform at least part of the time. Many of your cops expect it. You will find that many of your citizens do, too. You are not the mayor or the city manager; you're the chief. More than a few folks will expect that you look like it.

You are out to set a good example for your people. Be sure your uniform is clean and fits well. Be sure that your leather (or what passes for leather gear these days) looks good. Your shoes should not look like you just extricated yourself from a mudslide, either.

Wear your sidearm. In an emergency, you will be expected to respond as a peace officer. You will be hard-pressed to defend against a lethal threat if you are unarmed. Too many longtime law enforcement CEOs seem to forget where they put their firearm once they made chief. Maybe the weapon is too heavy; maybe it wears on the inside of their suit jacket. Whatever the case, they have set it aside for convenience or comfort and in the process exposed themselves to needless risk from criminals and unneeded ridicule from their own troops. They are setting a poor example that you do not want to copy.

If you are the leader of a small agency, you may find yourself handling calls along with your people. You obviously will want to set an excellent example for them in everything you do. Even if you are chief of a larger department, you should spend at least a little time on the street with your troopers. When you do, don't take over their calls for them or otherwise get in the way. Do not make it a daily practice to find situations or traffic violations that your officers will have to take over for you.

When you do show up on a scene, ask what you can do to help. Then do it. Show a high regard for officer safety, good judgment and basic courtesy in the process. You cannot rightfully expect your people to act properly if the chief himself abuses people physically or verbally. Doing either is absolutely never acceptable for you or anyone in your organization. It is up to you to demonstrate the *right* way to behave as a professional.

Your people will not expect you to be the best cop on the road. That is not your primary job. They *will* expect you to display the basic safety skills and demeanor of a competent patrol officer. They expect that you will not forget what it is like to be a cop.

Do not disappoint them.

YOUR OFF-DUTY CONDUCT IS AS IMPORTANT AS WHAT HAPPENS ON-DUTY

In the eyes of your employees and your community, the chief of police is *always* the chief of police. He or she is never really off-duty. Not entirely, anyway.

All of those eyes and ears focused in your direction mandate that you must never set anything other than a sterling example for all of them. As you know, you are always the leader and you are always "on." Bad behavior on your part almost certainly will be broadcast to everyone in the community, if not by the media then by the omnipresent unofficial grapevine.

You are the chief. There are now places you should not go where your presence in the past may have created no great stir, even though you were a cop. Downing several strong ones with the boys in a cop bar was very likely acceptable behavior for you as a front-line officer or even a supervisor. It is no longer advisable for you as the Big Boss. Too many things can go wrong in such an environment that you as the agency's CEO cannot afford to be a part of. As the agency's chief disciplinarian you may even be required to sit in judgment of behavior that erupts there. It is simply easier (and smarter) to stay away than have to explain your presence and your actions later, even though you may be innocent of doing anything wrong.

Sadly, there are almost certainly those in your community and organization who *want* you to look bad. It makes no sense to give them stones to hurl at you, no matter how poorly aimed they may be. Do not leave your good judgment and common sense at the office.

YOUR EMPLOYEES LOOK TO YOU AND WANT TO BE PROUD OF YOU

As noted, there are always going to be those who want you to fall flat on your face. That is just human nature. Fortunately for you, they are almost certainly in the minority, inside and outside the organization.

Although some may be loath to admit it, most cops want to be proud of the organization and the leader that they work for. They probably share that human need to belong to *something* that even a street gangster has. The good news is that most people really want to claim membership in something seen as worthwhile. Cops certainly fall into that category of humans. It is equally important to them that the leader of the pack is someone they can look up to.

More than one chief tells the story of a well-known leader of a large municipal police agency who seemed to have a knack for getting himself into trouble–and then skating out again, apparently unscathed. But his lengthy career as a frequently-in-trouble leader did not fail to cause damage. The damage was inflicted on his people, who repeatedly found it necessary to explain their boss's peccadilloes in their interactions with other officers around the state. Too often, the chief's name would come up in conversation, the eye-rolling and snickering would begin and the chief's employees would find themselves either defending their leader or joining in the levity. These cops were not proud of their boss; they were embarrassed.

Your people want to look to you as their strong, admirable leader. When things get tough, they *want* to believe that you have the answers that will see them through. They *want* to know that you are held in high regard both in the community and the profession. You are their leader and they *want* to be proud of you.

Your job as an ethical professional is not to let your people down. Not ever. The good news is that ultimate control of the situation rests in your hands. If you can state honestly that you are proud of your actions, chances are that everyone else who matters will be proud, too. Remember that.

DON'T ACCEPT FAVORS DENIED TO YOUR PEOPLE

It is important enough to say once again: members of your agency are watching what you do at all times. If you accept a benefit denied to them, you likely will lose their respect. At the very least you will surrender your right to expect them to forego special treatment and favors denied the general population.

Special privileges that have been offered to law enforcement officers run the gamut from free cups of coffee to sexual favors. Whatever rules you have imposed on your people in the name of professional ethics, realize that you must follow precisely the same guidelines yourself. If you expect your officers to pay full price for their meals and coffee (and you should), it is incumbent upon you to do the same. If you demand that your people pay out of their own pockets any parking tickets that they incur, you must pay yours, too. If you prohibit your cops from accepting free tickets to the ball game, then you must courteously turn down the same offer.

In other words, you should not expect the organization you lead to treat you as "special." Uniform and equipment regulations apply to you. So do the General Orders governing personal grooming and off-duty pursuits. The more clearly you demonstrate this reality to your people, the better it will be for your reputation as a positive role model.

One new chief removed the sign designating a reserved station house parking space for him. He realized he was quite capable of parking among the "regular people" and walking a few more feet to the back door. Another started wearing the uniform his troops donned, in stark contrast to his predecessor who routinely dressed for work as if it was his day off.

There are little things that you can do or refrain from doing that you may assume go unnoticed by your people. Chances are they do not. Being the world's greatest role model means following the same rules you set for everyone else.

NEVER CHEAT OR FUDGE ON THE RULES

Closely allied to the requirement that you must deny yourself special favors is the mandate not to cheat–ever. By cheating or cutting corners on the right way to do things you give up the moral high ground that an ethical leader must have at all times.

One chief severely punished any employee caught calling in sick when he or she was really quite healthy. Unfortunately for him, it was common knowledge throughout the department that the Big Boss also made liberal use of sick leave when he did not suffer so much as a sniffle. The chief's own sick leave abuse went unpunished.

You should not fudge on the rules because it is dishonest to do so. If you need more reasons than that, here is another. As noted previously, there are almost certainly people out there praying that bad things will happen to you.

By the nature of your job, you are going to sometimes make people angry at you for one reason or another. A few of your own current or former employees may be among them. These angry people are looking for the opportunity to publicize wrongdoing by the chief of police. They would like to unearth a major ethical error, but some little ones will do, if necessary. Little ones like rule violations. They are counting on a media always looking for muck to rake to help them get you. When you refuse to cheat you deprive them of fuel for your funeral pyre.

Do not bend the rules to your own benefit. Don't cheat the IRS or the Girl Scout cookie salesperson. Return the gift that your organization's ethics rules do not permit you to keep. If you received a ticket and you are guilty, pay it. All of these things a good role model does.

THE "LITTLE THINGS" ARE IMPORTANT, TOO

Little things, symbolic things, sometimes can be very important to your employees and the community. Seemingly minor, they can add up over time to help you form a reputation as a genuinely caring leader–or something else entirely.

There are a number of things you can do for your people. Many are "little things" that nevertheless can mean a lot for the employees you do them for. The point, of course, is that you are doing them because they are the right thing to do, not because you are putting on a show for an audience.

One chief opened his staff meetings with a prayer for the safety and welfare of his employees. Depending upon your staff's feelings about prayer and religion, this may or may not be a good idea for you to emulate. You do not want to give the impression that you are forcing your own religious beliefs on anyone else.

Another chief made it a point to remember all of his employees' birthdays with a greeting card or e-mail, while yet another recognized each one's hiring anniversary date with a congratulatory note.

You should appoint someone to keep you apprised of injuries, serious illnesses, deaths and births in your employees' families. Again, notes of condolences or congratulations are generally appreciated by their recipients, who may like the fact that their busy boss took the time to think of them.

Telephone calls from the chief are appreciated by most police people recovering from serious injuries, illnesses or surgery. Employees who have had spouses or children in serious straits generally appreciate a quick call from the boss, too. Your purpose in each case is to send your best wishes and hopes that things will soon be better.

No less a leader than the former mayor of New York City, Rudolph

Giulliani, has emphasized the importance of attending funerals as a chief executive. Chances are, if you find yourself wondering whether or not you should attend the services of an employee, ex-employee or close family member of an employee, you probably should be there. Funerals are the sort of thing where you may not get credit for being there, but you *will* be regarded less highly if you are absent. People, yours included, often notice those things.

Also deserving of your attention are the small celebrations of life that make up the collective life of an organization like yours. Be present at promotions, retirements and other special events if you possibly can. You do not necessarily have to play a big role or spend hours there. But a brief appearance often will fit your schedule and be appreciated by your work family.

The little things that show you to be a decent human being can add up to bigger things over time. As a good role model, you want your people to care. Setting the example for caring is your job.

LOOK AND SOUND LIKE WHAT YOU WANT YOUR PEOPLE TO EMULATE

A once successful chief relates how he began his climb to the top of his organization. As an officer, he picked out the individual he felt was the department's best sergeant and worked at learning and copying his behavior until he won a promotion to that rank. He did the same in his climb to lieutenant, and repeated his copying behavior throughout his climb to the top of the organizational ladder.

You want your subordinates to look at you in the same way. You want them to want to be like you one day, whether they consciously admit that goal or not. For that reason the onus is on you to project a great model for them to copy.

It sounds too simple to be true, but it is. If you expect your troopers to look good in uniform, you must, as well. If you want your supervisors and managers to set the example for exceptional command presence, you must set the example for *them* to follow. If you demand that your employees show courtesy and provide excellent customer service to those inside and outside the organization, you have to demonstrate the same. And if you require that your officers use language that portrays them as the decent professionals that they are, you cannot afford to curse like a monkey yourself.

It is all about what you want to be seen and heard to be. Once you have made that determination you can expect most of your employees to follow your lead.

That is what being a role model is about.

SUMMARY

You are the recognized, formal leader of your law enforcement organization. You have no single obligation as leader more important than serving as an exceptional role model for the members of the organization and the community you serve. As such you cannot afford to relax your vigilance and your efforts for even a moment.

Setting a good example says that you are never really "off" or out of sight. You do not have to be perfect. No one is. But you do have to guard against those unguarded moments in which you are tempted to do something that would expose you and your department to embarrassment. Slipups that are permitted the "average Joe" often are denied to you if you want to retain the moral high ground that authorizes you to demand much of your people. The requirement not to set a poor example ranges from your ethics to your moral behavior; your driving habits to your consumption of alcohol.

But you must do more than avoid bad behavior. You must set the standard in the positive things you do, too. You participate fully in your profession and your community. You display courtesy and professionalism to those you meet on and off the job. You follow the basic rules for being a decent human being. And you never forget how to be a good cop.

You are and always must be what you want your people to be. That is how you serve as the world's greatest role model!

POINTS TO REMEMBER

- Always handle your organization as if it is your personally-owned business.
- Remember that your every action is highly visible to your people, your boss and your community.
- As the leader, you should stay active in your community and profession.
- Do not do things forbidden to your employees; neither should you allow yourself special privileges that they do not enjoy.
- When you are wrong, admit it and, where necessary, apologize.
- Never lose the skills and outlook of a law enforcement officer.
- Know that almost as many chiefs have failed for their off-duty conduct as for their on-duty actions.
- Most of your people want to be proud of you; do not disappoint them.
- Being an excellent role model means that you never cheat or break the rules.
- Don't forget the small touches that make your people feel valued.

- Sound like, look like, act like the leader you want your people to emulate.
- Set your sights on serving as your profession's greatest role model.

Chapter 4

LEADING YOUR STAFF

No matter how noble your intentions, regardless of how great your abilities, you will not be able to do it alone. You will need a lot of help in leading your department to the place you have envisioned for it. The people closest to you–your command staff–will have a lot to do with whether or not the vision you have is realized.

One successful district attorney bragged about his "secret" to putting in place the staff he needed to fulfill his vision for his organization. Upon taking office, he required each attorney to submit his or her resignation, then accepted or turned them down as he saw fit in assembling his new team. It is unlikely that you have the same ability or desire to engage in a massive house cleaning. It is much more likely that, to a large extent, at least initially you will have to play with the cards you have been dealt, so to speak. That means that the staff members you have and how you lead them to share your vision will be the tools you must employ to get where you are going. Successfully leading your top team members is the focus of this chapter.

THE RIGHT PEOPLE IN THE RIGHT PLACES

Unless one or more of your top staff have demonstrated obvious illegal or unethical behavior, if you start chopping off the heads of your staff on your first day on the job you are asking for trouble.

You will need some time to assess the character and abilities of your top people even if you have worked with them before. If you are a chief from inside the organization you can lay out your expectations and gauge your staff's responses. It probably will not take you too long to see who needs to go, if anyone does. If you are an "outside" chief, a time period for observing your staff in action is even more advisable. Make it clear what you expect and hold your staff accountable for meeting those expectations. They may pleasantly surprise you.

Nonetheless, major changes in your command staff are often best made within the first few months of your new administration. This is the time when people inside and outside the organization are expecting change. You may encounter less opposition to change now than later. If you are to start making the alterations for the better that most want to see, you cannot afford to wait too long to remove those who are not supporting your efforts, either through incompetence or actual opposition. Do the unpleasant tasks now and get on with the re-building. Obviously, the need for prompt and radical staff changes will be less critical or even nonexistent if you have inherited an agency that is free of serious problems.

How to remove top staffers who clearly must go is your next challenge. A sheriff or a police CEO in charge of a truly "at will" agency has a relatively easy task. He or she can bring out the "we're going in a new direction" cliché, thank the selected staff member for his service and effect the needed personnel change.

For most law enforcement bosses it is not that easy. Depending upon the legalities of your local situation and your boss's desires, you may be able to buy out a surplus staffer's contract (if he has one) or offer a severance package to get him out the door. If he truly needs to leave right now in order for you to advance the organization, spending the money today will be worth the cost. Your boss likely knows that from his or her own experience. Expend the funds for a good cause and move forward.

Some chiefs have found that they only can remove even their highest-ranking officers via the performance appraisal or evaluation process. As long as the man or woman has received passing scores, he or she is immune from termination except for gross misconduct. If that is the situation you are faced with, resolve to use the performance review process properly and give the employee a fair chance to meet your clearly-outlined expectations. If he fails to do so he then can be removed without resulting litigation that ends badly for you. Once again, you must earn a reputation for fairness and honesty in the termination process. Do it the right way and you are much less likely to be handed back an employee you thought you had shed.

Once you have the right people on your command staff you will need to be sure that they are in the right assignments. Factors helping you determine "fit" include your needs and their skills and abilities. It is often said that you need your strongest leader in Patrol, as that is where the most visible and numerous problems frequently occur. That is simply due to the nature of the job. You may elect to put the man or woman you judge as your best there, even if he or she has had that assignment recently or does not want to go. At this point you are trying to secure results, especially if the department has been experiencing problems in that area. If there are big issues elsewhere in the agency, then that "strongest" leader may need to go there, instead.

Priority one is to get the agency moving forward on an even keel. The personal wants of staff can come a little later. From both within and without the department you are being watched for results, not the happiness quotient of your top staff. That you can work on together down the road.

At the same time, if you are the decent person you should be you have no desire to make people unhappy, even if you feel one or more of them has no place in your organization. No sane individual *wants* to create enemies or hurt people. Extend all the normal courtesies to anyone you must let go.

Retirement gatherings, going away parties and the like are traditions at most police agencies. Assuming they want them, allow departing staffers the dignities that you would expect if you were in their place. Face-saving is important to you; it probably is to them, as well. You may want the same courtesy one day. If an employee declines the attention, you have at least made a good faith offer.

As in so many aspects of your difficult job, it all really leads back to the Golden Rule of leadership: Treat others as you want to be treated yourself. Living and leading by that guideline can deliver big dividends.

DON'T GET TOO COZY TOO QUICKLY

It is a natural human trait to want to be liked, to belong. The new, "outsider" chief, coming into an agency full of strangers can be especially susceptible to the desire to be accepted as soon as possible. But coming in and seeking *too* much acceptance *too* soon can prove damaging to your effectiveness in leading the organization.

"I came in smiling at everybody and everything and wagging my tail a little too much," said one "outsider" chief. "Then, when I had to kick some butts, it made it harder for me to be taken seriously."

As in so many things, you should seek a balance here. You also do not want to be seen as the nasty, grumpy new boss that everyone wants to hate. Your best bet is to be openly friendly and gracious to your first-line people and supervisors while remaining a bit more reserved towards your top managers. It is not a bad thing for them to be just a little apprehensive about their new boss. At this point, it is alright for them to be more concerned about pleasing *you* than the other way around.

Even if you are an "insider" chief who has worked with these people for ten, fifteen or twenty years, it is appropriate for them to know that the relationship has changed somewhat. You can, of course, still be friends. But it is worth remembering that you may have to discipline one or more of these people or even let them go. If you are *too* close to them the task will be even harder.

Sincere and lasting friendships may well develop among you and your staff. Hopefully that will be your experience. But it is preferable to let those friendships build over time as opposed to trying to rush them.

It is unlikely that your own boss is going to go out of his or her way to curry favor with you. You should not do so with your subordinates, either. Friendly and approachable is good. Ingratiating and gushing is not so good.

ENDLESS RESTRUCTURING IS NOT GOOD

You naturally will examine your new organization to ascertain if it is currently structured in the most efficient and effective way feasible. You'll want to know if spans of control are appropriate and lines of communication make sense. You need to know who reports to whom.

With the input of your staff, you may elect to make changes in the organizational chart to improve the way the agency functions. But you should have clear-cut reasons for the changes you make. Things should be better as a result of the revisions. It is never acceptable to alter the organizational structure just so you can say that you have moved the boxes around.

Dogs mark their territory. You do not need to do that, at least not by changing the organization chart just to make it yours. You want to be known for the improvements you make in your organization's effectiveness and reputation, not for the way the boxes and lines are connected.

Too much restructuring too often confuses those both inside and outside the law enforcement agency. Do not hesitate to tweak the chart or even make massive changes to make for a better organization. Do not turn it on its head to satisfy your own ego. Follow the same advice that serves you well in your other roles as CEO: have a good reason for what you do.

If you do change the structure of your organization, watch carefully to see if the revisions are having the desired effect. Solicit the feedback of those most directly impacted by the changes. If, after a fair trial, you find the changes are not having the desired results, have the courage to alter your new arrangement. It is OK to admit an error. Hopefully your career will be long enough to permit you to confess to a number of them. Fix it and move forward.

HIRING AND PROMOTING: WHEN IN DOUBT, DON'T!

Selection and promotional processes are stressful affairs for everyone, including the chief who must "bless" the final results. Inasmuch as the process can be a tiring and even emotional experience, the natural tendency is to want to get it over with in order to move on to the next task.

As chief, you should not be rushed in your decision-making concerning *any* personnel matter. Chances are you will be stuck with the consequences of your hiring and promotional decisions for a long time. It is important to handle them well.

Doubtlessly you have been around awhile and have amassed more than a little life experience. You probably have seen both hiring and promotional decisions blow up, much to the embarrassment of those who made them. More than likely you have experienced the fallout from such a detonation yourself. As chief, you have a duty to the organization to keep those missteps to a minimum.

The best advice to you here is as brief as it is critical: When it doubt, don't. Move on to the next candidate. If you have no remaining, acceptable candidates, start the process over. But do not anoint if you harbor doubts about the wisdom of making an appointment. You have not been around this long without developing a sense for these things. If upon reviewing the facts your intuition tells you that something just isn't right, trust what your senses are telling you. One experienced police CEO put it this way: "The tie goes to the runner. In my book, the employer is always the runner."

Virtually all veteran police leaders can relate at least one horror story of an individual hired or promoted in spite of significant reservations who later failed to the detriment of the entire organization. It has occurred before and will happen again. You don't want it to happen to you.

It is not acceptable to appoint and hope that "training and experience will smooth out the rough spots." It is not OK to promote and wish that "she'll grow into the job." And it's certainly not advisable to do either and count on luck or divine intervention to come to the rescue.

When in doubt, don't do it.

DON'T MANDATE "YES" MEN

Bosses tend to like people who agree with them. They probably cannot help it. Many are sorely tempted to like less well those who habitually disagree with them, particularly in public. Therein is the trap for you, the boss.

It is reasonable for you to let your staff know that you won't appreciate their arguing with you in front of the troops or subordinate managers. That is a reasonable expectation that any boss should have in an effort to maintain discipline in his or her organization. Also let them know, however, that you want them to express their true opinions in the proper forum. That forum might be in a command staff meeting or within the confines of a private, one-on-one conversation.

You cannot run the organization alone. Your judgments and decisions really are *not* the only ones that matter. You need the views, thoughts, ideas and history of the organization that your staff members bring to the table. If it becomes clear to your staff that you will ridicule, belittle or otherwise disregard and disrespect what they have to say, they are likely to stop sharing what they really want to say to you. You will be the poorer for it. You also will be more likely to get surprised by something you could have had warning about.

Even if you vehemently disagree with them, thank your people in front of others for their dissenting views. Let them know that their advice has been weighed carefully, even though you ultimately may have decided to do something else. The goal is to keep your people talking to you about their honest ideas and opinions. Only in that way can you enjoy the benefit of their knowledge.

Remember: As good as you are, you cannot do it alone.

FIND OUT WHY THE FAILURE HAPPENED, BUT DON'T KILL THE MESSENGER

For the health of your organization, it is important that you hear all of what's going on there, not just the things that please you. You do not have to be a psychologist to realize that your people are much less likely to tell you the bad news if you are nasty to the ones who bring it to you.

Make it clear to your people that you want to hear about everything important that is happening in the department you lead. Make it equally clear that you will not punish those who deliver the report. At the same time, bad news must be followed up in an honest effort to find out what went wrong so that the disaster can be prevented from happening again.

In one legendary tale, a Human Resources type attempted to console a law enforcement executive that a recent, embarrassing incident involving police personnel was really not such a big deal, after all.

"No," the police boss said.

"You don't understand. This is the police department. Somebody has to pay."

This true story illustrates the way in which errors by police personnel have been looked at traditionally by traditional law enforcement bosses. In order to serve as an example for others, someone's head has to roll. Somebody's ears have to get boxed. But that's not always true.

More forward-looking police leaders make a distinct difference in the *kinds* of mistakes that are inevitable in any organization, and the appropriate response to them. They differentiate between "mistakes of the head" and "mistakes of the heart." The former are errors made accidentally because, for whatever reason, the employee made an honest mistake or just did not know any better. The latter category covers misconduct by employees who knew what they were supposed to do or refrain from doing, but consciously committed the transgression anyway. These police leaders visit much more severe sanctions on those who knew better but engaged in improper conduct anyhow.

You would do well to take to heart the examples set by your enlightened peers. Find out why bad news came to pass, but do not punish the bearer of the bad tidings. Invest the time and effort in finding out why the failure of people, equipment, policy or procedure happened. Then, assure that it's fixed with the minimum amount of figurative bloodshed possible.

You do not want to be punished by your boss for telling him the truth. Extend the same right to your people. Listen calmly to what they have to say and then rationally address the issue.

DELEGATE BUT HOLD ACCOUNTABLE

The true tale is told of a well-known chief of police who found himself unable to delegate decision-making to others. Although he grasped that he had a highly-competent group of managers, he found it almost impossible to delegate tasks, with the expected result that issues accumulated at his desk and languished, because he also harbored the tendency to put off decisions on even relatively minor matters. One of the chief's subordinates opined: "If we put one more thing on the back burner, we're going to need a much bigger stove."

The chief's inability to delegate and his proclivity to procrastinate cost him his health and then his job.

You cannot do it all, nor should you try. If you cannot trust your subordinate leaders, they should no longer be working for you. Get some you *can* trust. But make use of the people who work for you to carry out many of the tasks that come your way. It is the only way you can survive a demanding job with your physical and emotional health intact.

Routinely putting in 18-hour days won't prove your devotion to duty. The practice *will* contribute to the impression that you are unable to manage your time, delegate appropriately or both.

Size up your subordinates and their skills and abilities as you determine which one is best-suited for handling a particular project. That's something a good leader does. Explain what you want done and when the work must be ready. Allow the person assigned to ask questions and clarify the expectations you have placed on him, if need be.

Then, allow your subordinate room to work. It is alright to check on progress from time to time, but don't become an omnipresent pest. Let go of the project and let someone do it for you.

Your staffer may not do it precisely the way you would. He or she may not do it as well as you would have done. The question for you should be: Has the work been competently performed? Is the project complete? If so, you have saved yourself some time and effort and your subordinate has gained valuable experience. If the work has not been done to your total satisfaction, chances are you wisely inserted a time cushion in front of the due date so that there is time for changes to be made by you and your staff member.

It is fine to point out to your staffer where you want revisions made to his work product. But do not forget to thank him for his work, as well. He probably will do even better next time if it is made clear that his efforts were appreciated this time. Do not dispense false praise, but do recognize the completion of delegated tasks. Once more, you would expect no less from the man or woman who routinely delegates to *you.*

DON'T "DUMB DOWN" YOUR EXPECTATIONS

A commander from a West Coast mega-department took over as the new chief at a much smaller agency in the West. He immediately discovered that his new staff had not had the advantages of much of the training and experience he had enjoyed at a much larger agency. His people were by no means dumb; they simply did not share his background. Faced with this roadblock to his grandiose plans, the new chief promptly adjusted his expectations for achievement at his new home–downward.

You must not repeat that new CEO's error. Your assessment of your people may indeed tell you that they have a distance to go in getting where you want them to be. Your plans for the department may take a bit more time to implement than you initially believed. But none of that means it cannot be done. None of that means you have to settle for mediocrity.

Your predecessor may not have challenged his staff to do their best and push the envelope of their abilities. The status quo may have been good enough for him. He may even have been afraid of letting his top staffers grow to their full potential for fear that they would eclipse him. No matter what the cause, an unchallenged staff performing below their best is a staff that needs to hear from you that more is expected from them. Offer them your time and guidance.

Your top managers should now know that more is expected of them than may have been required in the past. If they need direction, you will provide it. Nevertheless, your expectations for personal accountability, competency and work ethics will not be lowered. Regardless of what happened (or didn't happen) in the past, a new day has dawned and there are objectives to meet.

Everyone will be expected to pull his share of the load. "I have not done this before" will not be a valid excuse not to do it now.

If your people truly do need training beyond what you have time personally to provide you are obligated to help them obtain it. They may require both time and funding to acquire the skills you want them to demonstrate. Having provided both, you now have the right to require performance that meets your expectations.

"I am not saying my staff was lazy," said one new chief.

"Actually, they were pretty competent people. There was simply a very laid-back atmosphere when I got here. No one had expected very much of them. I made it clear they were going to come up to my expectations; I wasn't going to drop to the ones they were used to. It took a while for them to understand that I meant what I said. Now we understand each other fine."

Your people probably have more strengths than they or you realize. Hold them accountable for excellence and you just might see more of it. Be willing to give them some time to get there, even though it may slow your schedule for change a little. You may be pleasantly surprised at the results.

START PREPARING THE NEXT GENERATION OF LEADERS

As chief, one of your jobs is to start readying your replacement to assume your duties one day. National and even regional searches for a new law enforcement chief executive are expensive, time-consuming and stressful for any headless police agency. If at all possible, staying inside the organization to pick its next leader avoids many of these problems.

Take the time to teach your command staff what you know. Lead by example and demonstrate for them the positive behavior you want them to copy. If they need additional leadership schooling, try to help them obtain it. There are good leadership schools available, including the FBI's National Academy and the Senior Management Institute for Police sponsored by the Police Executive Research Forum. There are others.

Take the time to explain *why* you embarked on a given course of action or made a certain decision, particularly when either was unusual or contrary to what you might have been expected to do. Your people are probably learning a lot more from watching you than either you or they realize. Be sure that what you are showing them is what you want them to copy.

You and your command staff also are responsible for developing your agency's next generation of first-line supervisors and mid-managers. There is not an American law enforcement agency that has too many competent sergeants, lieutenants, commanders and civilian managers. Again, it is your job to help assure a steady stream of quality replacements for today's leaders.

Over time, if you are doing that job really well the department's effectiveness, efficiency and character will not deteriorate when a veteran leader leaves. In the world that you are seeking, that steadiness should continue even when the top leader (you!) moves on.

Like the very old man who plants fruit trees, you are doing the right thing, the noble thing, when you prepare the way for those who come after you. It is what a leader does.

DEVELOP A REPUTATION FOR TRUST AND RELIABILITY

You know how important it is to serve as an excellent role model for those you would lead. No example you set is more important than the one you establish for your staff as a leader whose reputation for trust and reliability is beyond reproach.

It may sound outdated and even corny in today's world where what someone says is at times no more than a matter of convenience. But say what you mean and mean what you say. It still works for an ethical, trustworthy leader. That's what you are.

Your staff and diverse others must know you as someone who tells the truth, even if the truth is inconvenient or unpleasant. They must be able to trust that you will do what you say you will do and refrain from doing what you say you won't. You must, in a word, be *believable* without exception.

Your personal reliability also must be beyond question. If you say you are going to ask your boss for something for your people, the task must get done even if you know doing so will drive him or her right through the ceiling. In this case, your reputation is more important than your personal comfort in front of your supervisor.

When you say that you will or will not do something, your staff members must be able to count on it as a certainty. If they are to relay to their subordinates what you have told them, they have to know that you will not embarrass them by changing plans without letting them know. Once you "burn" your staff with untruths or false promises you will make it less likely that they will believe you in the future. That lack of trust will contribute to a slippery slope that you don't want to be on.

DON'T ASSUME THAT YOUR STAFF KNOWS WHAT YOU KNOW

Even if you have all "grown up" within the same law enforcement organization, your staff's experiences and training are probably at least somewhat different from your own. If you have come in as chief from another department, particularly one in another part of the country, your differences from your staff may be considerable.

One new chief assumed that his top officers knew the value of documenting field interviews of suspicious characters encountered on the streets. They didn't. Another assumed the staff knew how to review internal investigations and determine fault and, where necessary, recommend disciplinary action. They did not–the prior chief had kept those tasks to himself. Yet another chief thought his managers knew the value of conducting debriefings following major, critical incidents. That practice, as it turned out, had not been part of their prior experience.

You are already aware of the danger of making assumptions when it comes to officer safety. Danger of another kind also can be found in assuming that your staff knows what you know, and is willing to apply that knowledge to decision-making. In leadership as in officer survival, you cannot safely assume anything you do not know for a certainty. Doing so can be hazardous to your health–and the organization's.

Keep in mind that their failure to grasp something that you take for granted does not mean that your staffers are ignorant or lazy. That particular piece of knowledge or experience simply may never have come their way. You should only become really concerned if they fail to demonstrate the desired knowledge *after* you have made them aware of its importance. It is, after all, your task to let them know what is important to you if they truly do not understand. If you are unsure if they really don't know or are trying to pull the wool over your eyes, give them the benefit of the doubt–the first time. If they are being dishonest with you, that fact almost certainly will become evident soon enough. Then you can assess consequences for their poor choices.

Expect a lot from your people, but give them a fair chance to learn and perform to your expectations. The vast majority of them will not disappoint you.

LOOK TO YOUR STAFF'S TRAINING

Sometimes law enforcement bosses make the assumption that once an employee reaches a certain level in the organization–like captain or assistant chief, for instance–there is little more that he or she needs to learn. As you know, nothing could be further from the truth.

You have an obligation to obtain for your staff something more than additional experience. In today's era of tight training budgets, you may have to get really creative in sending your staffers to quality leadership schools. You also do not want to come across as favoring the brass over the frontline troops in awarding scarce training dollars. That's where the need for creativity comes in.

Let your staff know that you want them to further their leadership training, whether it comes via working on a college degree or attending conferences and seminars. Put it back on your staffers to find the session they are interested in and then identify the time and funding to get there.

Private as well as governmental grants are sometimes available to supplement local funds. Some law enforcement leaders are willing to pay their own way if their boss will give them "official business" time to attend. Be sure you are that kind of boss.

Innovative chiefs who have found themselves strapped for the funds to send their supervisors and managers away for specialized training have elected to bring the training home. You probably have considerable training expertise within your own department and geographic region. You may be a pretty good instructor yourself. Decide what you want your people to learn, organize the class and invite both instructors and students from nearby agencies. Become your own leadership training center. Learn from your first learning experience in order to do even better the next time.

Of course, when funds *are* available you should avail your managers of the opportunity to attend such top drawer schools as the FBI National Academy and PERF's Senior Management Institute for Police. Do not overlook the extensive course offerings of the International Association of Chiefs of Police, either. There are other high-quality regional as well as national courses out there. Government entities such as FEMA also put on good leadership classes from time to time.

Your leadership staff should not have trouble finding appropriate training and higher education, including on-line offerings. They just need to know that their boss values continuing education.

PERFORMANCE REVIEWS ARE IMPORTANT

If you are like most law enforcement CEOs, you have been known to rant about the importance of employee performance appraisals and the need to get them done on time–or else. You probably have told your managers and first-line supervisors that their people deserve to know how they are doing and how they can get better. And you probably have advised your subordinate leaders that their charges need to know that their supervisor considers these things important.

The performance review advice that you appropriately have given to your subordinate leaders applies to you, too. You should not assume that just because you have frequent contact with these people they somehow know precisely how they are doing and what you want them to do in the future. They probably do not, at least not to the extent that you may think.

A few law enforcement organizations still do not require performance reviews for top managers. That is a mistake. Even if your employer does not require it, complete annual, written performance appraisals for each of your "direct reports." Keep them permanently on file after sharing and discussing them with their recipients.

There probably will come a time when you want to reward exceptional performance or impose sanctions for inadequate work. The process will be much easier as well as more legally defensible if you have documented proof of performance in hand.

It is doubtful that you have advanced to this point in your career without experience in preparing accurate, comprehensive performance appraisal documents. This is not a book about how to do a performance review. There are, however, a few things to remember when recording for posterity the job performance of one of your top staff members.

First, remember that personal friendships must not enter into the performance review process. Be honest in your assessment. An evaluation that tells only part of the story may do more harm than good.

Second, let your subordinate know where he could do better. It is doubtful that anyone is beyond the possibility of improving his performance *somewhere,* so be honest and tell him what you wish he had already figured out for himself. After all, you have a personal interest in seeing him do an even better job.

Third, give your subordinate a chance to talk. An evaluation of job performance session should be a dialogue, not a diatribe. Ask him what you could do more or less of to better support your staffer. Ask your subordinate how you can do a better job. You are not bound to agree, but at least consider carefully what he tells you.

Finally, be sure that you and your immediate subordinates talk openly and honestly enough all the time so that the formal evaluation session does not spring any big surprises or "gotcha" moments. These are your people who are instrumental in helping you lead the organization. You do not want to antagonize them needlessly. The performance review session should result in an honest exchange, not a heated argument. Be prepared to take a break if anyone's emotions, yours included, begin to take control of the session.

Performance evaluations are indeed important. They are too important not to be undertaken as the serious exercise that they are. They are important for bosses, too.

DON'T ALLOW PERSONAL FRIENDSHIPS TO AFFECT YOUR DECISION-MAKING

The good news is that you can be boss and still have friends. The reality is that your friendships with subordinates are unlikely to remain exactly as before once you become the Big Boss.

The "outsider" chief probably has it easier than the man or woman who has spent a career rising through the ranks of the organization. The "outsider" is not saddled with the baggage that accompanies a career spent working with the people who are now to be subordinates. The outside individual's warts probably are not already known to his employees.

Certainly you can and should have friends from both inside and outside the law enforcement organization. You cannot and should not become a social outcast just because you are the boss. You still can go to dinner with your departmental friends and have a drink, if you want. You still can go fishing with your police buddies and have two or three. What you cannot do is go anywhere or do anything with your work companions and act like a fool. You are a role model, on-duty and off. You must not fail to act like one.

You also must remain aware that there are things inappropriate to discuss with your subordinates whether you are seated in the department conference room or in the corner booth at Joe's Pub. An obvious topic off-limits for discussion is your opinion of or your disagreement with your own boss. Another is the character or performance of another member of your staff who happens to be a peer or supervisor of your conversation partner. Your common sense and respect for common courtesy will aid you in identifying other topics for the not-to-be-discussed list.

Whether they are patrol officers or deputy chiefs, members of your department should not be singled out for special treatment because they happen to be your personal friends. They should not receive extra privileges and protection but neither should they be penalized in a well-intentioned effort to show impartiality. Reward their accomplishments and correct their shortcomings. Tell them the truth. When a friend is the subject of your decision-making, pause long enough to determine if your decision would be exactly the same for someone who did not enjoy a special relationship with the chief. Then, proceed with what your common sense and personal moral compass for fair play tell you to do.

REMOVE THE LIARS AND PLOTTERS– THEY WON'T GET BETTER

It is an unpleasant truth that oftentimes not everyone present in the organization has earned the right to be there. Sometimes people have to go to allow the organization to remain healthy or get better.

Law enforcement agencies cannot afford to tolerate dishonest people among their ranks. Dishonest people include those who are chronic liars. You know that applies to the cops who make the arrests, write the tickets and testify under oath in court. It holds especially true for those who would call themselves leaders.

A staff member or other manager who lies to you has forfeited your trust. He or she has no place in the organization that you are ultimately responsible for leading. Accidentally providing you with incorrect information is a mistake that could and should be forgiven. Deliberately engaging in the delivery of known-false information is an entirely different matter that points to a lack of character on the part of the purveyor.

You must have accurate information in order to do your difficult job well. You have no choice but to remove from your staff anyone who purposefully leads you away from the truth. He does not have the best interests of the agency or its leader at heart and has not earned the privilege of continued membership in the organization.

The tendency of most decent people, you among them, is to hope and pray that people known intentionally to have done bad things somehow will get better and not do bad things again. Sometimes that does happen. More often it does not.

To succeed in your role as leader you must have around you a corps of individuals you can trust always to do the right thing. While you cannot demand their loyalty to you as an individual, you must be able to require their loyalty to the position you hold, that of the leader of the organization. It has to be that way.

It is your job to let a misbehaving staff member know in a very clear way that he is not meeting your expectations and is headed for much more serious trouble. Depending upon the gravity of the infraction, you may give him the opportunity to prove that he has changed his ways and will not sin again. Then, if he does commit the same or a similar violation indicating lack of character or competency, it is time for him to go. He is not a wine; he probably will not get better with time. It is more likely that he will continue to sabotage what you are trying to accomplish.

There are many reasons why a staff member will plot against you. He wants the job you have. He never liked you. He's never liked *any* chief of police. He simply has a poisonous personality. No matter. Whatever the cause, the individual who clearly is actively opposing your efforts must go. Use whatever personnel machinery your employer has in place for removing an underperforming or nonperforming employee. Get HR and the employment law attorneys involved. But cut the cancer out of your organization before it sickens the whole body.

Removing incompetent or otherwise damaging people from the public safety agency is one of your most important roles as the organization's leader. The task becomes even more vital when the individual who needs removed is in a position where he can do the most harm: leadership.

Kind-hearted bosses have been known to shunt problem people whom they know mean them ill off to a remote part of the organization where it is hoped "they can't do much harm." Others have decided to continue to tolerate the offender because "he's a couple years from retirement anyway." These well-intentioned but ineffective strategies will permit the venom from these poisonous personalities to continue to weaken your organization. Do it right but do it now. Remove the incompetent, the unethical, the ill-intentioned leader from the organization that you will be held accountable for.

SOMETIMES CULTURE CHANGE MEANS SOME STAFF MUST GO

You already understand just how much damage truly ill-intentioned people can bring about for you and your organization. You know how much harm they can cause to the people you are responsible for leading. You also know that some of them cannot be "repaired." They simply are not going to get better.

Whether it is a restaurant or a police department, an organization is not changed radically overnight. Change in any organization starts with revisions in the way its human members think and do things, and that often requires basic change in the way they look at their jobs. You can instigate that positive change.

It is your responsibility as leader to both tell and show your people what you require of them. It is up to you to role model consistently the behavior you expect. You know that. But you cannot do it alone. If your employees observe you doing one thing while their other leaders are saying or doing something else, at least some of those employees are going to be confused. Some are going to do whatever feels right to them. If that does not happen to be what you want them to be doing, one or more of your staff members has just undone your efforts, intentionally or otherwise.

If you are advocating for the importance of, say, customer service, yet one of your staffers is saying or indicating by his actions that it's not that important, you should not be shocked when the action you desire fails to occur. Achieving an organizational goal requires that the leaders of the organization share that goal and make it clear that they do. If subordinate managers and supervisors cannot be brought via your honest efforts to advocate for what you want the organization to be, those leaders are an impediment to the progress you must have. Try again. If you cannot convince them of the importance of what you are all trying to do, they will delay or prevent the creation of the better organization you are building. You must deal with them effectively right now.

The truth is that complete culture change only occurs as some employees leave the organization. Although many first-line employees will alter their behavior if they hear and see a consistent message from you repeated enough times, others will not. You may be faced with waiting them out, assuming that they are otherwise performing their jobs in an acceptable fashion. Be patient and do not ease up on your efforts and expectations.

As noted, if you have evidence that members of your leadership staff are working to undermine your efforts, realize that they have to go. Understand, too, that your organization is not going to be transformed radically overnight. Be patient, but also be vigilant for detrimental conduct by your leadership staff that indicates intent to undo the good things you are doing. Act when you must to remove obstructions to doing the right thing.

Fixing is often preferable to firing. But not always.

SUMMARY

One of the most valuable tools you possess for leading your organization is your command staff. These people are your "direct reports," the individuals you personally supervise. Since you cannot do everything yourself (nor would you want to), you will depend on these top managers to translate your ideas, directions and hopes into reality. You need these people, and you need them to do a good job for you.

Leading your staff members where you want the organization to go is one of your most critical tasks as a leader. If they do not know where you want to go, they cannot guide their own subordinates in getting there.

The care and feeding of your staff members is critical if they are to carry out the mission you have set for them. You must be sure that they are in the right places to do the most good. You must assure that they are trained and supervised. You must guarantee that they have the right tools to carry out their assignments. And, finally, you must be willing to remove them if they prove to you that they cannot or will not do their important jobs.

Expect a lot of your staff. Take good care of them even as you hold them accountable. Do not accept that they cannot understand what is expected of them. Spend time with them as individuals and help them grow.

Also be willing to look past your current staff to the next generation of the organization's leaders. Help prepare them for increased responsibilities.

Always set an excellent example for them to emulate in everything you do. They are the future of law enforcement. One of them may replace you one day. You do not want all of your work to come to nothing because no one carried on the noble traditions after you were gone.

Your organization will rise or fall on the human framework you build to support and assist you. Be certain that you have built it strong.

POINTS TO REMEMBER

- Be sure that you have the correct people in the correct places to do the correct things.
- When you restructure or reorganize, have a very good reason for what you do.
- Allow your staff to disagree with you at the right time.
- Delegate but hold accountable those to whom you assign tasks.
- Do not expect less of your staff members just because they do not always meet your expectations.
- Be willing to teach and explain when your people do not understand what you want of them.
- Look beyond your present staff to begin preparing the agency's next generation of leaders.
- Be certain that your actions prove to your staff that they can trust and rely on you.
- Evaluate your staff members' job performance; be honest with each one when you do.
- Never allow personal friendships with staff members to influence your decisions about them.
- Accept that sometimes high-ranking officers cannot or will not support what you are trying to accomplish and must go.

Chapter 5

YOUR RELATIONS WITH YOUR EMPLOYEES

You can have a huge impact on the future of your law enforcement agency all by yourself. You must have a solid command staff and strong first-line supervisors to get where you want to go. But neither you nor all of these people put together can move the agency forward without the cooperation of the sworn and civilian employees who actually do the work of policing, day in and day out. You cannot reach your destination without them.

In virtually every law enforcement agency the vast majority of the employees wants to do the right thing. They may not all agree on exactly what the right thing happens to be, and that's where your role as their leader comes into play. It is up to you with the aid of your subordinate managers to show and tell them where the department is going and how you will all get there.

Police people do a good job of achieving the goals they are assigned *if* they understand what those goals are. With today's work force, it is also important that those asked to achieve the goals know why the goals are important. As their leader, you will make that clear to them. That is part of what a leader does.

It is doubtful that your people are going to help you reach your goals if your relations with those same people are poor, whatever the reason for the friction. If many of your employees either dislike or distrust you, your task of leading them is going to be difficult. It is certainly not necessary or likely that every one of your people will love you. But if a substantial number of them oppose what you are trying to do your job can become nightmarishly trying.

It is unreasonable to expect that you will have the active support and affection of every one of your employees. Few chiefs have ever enjoyed that distinction. Some of your people will actively support you and a few will just as energetically oppose you. For many, however, who the chief of the moment happens to be is not terribly important. They just want to be allowed to go about their jobs and live their lives without too much interference from the Big Boss. They are probably more concerned about the wants and foibles of their first-line supervisor than they are yours. Nonetheless, it is these people you will need to influence to get your own job done well.

No special magic is required to help you relate to and lead your employees. The skills you have honed as a caring, competent leader will be sufficient to get the job done. What follows is some common sense advice for getting your difficult job of leadership accomplished. Good relationships are, after all, the bread and butter of a good leader.

DON'T TRY TO BE A SUPERHERO

Just be yourself. It's plenty good enough. Except in the smallest of communities neither the citizens nor the cops expect the chief to be a street officer, detective, undercover operative and SWAT guy all rolled into one. They will not expect you to spend your days at your desk and your nights working the street. You simply cannot do all of that stuff and retain either your physical or emotional health, so don't try.

Once upon a time in the Western U.S. there was an incredibly popular chief who had taken over a medium-sized police department from a rather lackluster predecessor. The chief seemed to be on-duty around the clock. He attended the expected official functions during the day and then rode with the vice cops or narcs at night. He led the way on SWAT callouts and answered many calls with Patrol. The cops loved it.

Then one day the overstretched chief had a massive heart attack. Before long he left the department on a medical disability and shortly thereafter he died. The poor man was mortal. He was not a superhero. His people missed him terribly.

Credit your employees and your citizens with enough sense to realize that today's chief of police has a job that is more demanding and more complex than ever before. While all of them will expect you to have a cop's street sense and be capable of doing the job of a front-line officer in a pinch, few will expect you to chase felons and kick down doors on a daily basis.

Do not set higher standards and expectations for yourself than are reasonable. Do not expect to be everything for everyone 24 hours a day. Being an average cop who happens to be a great leader should do just fine. You are being paid to lead your people to, among other things, catch crooks. No one expects you to catch them all by yourself.

DON'T ATTEMPT TO PLEASE EVERYONE, ALL THE TIME

As the new chief you will hear a lot from many people, both inside your organization and out. You will hear some good ideas and a lot of not-so-good ones. You will get plenty of advice from your first day on the job until the last hours you spend there.

People will want you to do things for them. Some of those things will be the sort that a good law enforcement leader *should* do. Others won't be. A few requests may be downright unethical or otherwise improper. It will be up to you to sort your way through all of these requests and entreaties in deciding upon a proper course of action.

Experience likely has taught you by now that you will be unable to please everyone on the inside of your organization, much less those on the outside, too. You already know that the act of giving one person something he wants may greatly anger another, who wanted the chief to do something else. That's just life in the real world.

Do not try to give everyone everything he or she wants. It is neither possible nor desirable. Some of what they want may, in fact, be bad for the organization or even the person who wants it.

If you are the new chief, expect some old suggestions that have been brought forward and rejected previously to be trotted out again and presented to the new guy. That's alright. There may be some good ideas you want to try out among the swarm of proposals you are presented. There may be a few that were rejected for the wrong reasons. Others probably were quite properly turned down. You will not know which is which until you listen attentively.

Life has taught you by now that you can never please everyone. Nor should you try. Some always will be happy with strawberry while others want vanilla. If you have determined through honest evaluation that "strawberry" is best for the organization and the community you serve, go for it. Don't feel obligated to offer "vanilla" the next time. That flavor may never be the right choice for your local situation.

DON'T TRY TO FIX EVERYTHING ANYONE EVER COMPLAINS ABOUT

It is important to hear what your employees, commissioned and civilian, have to say about themselves, their organization and their role in that organization. They all need a chance to vent their feelings to the boss every now and again.

It is especially necessary that a new chief establish and communicate an open door policy for each of his employees to spend half an hour or so with the boss. Unless you are head of a really small department, you may want to have a secretary or aide schedule the appointments around your busy days. You cannot handle all of the details by yourself.

Listen to what your people have to say. Many will not necessarily expect action on their gripe. They just want to know that they have voiced it to the person at the top. Listen attentively and without becoming defensive. Your role is to listen more than talk. If you need to get back to an employee with an answer to a question or request, be sure that you keep your word to do so. Respond immediately where you can.

Don't promise to change most things until you confirm with your staff that the situation actually *is* as reported. Also, first confirm that a requested change really would have the positive results claimed. Beware of unintended consequences. Removing a given task from Patrol may unacceptably increase the workload in Investigations. Shortening report narratives may save time for patrol officers but create more work for detectives, who now have insufficient data to work from. Think and consider before you leap or even promise to leap.

You have heard the old saying that the boss only needs to worry when he fails to hear *anybody* complaining about *anything*. That happy state of affairs is simply not normal for most human beings. If they are voicing no complaints at all it may be that your troops have given up on your ability or willingness to help them. That bodes ill. Some griping, then, is natural and to be expected. It does not signal that a "no confidence" vote for the chief is just around the corner.

Trying to fix anything and everything that anyone complains about is impractical and inadvisable. It is unlikely that you or anyone who eventually replaces you can ever satisfy all hands all the time. Find out how many others appear to share a complainer's issue and evaluate it for its degree of actual impact on the organization. Be prepared to let some of the "little stuff" go, at least while more important issues are addressed first. There may be time to take another look later.

Trying to fix everything could lead to a shotgun problem-solving approach that causes you to neglect the urgent things that really need fixing. Don't do it.

SEEK RESPECT, NOT LOVE

You have heard it before, and it is still true. No matter how wonderful a person you are, no matter how close to sainthood you may be, it is highly unlikely that everyone will think favorably of you. Both inside and outside the law enforcement organization there probably will be people who wish you ill. A rabid few may literally wish you dead. Some people really can be that mean-spirited.

Do your best to be a fair, honorable, decent human being. You owe that to yourself, your employees and the greater world at large. Having done so, try to be content. Recognize that not everybody will grant you their affection, no matter how much you may deserve it.

What you *are* seeking both inside your organization and beyond it is recognition that you have treated others in precisely the manner you would wish to be treated yourself. You want to be seen as someone who is just and fair in the way he handles people issues on the inside and outside of the police department.

One chief put it thusly:

> When I got here my mostly-young cops did pretty much what they wanted because the old chief was too engrossed in his retirement business to rein them in. It was obvious to me that some of them actually wanted some boundaries set. I did that and enforced them. It cost a few of them some time off before they figured out I meant business. Now they follow the rules and we've got a much better department. I can't guarantee you any of them love me, but I think I have got their respect. I treated every one of them the same when it came to discipline, and they know that.

If some of your people do love you, consider that to be a major bonus. You may indeed be a special person. But be willing to settle for their respect. That, too, will take you a long distance down the road to building a solid, professional police agency.

REALIZE SOME WILL SUPPORT, SOME WILL OPPOSE, MANY JUST DON'T CARE

As a brand new police officer you had your own list of things that really interested and motivated you. You probably found the job exciting and wanted to catch bad guys. You wanted your peers to know that you were courageous and could be counted on in a fight. You probably sought to please your sergeant and dreaded the prospect of disappointing him.

As for the chief of police, he probably was not all that important a figure in your young life. You did not see him all that often and were not all that excited about what he did as long as whatever it was did not reach out and touch you in a bad way. The chief was, in a word, *irrelevant* to you most of the time.

Thinking back on your own early days as a cop, you should not be too surprised to learn that's the way many of your people see you now. Their first-line supervisor is a lot more important than you are in their world. Many of them simply don't give a fat fig about you, one way or the other.

There are exceptions, of course. The conversation you had with a young officer or the note you sent him about the good work he did may have transformed him into a friend and supporter for life. That's great. Keep providing those personal touches.

There is the other side of the coin, too. There is the employee who you, in his mind, unjustly corrected or otherwise "mistreated." He is willing to be your enemy for life. He'd be happy to see you fired, but he'd be downright ecstatic to see you run over by a truck. He does not like you, and never will.

Your top staff and managers likely can be divided up the same way. Many support what you are doing with the department and will strive to help you. A few, perhaps among them one or two who want your job, would not be distressed to see you fail. Most, like the mass of your employees, may be somewhere in the middle of the pack. They will support you as long as things look to be going pretty well. They will back you as long as you appear to be in firm control of the department. That is a particularly good reason for not only being in control but looking like you are. You should never give the impression that you are planning to leave anytime soon.

The key for you, of course, is not performing in such a manner that the police people in the "big middle" will be motivated to oppose you. By being fair and showing sincere interest in the welfare of your employees you help to ensure that the "big middle" stays with you, or at minimum does not actively oppose you.

That same scenario can be applied to the community as a whole. Many people who have had the opportunity to meet you like you and support what you are trying to do in the community. Some may even be quite vocal with their support. Another, smaller group does not care for you. Whether each of these folks received a traffic ticket or their kid got busted really does not matter. They didn't like the last chief and won't like the one that follows you, either. A few of them are plenty vocal, too.

Again, most of the people are in the middle and are relatively indifferent on the topic of their chief of police. Many do not know who their police chief is, and just as many don't care. As long as you avoid doing stupid things most of these people will leave you alone. They just want to be allowed to live their lives in relative safety. They want the cops to come instantly when they call and give the tickets to the other guy who richly deserves them.

The good news is that, like most of your employees, this last group can be motivated to assist you and your officers for a good cause, well-publicized and explained by you and your department. Many of these people want to help the good guys by doing their civic duty, if you'll just channel their energies in the right direction. Do not overlook these "uninvolved" citizens. They have the potential to help you.

Realizing the variety of audiences you have watching your performance should provide you with plenty of evidence of the political nature of the world you work in. But none of those audiences have quite the potential for doing you good or ill as the group you know as your employees. Staying in close touch with the members of that audience can mean all the difference between success and failure for your plans–and yourself.

DON'T BECOME INVISIBLE WHEN THE NEWS IS BAD

When things get tough, people want to see their leader acting like one. That means you need to be seen at the front of your organization anytime things get dicey. Your employees have a right to expect it.

At times, being out front can be taken literally. If there is civil unrest in the streets, you should be out in those same streets with your officers. That does not necessarily mean you must literally lead them–you may have tactical unit commanders who can perform that task better than you. Nonetheless, you must be visibly present with your people, prepared to make or approve key decisions if called upon.

You also must be highly visible and out front as the police department's primary spokesperson when bad news touches your department. This negative news media reporting could result from a "bad" police shooting, a high-speed pursuit that ended tragically or unlawful or immoral behavior by a police employee. While you may use a police Public Information Officer to report run-of-the-mill cop shop news, bad tidings involving your agency and its people merit your personal handling.

As uncomfortable as it may feel, it is your job to face the cameras, microphones and tough questions. At such a moment, your employees and your citizens won't like it if their police leader looks like he is hiding behind his people. They will be even less happy if it appears that the chief literally is hiding and refusing to meet with the press at all.

Regardless of what caused the bad news, you are the one who should stand in front of the bright lights and answer the tough questions. It is you who should take the calls of reporters who are uniformly insistent and sometimes rude. You are the leader, and effectively responding to bad news is part of your job. Once more, your employees expect it.

If the negative news reporting involves your own actions, responding honestly and openly becomes even more difficult–and important. It must be done. Be sure that your boss knows that the bad news is coming and what caused it. You do not like front-page surprises; odds are your supervisor doesn't, either.

Here is another piece of absolutely essential advice for responding to bad news: Tell the truth. Always. If you cannot or will not answer a particular question, say so and explain why. (The investigation is continuing, it's a personnel matter, or whatever the case may be.) Never say "no comment." It makes you sound like a gangster in front of a Congressional committee. There are better ways of saying essentially the same thing.

Get out front. Be seen as being out front. Stay there until the crisis has passed. Act like the true leader you are. Confront hard times or bad news head-on. And realize that both *will* pass.

WEAR YOUR UNIFORM A LOT

To repeat: It is important that you act and look like a leader. You are the police chief, not the water department director or the city manager. Police chiefs traditionally wear a uniform, at least some of the time. Plan to wear yours a lot.

Your community may have an expectation about how often they will see the chief in uniform. Some people don't care one way or the other, but many do. From your interactions with your citizens you will be able to gauge their expectations to at least some extent. It's likely quite a few will want to see their top cop *looking* like a policeman, at least much of the time.

Your officers probably care more about how you look than they may be willing to admit. Especially your patrol officers want to see you donning the same duds they have to wear. If you are a working chief in a small department, it is even more important that you put on the clothes that announce you as an officer of the law. Quick recognition could even contribute to your personal safety.

Your officers and your community should not see you in uniform only when you have a funeral or other official function to attend. Rather, they should get accustomed to seeing you dressed that way.

You have heard the bit about dressing for success. For you, the police chief, that means wearing your uniform often.

RESPOND ON SOME CALLS, BUT STAY OUT OF THE WAY

Your people want to know that you are interested in what they are doing. They will not, however, appreciate your finding extra work for them on a regular basis. Stop by and offer to help out if your officers are handling a call and you happen to be near. If it's clear that they don't need you, touch base and be on your way. But do not make a habit of pulling over drivers for minor traffic violations and then calling for an officer to deal with the infraction. That sort of help probably won't be appreciated if it happens too often.

Expectations for what you do on the street change, of course, if you are a working chief in a small department. There you will be expected cheerfully to handle your share of the work without pulling rank to get out of it. You will be expected to role model the officer safety, customer service and work ethic that you demand of your employees. You will, in other words, have an excellent opportunity to show your officers how the job should be done. You cannot afford to miss such a teaching moment.

As the leader of a larger department you still have the important responsibility of demonstrating for your people exactly what you mean when you insist on "exceptional customer service" or "excellent street survival skills." Be sure to do it right. If you realize that you have fallen short in some area (skills *can* get rusty) let your watching personnel know that you realize you erred. Maintaining your credibility with your employees requires such brutal honesty on your part.

Realize, too, that your presence on an incident scene may cause the officers or citizens involved to assume that you have taken charge. If you are assuming command, whatever the reason, say so. (This should not happen often.) Otherwise, make it clear that Officer X or Sergeant Y remains in command and you are simply there to assist with the grunt work. You really *can* still direct traffic or man the corner of a perimeter, you know.

MAINTAIN CONTACT WITH THE UNION, BUT DON'T PANDER

If your agency has a union or police officers' association it is vital that you maintain good communication with its leaders. Some chiefs have chosen to join the local organization as a show of support, but you will have to assess the jurisdiction's politics and your boss's feelings on that one.

Make it plain to the union's leaders that you want to meet on a regular basis. Then, stick to the schedule as a clear indicator that these exchanges of information are important to you. By hearing about the issues that are of current interest to your people you will help yourself avoid at least some of the surprises that chiefs don't like. Consider bringing your top staff to these meetings so that they do not feel left out. They also should be able to answer some of the union representatives' questions on the spot whereas you might have to return with an answer later.

If you do need to do some research or checking with your staff before you can respond to a union query, say so and promise to get back in a timely manner. Then, keep your pledge. These sessions and your follow-up to them will help build your reputation for trust and credibility–or your lack of same. Be sure the impression you leave is a positive one.

Naturally, you cannot and should not attempt to satisfy every request or demand your employee group makes. Some of their wants simply won't make sense from an organization-wide standpoint. Others will not be financially affordable or would, if granted, strip away an employer's right that you want to keep. Your union's officers will not expect that all of their requests will be granted.

Remember that is neither necessary nor desirable to give your union reps everything that one of their members asks for. They don't expect that you will. They, too, realize that some requests are unreasonable. Some issues they are bringing forward only because they feel it is their job as ethical representatives of the membership to do so. The union's officers will not respect you if they sense you are trying to pander to the membership.

Stand up for what you believe to be right. Do not waiver on the important things you expect from the organization and its members, union-affiliated and otherwise. Remain courteous and respectful to the employee association's representatives at all times, even if the people across the table occasionally fail to follow your lead. As you already know, when it comes to your relations with *all* of your employees respect is to be sought ahead of affection. A successful chief must have the former; the latter is an add-on bonus.

REALIZE THE IMPORTANCE OF OFFICER SAFETY AND GOOD EQUIPMENT

If you were like most street cops, going home at the end of your shift with no additional holes in your body was your most important objective. You probably believed that the equipment you were issued to get your job done safely had a lot to do with whether or not you made it home without added bodily apertures. You expected your department to supply that equipment and the street survival training that went with it.

As chief, you can assume that your officers want the same assurances that you did. They want to know that they are properly equipped to do their jobs as safely as possible. They want good cars and top-notch body armor. They expect good weaponry and reliable radio communication. And they expect you to guarantee all of this for them.

Many of your cops will take for granted that their employer will get the best he can for them. They may not grant you any points for doing so. But they certainly will hold it against you if they decide you are cutting corners at the expense of their well-being. They also will take note if you spend instead for what they see as frivolous things that only benefit the brass or "community relations."

In tough budget times it is harder than ever to run a law enforcement agency. You will find yourself pulled in several different directions by real needs that you simply do not have the dollars to meet. As you make the difficult decisions on where to spend and where to defer spending know that your people are watching you. Next to salary and benefits, how they are equipped to do their jobs occupies a high spot among the concerns of your first-line officers and their supervisors.

It is the unusual chief who can purchase everything that his people desire. That seldom happens. But your employees will expect that you do as much as you can with the funding you have. You may not be able to buy everyone new body armor this budget year, but you can begin by replacing the oldest vests. You may not be able to afford a personal patrol rifle for each officer, but you may be able to establish a pool of weapons that can be checked out for duty. Always do the best you can with what you do have.

Do not overlook the expertise that exists in your own agency when it comes time to buy or replace equipment. User input is important if the majority of your people are going to support the choices. Every agency has its share of "equipment geeks." Get their opinions, but all of you should realize that their every wish is unlikely to be granted. Again, do the best you can with the financial support you have available. Next year, try to do more.

Taking care of their legitimate equipment needs is one way you can provide your people with tangible evidence that you mean it when you say you will support them. Always do the best you can in this crucial area.

MEET ALL YOUR PEOPLE–SET EXPECTATIONS EARLY

It has already been noted that you need to sit down with as many of your employees as you can as early in your tenure as possible. You are there to listen more than talk. But it is also important for you to use this time to lay out where you are taking the department and each employee's role in the journey.

Let your employees know your goals. They are now the department's goals. Let them know how they can help the department achieve those goals. Let them see that you'll be role modeling the behavior you expect and what that behavior is. Allow time for questions and clarifications. Not everyone will buy into it right away, particularly if what you are expecting is different from what was expected in the past.

One new chief learned from one-on-one meetings with his employees that his predecessor expected only that his people stay out of trouble and thus not focus attention on him or the department. Enforcement action was not encouraged, as it might lead to complaints. The new chief had to repeat time and time again that he wanted to see active but courteous cops who made lots of solid arrests and wrote good tickets.

Repetition will be a valuable tool for you. Be prepared to state over and over the goals of the department. Be ready to repeat often the attitude and values you expect your employees to demonstrate. Be sure you constantly role model both. Speak it, write it, advocate for it. Do each many times over. Require your staff to do the same. Do not let up. Reinforce your message every time you have a new opportunity to meet with an employee. Do the same in front of employee groups.

Be consistent in your message. Do not tell your sworn one thing and your civilians another. All are equally capable of delivering, for example, courteous customer service. Do not exempt any individual or group from your high expectations. Demand it, expect it, reward it. But the whole process begins when you meet with your people.

Do not limit yourself to meeting with your people only when you are their new leader. Tenured chiefs need to know what their people are thinking, too. Set up opportunities to meet with your personnel both one-on-one and in groups from time to time. Getting too comfortable by *assuming* you know what they are thinking can get you into serious trouble. Do not interpret apparent apathy as a sign of support. It isn't. Keep communicating with your people, instead.

DON'T IMPLEMENT CHANGE MORE QUICKLY THAN YOUR PEOPLE CAN ABSORB IT

People find comfort in the familiar, even if the familiar is sometimes less than an ideal state of affairs. All change–even change for the better–is potentially stressful for those who will be directly affected by it.

You are almost certainly going to make changes in the organization, regardless of whether you are a new chief or a veteran leader. You will require your employees' help and cooperation if those changes are to work out as intended. To accomplish that, you need them to be as comfortable as possible with what they are being asked to do. If you want them to support change, you would be well-advised to let them know exactly how it will make their lives better. The work will get done quicker. There will be fewer errors to fix. There will be fewer citizen complaints. Fewer officers will be injured. Whatever the case, let your people know how change will affect them, hopefully in a positive way. Be prepared to repeat the message–a lot.

Using the chain of command, let your people know beforehand when change is coming. Tell them why it is needed. Let them know the results you expect. Do your best to be sure everyone understands. Then, go ahead. Monitor the results for needed revisions or additional clarifications. Have the courage to abandon an adequately-tested change that clearly does not work well.

A little grumbling is normal in any organization. But if the grumbling about change(s) is building to a dull roar you may have trouble on your hands. If significant numbers of your people are confused about what they are supposed to be doing and don't seem to be getting any less confused over time, additional action may be required. That action may consist of more detailed explanation, clarifications or revision of the original change. But it also may call for more than that.

Continuing confusion in the organization that includes obvious employee resistance may indicate that it is time to slow the pace of change. That does not mean that you should abandon your mandate for continuing, positive change. It *may* mean that you should slow down until your people catch up with you.

Rely on your managers and supervisors to tell you if change is moving faster than the employee on the front-line can assimilate it. But do not assume they will come to you voluntarily with this information. They know you expect change and may be reluctant to tell you that there's trouble in paradise. *Ask them* if change is stirring up major people problems and serious dissent. Weigh carefully what they tell you.

Be willing to apply the brakes a little as opposed to confronting a full-scale revolt. Slow the pace of change even as you continue to move the organization forward. Be prepared to take a breather before resuming the journey at a little lower speed.

TAKE TIME TO LISTEN

You have a lot of things to cram into your very busy work day. As a consequence, the temptation may be strong to brush off the employee who wants a moment of your time in the parking lot, the hallway or over the telephone or e-mail.

It is very important that you manage your time well. Lengthy gossip and bull stuff sessions can indeed keep you from the more important tasks you must handle. At the same time, reliable information is power. It is hard to get too much of it. That is especially true for the chief law enforcer of the community.

Even as you manage your minutes, it is important to give some time to those who want to talk with you. Do not avoid them. Find out where they are going with the conversation as quickly and courteously as you can. You may want to connect them with someone else for what they need. It's to their advantage and yours that you find this out as quickly as possible.

Listen, but try to keep your communication partner on topic. Steer a wandering speaker back to the subject at hand. Ask questions, as necessary, to clarify his or her meaning. Find out, in other words, what it is the individual wants you to know or do. Then you can start to bring the conversation to a polite conclusion. Realize that the speaker may be quite pleased by his audience with the chief and will be reluctant to surrender your attention. For that reason the burden may fall upon you to end the conversation eventually by begging off for a waiting meeting or appointment.

Try to answer personally as many phone calls and e-mails as you can. You will realize from the subject matter of some that they were meant for someone else in the organization and can be delegated. (Salespersons' messages fall into that category.) Recognize, however, that you will build support both inside and outside your department by granting as many people as you can some time with the chief, even if that time is closely measured. You must avoid isolating yourself in your office.

Good ideas and revelations can come from the least-expected places. For that reason you will be doing yourself a favor by taking the time to really listen to what you are told. It is also the *nice* and right thing to do.

DON'T FORGET THE PERSONAL TOUCHES

To be a successful chief, you must be more than a figurehead perched on the top limb of the organization chart. Your people want to see you as a likeable human being, too.

There is no requirement that you be the best friend of each of your employees. It is not even required that all of them like you. But it will make it immeasurably easier for you to lead your people if they see you as a person who does some things that they deem positive.

The list of things you can do to assure people that you really are interested in them as individuals is practically endless. Books have been written on the topic. You doubtlessly will be able to come up with things that no one else has even thought of yet. The idea is to treat others–your employees, in this case–in a manner that tells them you really do care. It is the old Golden Rule principle all over again.

Employees like to hear you use their names. They like for you to at least acknowledge their existence when you encounter them in the hallway or parking lot. Many appreciate a smile or a wave when conversation is impractical. And virtually all like to hear a kind word when they are having a tough day.

You naturally should attend the services when the spouse or child of one of your employees passes away. You should send a note of condolences when you learn that a parent or other close family member of one of your people has died. Visits to the hospital are a good idea when one of your people is there for more than a day or so and visitors are allowed. A trip to the emergency room is advisable for you when one of your people is there with significant injuries.

Allow your common sense to guide you in what you need to do and when. Personal notes from the chief are a good idea when an employee has done exceptional work or overcome a major challenge. With today's generation of new employees, an e-mail message from the boss can serve much the same purpose. The point is that you have cared enough to make the contact or do *something* you otherwise would not have done for someone else.

Be as innovative as you want in letting your people know that you are thinking of them and are aware of their triumphs and tragedies. Never overlook the value of the personal touch from the heart.

BE FRIENDLY, BE APPROACHABLE, BUT DON'T SELL USED CARS

One police administrator was known to wear an almost-perpetual frown. If he spoke to his line-level troops at all, it was in brief, clipped exchanges. In sum, he was not a very pleasant fellow to be around. He apparently felt he needed to don that persona to distance himself from his officers. He succeeded.

Every leader has his or her own personality, his or her own way of approaching and responding to others. It is doubtful that you are going to change yours to a radical extent now. It *is* possible, however, to reinforce the good things you are doing and minimize the distracting ones.

Unlike the ill-advised boss referred to previously, you must be approachable to people inside and outside the police department. Your employees and your citizens both expect and deserve that. While it should not reach the dimensions of a clown's, a sincere smile from you is probably not too much to ask, either.

Inasmuch as you are the designated and formal leader of your organization, people must be encouraged to approach you. Your demeanor, expression and manner of speech all can help answer that need–or frustrate it. Frustration is not what you are seeking in the people who follow you.

At the same time, you do not want to come across as a carnival barker or the slicer-dicer sales guy in the late-night television commercial. Most people, especially cops, are quick to pick up on insincerity. Being labeled a fake is the last thing you need as a leader. Smiling is good. Shaking hands and patting people on the back is nice. Remembering their name and using it is appreciated. Just do not overdo it and let yourself be transformed into a uniformed used car salesman by overexuberance.

Most people, your employees included, have an image in mind of what the top cop should look and sound like. Command presence and a military bearing can contribute to a very favorable impression for many. A courteous manner and a pleasant smile that says "you can approach me, I don't bite" will help, as well. Anything and everything that transmits "I am a decent human being and a nice person" contributes, too.

You do not have to overdo it. Leave that to the guy with the bad hair and cheap suit who sold you your last clunker. Just be nice!

SUMMARY

More than a few police leaders who had some excellent ideas for the betterment of their agency and the profession failed to accomplish them. Some of those CEOs were shown the door following relatively brief and tumultuous careers at the helm of an organization. Some left due to politics, others departed due to events beyond their control. But more than one or two exited because of poor relations with their most precious resource: their employees.

Getting along reasonably well with the people you lead requires neither luck nor magic. It *does* require a good supply of common sense and the willingness to treat employees in the manner in which you would like to be treated yourself: with fairness, empathy and a genuine willingness to engage in two-way communication.

This chapter has discussed some "little things" you can do to improve the connection you have with your people. Memorize them, do them. Taken all together, they paint a picture of you as the caring, competent police leader that you are. Performing in this manner also identifies you as a very decent person. In a field where serving as a positive role model means everything, you can hardly go wrong.

Your organization can never be any better than you are. Assure that your employees always experience you at your best.

POINTS TO REMEMBER

- Your people will not expect you to be the sharpest cop on the street, but they will expect you to be able to function as a law enforcement officer when required.
- You will make yourself crazy if you try to please everyone and fix everything anyone gripes about.
- You should work to earn your employees' respect, not their affection.
- Always be out front when controversy erupts or the department is under attack.
- Looking and acting like a cop means that you should wear your uniform at least some of the time.
- Show up on the street on occasion but allow your officers to maintain control of their calls whenever possible.
- If your department has a union, meet regularly with the leaders to maintain open communication.
- Realize the importance of officer safety and good equipment for your people. Assure that both are emphasized in your department.
- Meet one-on-one with as many of your people as you can. Listen to their concerns and tell them your expectations.
- Remember the "little things," like attending funerals and sending notes of appreciation or condolences to your people.
- If you sense that your people are very uneasy with rapid change, slow things down but keep moving forward.
- Be friendly and approachable to all, but do not overdo it and come across as insincere.

Chapter 6

PRIORITY ONE: YOUR EMPLOYEES' WELFARE

You have important obligations to your community. You have equally vital responsibilities to your boss. But there is nothing that you do or will do that is more urgent than looking to the well-being of the members of your organization.

Taking care of your people extends well beyond pursuing fair salaries and benefits for them, as important as these considerations are. You also must be aware of their equipment and training needs as well as their physical and emotional health requirements. You must stand up and represent your employees when they are under attack in the press or the community, too.

Supporting your people at all times does not mean lying for them or insisting that they were correct when you know for a fact that they erred. You also support them when you tell the truth and thereby help maintain the integrity and credibility of the agency. That is just as important as getting them an extra patrol car or a pay raise.

In this chapter some of the subjects from the previous one will be revisited. That is not by accident. What you do to keep your employees safe and see to their other needs is *that* important to their welfare–and your own future as their leader.

OFFICER SAFETY IS VITAL

The very first rule of officer safety is treating other people properly. You know that. Officer safety and good police-community relations are not polar opposites but actually work hand-in-hand. You know that, too. It is up to you to make both of those realities equally clear to your officers.

At the same time, your experience has taught you that for a small segment of society not any amount of good will and courtesy will dissuade them from their willingness to cause harm to a law enforcement officer. It is for those individuals that your officers' survival tactics and techniques must be well-honed. Your officers' need to go home in good health at the end of their watch must always trump the bad guys' plans to cause injury and mayhem.

You should make it clear to your staff and subordinate supervisors that your officers' safety always takes precedence over the need to save on manpower, reduce overtime or clear a contact quickly in order to go on to the next one. Street supervisors as well as dispatch personnel must be aware of the importance of assigning back-up help any time an officer is involved in a potentially hazardous call. This requirement for adequate back-up or cover must be built into your agency's policies and procedures and enforced by patrol sergeants and communications center bosses.

Likewise, your training staff must be conscious of the critical importance of officer safety tactics and procedures and the mandate that they stress the importance of officer safety to their charges. This is especially important for those who serve as field training officers and supervisors. It must be clear that speed in handling an assignment or the "need" to prove one's mettle are always subordinate to good officer survival practices. It is also vital that supervisors hold veteran police officers to the same officer safety expectations placed on slick-sleeved rookies. Indeed, you have a right to expect more, not less, in officer safety from these "old salts." Seniority carries with it the obligation to set a good example, not a poor one. You have both the right and the obligation to come down hard on the veteran officer or supervisor who is not serving as an excellent example for officer safety as practiced in the real world.

ROLE MODEL THE SAFE BEHAVIOR YOU EXPECT

You know that your people are watching you. You realize that you must set a good example of the behavior that you want to see repeated. In no aspect of your work is that more important than in the safety practices that you display for your officers to witness.

You are responsible for handling and carrying safely the lethal and less-lethal weapons that you are issued as a part of your job as a peace officer. That holds true both at the training site and in your daily activities. If you are going to bark at your investigators or staff personnel for not carrying their weapons, you can ill-afford to go around unarmed on-duty yourself. Bad guys seldom announce that they are coming, nor do they excuse the chief from becoming a target of their ill intent.

If you back-up your officers on the street on occasion, be certain that you are on your very best safety behavior. Watch your approach and positioning.

Stay alert for the danger signs. Don't make dangerous assumptions or otherwise become careless or complacent. Follow excellent weapon retention practices. Don't get too close, too soon. It's what you expect of your people. You cannot afford to do less. Expect them to ridicule you if you do.

Role model excellent accident prevention behavior, too. Handle all weapons in a safe manner. Take no foolish chances around suspicious items that could be explosive devices or biological threats. Operate your police vehicle in a cautious, safe manner that you want your people to see and emulate. Wear your seat belt when driving the vehicle.

Wear your body armor when you are working the street. Do not take any chances with *any* situation that you would not want your people to take. You are the role model and your behavior for good or ill always is on display.

MAKE SAFETY EQUIPMENT A PRIORITY

You will not be able to purchase everything you or your people would like to have. No chief is ever able to do that. The various demands pulling at the leader of a modern law enforcement agency are simply too numerous to permit it. As a result, it will fall to you, the leader, to determine what you can obtain, and in what quantity and time frame.

You may, for instance, decide that the purchase of the latest body armor for your SWAT team is something you must do. Next you will have to determine if your available funding, grant-assisted or otherwise, will permit you to buy it all at once. Otherwise, you may be forced to buy some of this vital safety gear this year while the rest will have to wait for the next budget cycle.

It is fair to assume that your employees most at risk (for present purposes, your SWAT operators) will want the best that money can buy. They will, for instance, want a set of new body armor for everyone and they will want it now. There should be no greater concern for you than your peoples' safety. If you can get the gear they want and get it immediately that obviously will be your first choice. If you cannot do it that way, whatever the reason, you should let your troops know that. They need to know the prohibiting reason(s), as well.

Obtaining the best weaponry, armor, vehicles and other safety-related gear always should be your priority as the agency's leader. Do it whenever you can. Give your people an honest explanation of "why" when you cannot. When you can't, be sure that you are not spending the money instead for a pet project of your own. In your troops' minds, doing so will make it appear that you value their safety less than you do your personal desires. Leaving that sort of impression with your employees almost certainly will return to haunt you.

If it is truly something that your people need to be safer, be willing to argue your position to your boss if you are prohibited from spending what you need to obtain it. Do it away from the presence of your employees. Avoid emotional arguments and implied threats. Rely instead upon facts and logic to make your point. No one wants to see an officer harmed if reasonably-obtainable safety equipment could have avoided that outcome. Your boss doubtlessly shares that view.

But pick your hill to die on. You will require your boss's support another day, perhaps to acquire some other item that will benefit your employees greatly. Do not burn your bridges or hopelessly alienate your supervisor. Reason, not emotion, should be your personal tool of choice for obtaining what your people really need.

FULFILL YOUR ROLE AS A RISK MANAGER

In addition to the many other hats you wear as chief of police, you are also a full-time risk manager for your organization. With others in your agency you share the responsibility of saving both lives and money by preventing or correcting unsafe behavior. It is the right thing to do in order to prevent human suffering. It is the practical thing to do because preventing accidents of all kinds as well as keeping people healthy on the job can save a lot of cash for your agency and your employer.

Once more, you cannot do it all by yourself. You must make your top managers and first-line supervisors aware of their duty to look out for hazardous equipment, procedures, policies and practices throughout the department. Just as important, they must remain on the alert for "hazardous" personnel. The latter could include officers who drive too fast, display poor officer safety practices or tend to start fights or escalate situations that they are part of.

Detecting "risky" behavior is only the first part of your risk management job–and your staff's. Bad behavior permitted to continue sets you and your agency up for civil liability. As the opposing lawyers will argue, you were aware of unsafe or otherwise bad behavior but allowed it to continue unchecked. That means you and your subordinate leaders must strive to immediately correct malpractice anywhere you find it. Unsafe equipment must be fixed or replaced. The same holds true for your department's policies and practices, and its people.

You cannot afford employees who are causing increased, unnecessary liability for your agency and your employer. They ultimately will cost you money and get you in trouble. Depending upon what their bad conduct happens to be, they also may endanger their fellow employees and the citizens you all serve. That, of course, is the most compelling reason of all to repair or remove these human time bombs. If you wait until they detonate to address their issues, you will have waited far too long.

Unfortunately, there is no shortage of examples of police employees who brought negative consequences upon their employers and their bosses by blowing up after giving obvious warnings of their tendencies for bad behavior. These "tendencies" have included behavior ranging from reckless driving to anger management issues; immoral conduct to outright criminal behavior.

In one department, an off-duty officer fired on law enforcement personnel who were making a mental health welfare check on her. After the incident, it was learned that the officer was still armed and on active duty following an earlier episode in which she had shot up her own home. You do not want to appear on the evening news or on the local newspaper's front page to explain why that officer was still on your payroll.

DEFEND YOUR PEOPLE WHEN NECESSARY

You would look foolish indeed if you adopted the posture of defending the actions of your people even when they were clearly and seriously wrong. Your credibility in the community would be unlikely to survive such a performance.

Fortunately, you are more likely to be called upon to answer questions in situations where your people basically did the right thing, even if their performance may not have been flawless. Things seldom go perfectly in the real world, and law enforcement operations are not an exception to the rule.

It will fall to you from time to time to explain publicly why your people chose Plan A instead of Plan B, why they arrested John instead of Sally, why an obnoxious 14-year-old ended up in cuffs. Many of the situations that your people handle are far from being black and white decisions. Not infrequently there is more than one way to achieve essentially the same outcome. Always be ready honestly to explain and, where necessary, defend your people when they are under siege from the media or others when they were simply doing their jobs in good faith. Your people will expect you to do this and will be quick to blame you if you do not.

This is a task you must handle personally. Do not shove the public information officer or some other subordinate out front to deflect the heat. Both your own people and the community have a right to see you in this role. Do not hide from questions or controversy. Doing so will, in the long run, hurt you more than the temporary sting of some hard questions and tough publicity. Most especially your own people will not forgive you if you go into hiding at a time when they believed you needed to stand up for them.

It is neither necessary nor advisable to stretch the truth in explaining the actions of your people. That advice does not change whether you are talking about a "questionable" officer-involved shooting or a high-speed car chase that ended badly. It is OK to admit that something could have gone better. It may be worth saying publicly what you know to be fact: Few law enforcement operations, if any, are ever perfect. It is alright to say so when something clearly went wrong. You can do all of those things and still back your personnel for their handling of an incredibly difficult situation. It is also quite acceptable to remind the public of how incredibly hard the job of a street cop is.

Tell the truth. Praise your people for what they did right. Acknowledge that things can almost always be done differently. Not necessarily better, but differently. Explain police practices and procedures when doing so would bolster the public's understanding of what happened and why. Emphasize again the difficulty of the law enforcement officer's job in a world of split-second decisions and months-long second guessing by "experts."

Do not abandon your people for political expediency. If you do, don't be surprised when they abandon *you.*

ADVOCATE IN THE COMMUNITY FOR YOUR PEOPLES' WELFARE

As the police chief you will attend a lot of rubber chicken lunches and early morning civic club affairs. You will be asked often to speak on the state of crime and law enforcement in your jurisdiction. You will be asked questions on those same topics (and many more) in one-on-one conversations and casual encounters in the community.

In your numerous opportunities to share your expertise with diverse others you will have a terrific chance to advocate for your employees and what they need to do their jobs safely and well. The idea is not to frighten the public into believing that there is a killer hiding behind every tree. That kind of scare talk is often counterproductive. Instead, present an accurate picture of the local public safety situation. Then shift into what your people are doing to keep the community safe. Move from there to what you and your employees need to do an even better job. Do not exaggerate or create paper dragons. Your credibility and integrity are at stake here.

Know that danger can accompany these open discussions and pronouncements. If you already know that your manager or elected board is presently unable or unwilling to grant you additional resources due to financial or other constraints, you risk getting yourself sideways with your boss or bosses if you beat the drum too loudly for things you cannot have.

Here you are doing a balancing act of sorts. You want to get your people what they need to do their jobs safely and well. You want to give your audience an accurate picture of the local scene. At the same time, you cannot afford to anger the people who ultimately will decide on the resources you will receive this year, and the next. They also will decide, in many cases, on your personal future with the organization.

At the very least, let your boss know if you plan on making a statement (or already have made one) that puts you at odds with any position held by your employer. You don't like surprises, and neither does he. Be prepared not to be praised for your pronouncements. Nevertheless, being honest and forthright about your public statements and actions is always the right way to go. Bosses tend to get feisty when they hear about their subordinate's "controversial" public stands from persons other than the outspoken employee himself.

None of this political reality should prevent you from sticking up for your people and responding to their legitimate needs. Be honest when you do. Let your boss know what you are up to. Neither underestimate nor exaggerate your needs. Do not assure your audience that all is well when you know for a fact there are wolves out there. But do not seek to senselessly frighten people, either. As in all things, openness and honesty are your best policies.

Advocate for your people. Expect some tough questions and some opposing viewpoints when you do. Realize that your boss may seek to rein in your advocacy from time to time. Work within those constraints while maintaining good communication with him or her. All of this amounts to serving your employees' best interests while protecting yourself, too.

EMPLOYEES' EMOTIONAL HEALTH IS IMPORTANT, TOO

You probably will find yourself preoccupied with attending to the physical and material needs of your employees. You rightfully will work hard to get them the salaries, benefits, equipment and other "stuff" they need to do their tough jobs. If you are thoughtful, you will not neglect the needs of your civilian employees as well as those of your sworn cops. All of these things are appropriate for you to do, and do well.

Your employees have other needs that also will need addressed. Their mental and emotional health must be equally important to you, their leader. Policing can be an extremely stressful way to make a living. You know that. As chief, you feel the stresses of your very difficult job as intensely as anyone. The daily stresses of your people may be a little different than your own, but your people feel them intensely, too. You do what you can to protect your own mental and emotional health. It is right that you endeavor to help your people stay equally healthy.

Alerting your supervisors and managers to keep an eye on the apparent mental health of their subordinates is one way you can help your people stay healthy. You can do the same for your own "direct reports." What you are all looking for is out of the ordinary behavior that might indicate that the person displaying it is undergoing one kind of crisis or another. At times, a patient ear may be all that is required to detect or even address a festering problem.

Problems can, of course, range from family illness to financial difficulties to marital infidelities, and can cover all of the ground in between. There also may be physiological reasons for unusual or troubled behavior. The supervisor's role is to make known to the employee the concern of the organization and proffer help where it is needed.

Professional assistance might be recommended where help beyond a non-judgmental ear is required. Most employers offer the benefits of an employee assistance program that includes help for marital, mental health and substance abuse issues. Yours should, too. Trained police psychologists, where available, also can offer a lot to your people. Take advantage of their services and find a spot in your budget for securing the regular services of a competent one.

Beyond the effects of the daily stresses of the job you must be prepared to deal with catastrophic incidents that can drastically impact the emotional health of the entire organization. Officer-involved shootings and the death or serious injury of a police employee can be expected to have devastating effects on the psychological health of the entire organization. The families of your employees also may be severely impacted by such occurrences. It will be up to you as the organization's leader to keep these members of the organization's extended family informed when tragedy strikes. That will mean meeting with them as often as needed to convey information, condolences and assurance.

For your organization, nothing can compare to the stress generated by the on-duty death of one or more of your law enforcement officers. You must prepare now for such an eventuality, even as you pray it never occurs. Talking with law enforcement CEOs who have gone through such tragedies and their aftermath can help prepare you. Your colleagues should be willing to share the lessons they learned in responding to these crises. The national Concerns of Police Survivors (COPS) organization can provide you with invaluable advice for responding to the emotional aftermath of a law enforcement officer's death. That organization's website can help you get in touch with a COPS representative in your area. Do not overlook this vital resource before and during an emergency.

Following the violent death of one of your officers, you as the department's leader will have three key responsibilities to execute. First, you must be readily available to offer condolences and personal support to the family and friends of the deceased police officer. Second, you must assure that all of your employees receive accurate information about what happened and what is going to occur next. You will need to deliver this information in person to the extent possible. Rumors run rampant at such times and it is important that you are seen and heard throughout the organization, across all shifts. Finally, if the death was the result of a criminal act it will be your task to assure that those responsible are identified, arrested and prosecuted as a result of lawful, proper police procedures. You must help guarantee that there is no doubt that the offenders were handled ethically and professionally by your personnel.

You will be wise to remain alert for the delayed emotional effects of a tragedy that may show up days, weeks or months following the event. These crises could appear in employees far removed organizationally from the victim officer. Dispatchers who listened to the critical incident unfold could have emotional, even hysterical reactions much later that will require professional, follow-up care. A Records Section employee emotionally linked to a sworn participant in the incident could experience an equally bad reaction requiring relief from duty and professional intervention.

Of course, you also will want the supervisors of personnel involved in a critical incident to watch for indications that things may not be good at home for an employee because of a significant other's reaction to an on-duty incident. You must be willing to provide whatever assistance you can to help an employee and his or her loved ones get through the after-action trauma of an emotion-charged incident. Finally, you must watch the supervisors and managers themselves for any indication that they are feeling the strain and need assistance. Don't overlook your own mental and emotional health needs, either.

The mental and emotional good health of your employee family always should be of great concern to you, the "head" of the organizational family. Paying attention to big and little issues in your peoples' lives does more than contribute to the effectiveness and efficiency of the organization. It also reveals you to be the caring leader that you are. More important still, it is once again *the right thing* to do.

REALIZE THE VALUE OF "LITTLE THINGS"

Small matters sometimes turn into bigger things that no one anticipated. An offhand comment, action or gesture on your part can grow into something garnering major praise or condemnation from your people. Little things really *can* mean a lot.

You are already aware of some of the small touches that can very favorably impress your people by showing them they are something besides an employee number to you. Birthday greetings are a nice touch. So are congratulatory notes on the birth of a child or other life-changing event. Notes of condolences are appreciated when one of your people has experienced a personal loss. A phone call or a hospital visit from the chief is often appreciated when an employee is seriously ill or has suffered a significant injury.

All of these things and more that you will think of yourself can help send the message that the boss really does care, after all. But you cannot do any of these things if you do not know about the events that instigated them. Require your staff to keep you advised of these significant occurrences in your peoples' lives so that you can acknowledge them. In some departments this duty resides with the chief's administrative assistant or secretary. Just be sure that someone is doing it for you.

You should be sincere when you express an interest in your employees' ups and downs. Most people are pretty good at sniffing out insincerity. Do nothing at all as opposed to sending a message that you don't really mean. If you are going to praise performance, be sure the performance really is praiseworthy. Nothing rings as hollow as praise tendered for simply doing one's normal job. Be sure what you are acknowledging truly deserves the recognition. Be certain that praise is honestly distributed throughout the organization and is not reserved for the "boss's pets." Hopefully you do not have any of those.

Employees generally like to hear the boss use their name in a positive way. Greet your folks by name when you can. Go out of your way to go by where they work or hang out in your building. One chief routinely entered and left the police station via a door that assured him the least amount of contact with his employees. Another CEO regularly took a longer route between the parking lot and his office to assure him of encountering the maximum number of his people. In each case, the employees noticed and commented accordingly. Guess which leader enjoyed the most employee support!

Stay attuned for additional little, inexpensive, seemingly-trivial things you can do to show your employees that you care about them as human beings. Chances are they won't regard them as trivial at all.

WALKING THE TIGHTROPE BETWEEN YOUR PEOPLE AND YOUR BOSS

A veteran city manager tells the story of one of his career's police chiefs who endeavored above all else to show his people that he was on their side. As a routine, the chief would double whatever it was his employees asked for when he took the request forward to his boss. It appeared to the manager that the chief was not only trying to ingratiate himself with his people, but also was trying the old trick of "ask for twice what you need so you'll get what you want."

The manager questioned the chief's loyalty to the larger organization as a team player, since the other department heads had needs, too. The pair argued incessantly over the chief's "doubling" practices. Eventually the chief departed the organization before his boss could fire him.

What your people want and what the larger organization can afford to give you for them often will not be the same. It will be up to you with help from your staff to determine what your people truly *must* have to do their jobs safely and well as opposed to what they would *like* to have. You owe your people your best efforts and arguments in obtaining the things they really need. But you owe your boss and the larger organization the loyalty required to trim excessive wants down to affordable reality. You should not blame your people for asking. Neither should you be surprised if on occasion they attempt to push you out front to lead the charge for something they actually can live without.

To do your job well you must see the big picture that is the whole organization of which your own department is only a part. That may sound trite but it's true. Your boss will expect you to realize that and will be plenty grumpy if it appears that you don't get it.

Never fail to represent your employees' legitimate concerns. Tend as best you can to their real needs. But have the backbone to tell them when their wants are frankly beyond what their employer can give at the time due to financial or other constraints. Don't blame it on your boss. (That can be fatal!) Rather, give them the facts. That's your job, too.

REMEMBER WHAT CONCERNED YOU AS A FRONT-LINE COP

If you are not careful the duties and crises of your administrator's day will consume all of your waking moments. The political intrigues, personality clashes and power plays that worry you will eat up the time you might otherwise have used to spend with your employees. Listening to the concerns of the community and its power structure may, if you don't watch it, occupy the time you could have spent listening to the ideas and concerns of police people.

In spite of all the concerns you will have as the police *chief,* try really hard not to forget the concerns you had as a police *officer.* Try to recall the things that most occupied your thoughts as a first-line enforcer of the law. By staying in touch with what concerns your people you can better serve their interests. You just might save yourself from some nasty surprises in the process.

If your agency has a union, listening to the concerns that the representatives of the organization bring forward can keep you connected to the mind-set of at least some of your department's members. Listen to your agency's non-union employees, too. They may have an entirely different set of concerns, or a different take on the ones worrying the union. Do not overlook the views of your front-line supervisors, mid-managers and top staff. Listen to all of these people and meet with them or their representatives periodically. But, above all, do not lose track of what your front-line cops are thinking and saying.

When you were a young officer it's likely that you focused your thoughts on having a good patrol car, decent equipment, a fair supervisor and support from the brass when things got tough. It is equally likely that your troops want pretty much the same things today. Yes, salary and benefits are important to them. They want you to secure for them what the organization can afford, and then some. Chances are, however, that they are even more focused on what they might term their "working conditions" as police officers. If you will recall, you were, too.

It is almost a given that your officers also expect fairness not only from you but from the intervening layers of supervision between you and them. They will hold you responsible if they don't get it, or think that they don't. They expect you to defend them in public when they are attacked for doing their jobs. They expect you to be there when a critical incident erupts and emotions run high.

Many won't admit it, but your people need you. Do not let them down.

NEVER STOP TRYING TO IMPROVE THE LIVES OF YOUR PEOPLE

You've likely promised yourself that you will never cease in your efforts to make your organization better. You probably have said to yourself that you'll never accept the status quo and rest on your laurels. All of those promises have helped make you the good leader that you are.

Make yourself one more promise. Pledge to never stop trying to make things better for your employees, sworn and civilian. It goes beyond pay and benefits, as important as those happen to be. Improve your employees' working environment whenever you can. It may be something as simple as improving the lighting in a dimly-lit area of your facility or getting the patrol cars' interiors cleaned more often. Or it could be something as major as changing the department's weaponry or getting the police facility remodeled or replaced.

Many of the improvements that you can make will cost money. Budget will control much of what you can do. But not always. Try to become an expert in devising low-cost and no-cost measures for making things better. It may be a revised work schedule or the relaxing of a particularly onerous rule. It may involve a minor uniform change or a decal revision on the police cars. Keep listening to the ideas and concerns of your people. You almost certainly will come up with some fodder for positive change.

Successful CEOs from the private sector sometimes talk about their goal of keeping their employees happy for the benefit it brings their bottom line. While you may not be concerned about profit margins, you are no less involved in running a complex business. Your business, too, works better when its employees are reasonably content. Always striving to find ways in which to better their lives is without a doubt one of the ways in which you can keep the majority of your people positive and productive. That's good business, too!

SUMMARY

When you signed on as police chief you accepted the responsibility for attending to the needs of your people. Their safety and general well-being should always be foremost in your mind and figure into your decision-making. Assuring their physical safety requires that you buy them the equipment that they need to do their jobs safely. It also mandates that you personally role model proper safety practices and good risk management at all times.

It is your job to represent your employees in the community when they are attacked. You must advocate for them in a continuing effort to get them what they truly need to do their jobs safely and well. But you also need to recognize that representing your peoples' interests may on occasion put you at odds with your boss. Walking that tightrope will require all of your human relations skills as a negotiator and mediator. Your earned reputation for credibility will help you, as well.

Try to recall the issues that concerned you as a street cop. Your people are probably expecting you to solve some of those same issues–and some new ones–today.

Do not ever forget your vital goal of trying to make things better for your people without bankrupting your employer in the process. It is unlikely to be an easy undertaking. But it is one that you must take on as the leader of the people who make up your organization.

POINTS TO REMEMBER

- Emphasize officer safety in all of your department's policies, procedures and practices.
- Always serve as an excellent role model for officer safety.
- Always seek to obtain the best officer safety equipment for your personnel.
- Strive to be an always-alert risk manager.
- Defend your people when they have drawn criticism for doing their jobs.
- Represent your peoples' needs to the community.
- Recognize that representing your employees' interests occasionally will put you at odds with your boss.
- Look to your employees' mental and emotional health needs, too.
- Try to remember the things that most concerned you as a front-line officer and address them as the chief.
- Never stop trying to make the lives of your employees better.

Chapter 7

MANAGING YOUR RELATIONS WITH THE COMMUNITY

You need the support of the majority of your employees to succeed in your difficult role as chief of police. In a best-case scenario, you also need the backing of the local political structure. At the very least, the local political powers should not be working to oppose what you are trying to accomplish.

A successful law enforcement CEO requires an additional source of support. To the extent possible, you need the backing of most of the people you represent. You want the maximum number of "regular" citizens behind you. You desire the support of your community's service clubs, civic groups, professional organizations and other entities, also.

It is all about the members of the community. These people and how you interact with them will help define your degree of success or the lack of it working within your community. You will need to interact with them individually and in groups, large and small. Sometimes they will agree with what you are trying to do and at times at least some of them will oppose. Other times they will have questions. All of these people you will have to work with at one time or another.

Managing your sometimes complex and always varied relationships with the various members of your community is the subject of this chapter. It is something that a successful leader (like you) must do well.

SET UP A KITCHEN CABINET OF WELL-CONNECTED PEOPLE

If you have done your research well, you already have identified many of the local citizens who make your community work. They are the bankers, school leaders, doctors, lawyers and "chiefs" of your town or city. But there are also the less well-known people who may not hold "power" positions but are nevertheless extremely active in their neighborhoods, civic groups and affairs of the community. These people may be less known, but they are important to you, too. Your boss, your staff and your fellow organizational department heads can help you learn who they are if you don't know already. These lesser known but highly active people can assist and support you in what you are trying to do with the community and the department.

If you are moving into a new department as its leader you may find that you have inherited a "kitchen cabinet" group assembled by the prior chief. You'll be wise to meet with this group as soon as possible and let them know that you intend to continue their existence as a valuable source of advice to you. Tell them your goals and plans for the department. Let them get to know you and enlist their backing. You can, over time, add your own members to the group so long as the group's size does not become unwieldy. In that way you gradually will make the group "yours" as opposed to someone else's.

If such a group does not already exist, you probably will want to create your own chief's advisory committee, or whatever you choose to call it. You need a group of smart people to examine your ideas and provide their own suggestions for the betterment of the agency. You need to hear from well-placed people as to what the community is saying about you and the department and its practices. You need people you can call together when a controversial incident occurs that brings the department under attack. At such times you must have friendly ambassadors to spread what you have to say throughout the community. You require their help in disseminating the true story when a lot of incorrect information is flying about. These people can help you explain and defend, when necessary.

Such an advisory group can be of just about any size you wish. You may find that a group of a dozen or so influential people is a good size. It will be big enough to give you a variety of views and small enough to be manageable. How often you get the group together is up to you. These are probably very busy people, so one meeting per quarter may be about right. You always can bring them together for a special session if the need arises.

If you have the money, consider meeting at noon over a light lunch of sandwiches or pizza. Establish an agenda of what you want to discuss but also leave some time just to talk. The idea is to let these influential people see and hear for themselves that you are an honest, intelligent, likeable person who is doing a good job and has some ideas that will benefit the community.

It also will be a good idea to represent your community's diversity in your kitchen cabinet. Women should be there along with ethnic minorities. You will want your group to be nonpartisan to the extent possible, so try to assure that more than one political viewpoint is represented. Some chiefs like to assure that the educational and religious communities are represented, too.

In some jurisdictions police chiefs maintain a separate advisory group of young people in their teens as a sort of "youth commission." The chiefs consult with them on laws or police policies and procedures involving younger citizens. Some law enforcement leaders in communities with substantial racial or ethnic minority populations have established advisory bodies from those communities, too. Rely on your knowledge of local attitudes and issues to tell you if you need to form one or more additional advisory groups to provide advice to the chief. Doing so can bring you direct support from the members of the body as well as at least some support from the community they represent.

Think really hard about it before you decide to disband an existing advisory group, even if you question its overall value. Doing so is likely to send the message that you do not care about that community, even if that is not how you really feel. Some of the group's former members may feel disrespected and obliged to criticize you publicly. Dissolving such a group also diminishes the number of voices you hear, making it easier for an unpleasant surprise to overtake you.

ACCEPT EVERY INVITATION YOU CAN

You are going to be plenty busy as the chief of police. You will need to ration your limited time carefully. You will have to leave some personal time for you and yours, too. But know that it is important to obtain maximum exposure concerning who you are and where you are taking the police department and community. You will do that best by getting in front of your public as often as feasible.

Do your best to grant every reasonable interview or meeting request and accept every speaking engagement that you possibly can. Get used to cardboard lunches and breakfasts that are cold before you have a chance to touch them. Steel yourself to listening patiently to tales of how a constituent was wronged by your officers or aggravated without end by the local kids, dogs, motorcycles, bad drivers and/or hooligans. The speakers are your citizens and potential supporters. To the limits of human patience and endurance you should listen to them and express appropriate interest and empathy. All of that is part of your job, too. Doing it well can bring you support that may be useful later when you and the department are under attack. People tend to remember how they were treated during their personal moment with the chief.

Consider putting together one or more presentations in printed, slide or

PowerPoint format to take with you when you visit these groups. Possible topics are practically without end, but you hardly can go wrong with a presentation depicting the mission, goals, operations and programs of the department. Include some interesting pictures. If you are seeking support (including financial aid) for a special undertaking, have a canned presentation on the topic ready and be prepared to supplement the program by answering questions. If there is a particular issue (increasing numbers of traffic accidents, rapes, burglaries, etc.) worrying the department or the community just now, have your people prepare a "prevention tips" presentation for you to narrate on the subject.

If you really seek to increase your public exposure, send a letter in which you offer a chat with the chief to each of your community's civic, social, political and other groups. Be prepared for a big response when you do. There are a lot of program chairs out there who have schedules to fill. It will be hard to pass up a chance at a presentation by the local top cop. Once you have solicited an invitation, try not to turn anyone away.

DON'T GET LAZY AS YOUR TENURE GROWS

You have a lot to do as police chief. You will become more and more comfortable in that role as your tenure increases. Hopefully, your comfort level with the job will increase as you feel a corresponding increase in the support you get from your boss, your employees and the community as a whole.

In that growing amount of comfort there lies a danger for you. It is good that you are no longer as ill at ease as you were as a new chief. That amount of nervousness was not very good for your physical or emotional health. At the same time, you do not want to permit your growing degree of comfort and familiarity with your situation to lull you into complacency. In other words, you cannot afford to get lazy.

Some leaders in all kinds of work have mistaken apathy for a lack of opposition. The truth is that there still may be unhappiness out there in either the department or the community that simply has not yet become intense enough to surface as active opposition. That could still happen. One more incident or grievance, real or imagined, could be all that is required to activate the boo birds.

You are not as likely to be surprised by dissention if you stay active in community affairs where you will be exposed to what people are saying. Some chiefs have even discovered discontent inside their organization by listening to community members. Cops, it appears, are not overly restrained about *who* they complain to when they are unhappy. Self-survival is another good reason for remaining very accessible in your jurisdiction.

Maintaining a very active presence in your community will help you demonstrate to the movers and shakers that you are a force to be reckoned with and not someone to be taken lightly. It will demonstrate the same thing to your own employees. That is important if you are to retain your status as a community leader in your own right.

BE OUT FRONT WHEN CONTROVERSY ERUPTS

Your employees expect that you will act like a leader when controversy breaks out and the department is under attack. They will expect that you remain visible and serve as the department's primary spokesperson in answering questions or deflecting criticism.

The members of the community also will expect maximum visibility and participation from you when tough times of any kind confront your town or city. This is not the time for you to send a chief-surrogate out front to represent you. The citizens who are paying your salary expect to see and hear the real thing.

Of course, there are many different versions of what might be termed a "controversy." One such situation may arise from the actions of your own personnel involved in a use of lethal force. Controversy might develop over a fatal crash related to a high-speed police pursuit. It might grow out of an in-custody death or even an off-duty misadventure of one or more of your officers. It might even result from something the chief (that's you!) did or didn't do. Regardless, you and your agency have become the focus of strong opinions and emotions in the community. It will fall to you as the leader to speak for the law enforcement organization.

Whatever the cause of the furor, be sure that your boss is briefed on the cause and nature of the flap and how you intend to respond to it. He may ask you to fill in the members of your community's governing body, as well. Once you have command of the facts and have devised what you want to say, do not wait too long to say it. Putting off a response until people are clamoring to hear from you detracts from your image as a leader who is willing and able to take on a crisis. It also can make it look like you are hiding.

Events not brought about by you or your department also will demand your visible leadership. Natural disasters, serial crimes and civil unrest are examples of situations requiring highly visible leadership from the community's top law enforcement officer. By personally "showing the flag" of your organization you can help assure nervous citizens that authority is in control and the problem, whatever it is, will be addressed successfully. What you are providing here is psychological support for an ill-at-ease populace. By remaining visibly calm and confident you can transmit that attitude to others. After all, things can't be so bad if the chief says they're not.

Do not lie, but be reassuring. Let your citizens know that their government is functioning and will provide for their needs, most especially public safety services. Radiate confidence and hope, not gloom and desperation, even if you have to rely on your acting skills just a little.

Once again, maintain your integrity by telling the truth. The average person will not expect a gentle rain of honey when the outhouse blows up. But he'll feel better if the chief assures him that the fallout will be short-lived and survivable. He also will be favorably impressed if he sees that the chief is out there getting spattered, too!

DON'T LIMIT ACCESS UNREASONABLY

Except in the smallest of law enforcement agencies it is probably not reasonable to expect that every individual with a point to make or a grievance to air will get a personal audience with the chief. You simply have too many responsibilities to your community for that to happen. There are certainly others in your organization who can competently service those complaints and demands, often more quickly.

You will have to use your best judgment in determining how much you want to limit the public's access to their chief law enforcer. As a general rule of thumb, you'll want to see as many people as you can and talk with many that you cannot meet in person. By listening to their concerns and trying to help them you will make supporters out of at least some. You also will reduce the likelihood of stirring up active opposition and instigating complaints to your boss that you have turned a deaf ear to the community's concerns. From a slightly more selfish point of view, by seeing as many of your citizens as possible you will reduce the likelihood of being victimized by a nasty surprise that you did not see coming.

It is indeed important to remain accessible to the maximum number of people. At the same time, you will accomplish little beyond personal frustration by making yourself always available to every wing nut in the vicinity. (Yes, your community has some.) Your staff will know who many of these folks are. You will identify others yourself. Allow your staff to screen these people away from you to the extent feasible. Granting them an extended audience will eat up your limited time that could be better spent in more fruitful work. Lavishing a lot of time on these troubled souls will bring you virtually nothing worthwhile in return. It probably won't even help them. This approach may seem harsh, but it is necessary if you are to reach your full potential in helping the community you serve.

DON'T BECOME ALLIED WITH A FACTION OR FRINGE GROUP

And speaking of wing nuts, you will want to be cautious about choosing the groups with which you will associate yourself closely. Leaving the Democrats and Republicans out of the mix for the moment, your community probably has a few collections of individuals who are seen as just, well, strange. These are probably not good associates for the chief of police. You have a right to believe in pixies, flying saucers and that Elvis is working in the local diner if you want to. But keep those particular feelings to yourself. And don't hang around with groups that publicly share those beliefs.

By virtue of being the chief you will attract the attention of people and groups who either want something from you or want to boost their own ego or standing by their claimed association with the chief. That is normal behavior that you should expect. That's why most of the people you ask to share a cup of coffee or a lunch accept the invitation. You are *somebody,* and you just might be able to do something for them.

But be careful of those whose motives for wanting to know you better are suspect. Rely on your own good judgment and common sense as well as your staff's knowledge in avoiding close associations with these individuals. A meeting in your office with one or more of these folks is acceptable unless they are clearly *way* out there. (You may want to have one of your staffers join you for the appointment.) But going to meetings or other events with them is something you probably want to avoid.

As a general rule of thumb, avoid participating in the affairs of organizations that are off of either the right or left ends of the political scale. Avoid associating yourself with known hate groups or racial supremacy organizations. Stay away from extremists of all varieties and looney groups of all types. Joining the local band of UFO fanatics who believe that the mother ship is returning for them next Wednesday would not be a good move for you.

You even will need to be a bit cautious with your associations with the established and respected political organizations. Your actions will have to be guided by your knowledge and understanding of the local political scene. Knowing the lay of the political landscape is one of your responsibilities as chief. But remain mindful that you are everyone's chief of police in that jurisdiction. You are not just the Republicans' guy or the Democrats' pal. You are bound by the law and your ethics to see that everyone is treated equally under the law. Doing anything else could cut your career short, and should.

None of this means that you do not have a right to express your personal political beliefs. It does mean that you should show common sense in doing so. If you want to hang political flyers on doors, have at it. But do it on your own time and out of uniform. Feel free to attend the formal breakfast for the party of your choice, but consider doing so while not wearing your "chief costume." It's likely that not every one of your elected bosses shares your political views.

Be sure that you listen equally well to all camps of political views and opinions. Do not totally shut out the ones you disagree with. As chief, you must serve the interests of their members, too. Besides, keeping them talking with you lets you know what the rascals are up to!

LISTEN TO CONCERNS: DON'T BE TOO QUICK WITH PRONOUNCEMENTS

As a leader, you are probably an action-oriented person. You want to know as quickly and succinctly as possible exactly what the problem is so that you can get on with solving it.

As you are doubtlessly learning every day from personal experience, sometimes your own people as well as many others really do not expect you to *act* on their concerns. At least, not right away. They just want to *tell* you about them.

You often will find the same to hold true when you are dealing with diverse members of the community. The persons conveying the information to you want the chief of police to be aware of the situation. They may or may not expect the chief to act on it. The challenge for you will be trying to figure out the appropriate response. When you are in doubt, there is one fairly reliable thing you can do to cut your way through the fog of uncertainty: Ask questions. Listen carefully to what you are hearing before either replying or committing yourself and your organization to a course of action.

Your law enforcement experience has taught you that there is almost always another side to a given story, no matter how convincing the original telling sounds. Chances are that you are only hearing part of the tale when you are cornered by a citizen or group with an "issue." Promise him or them that you will look into it. If you absolutely know enough about the circumstances to accept that you are being given the straight facts, it's OK to go ahead and answer or commit to a specific course of action. Otherwise, hold off on a final decision until you know more. That is preferable to promising something and then having to break your promise after you learn the whole story.

People naturally want you to concur with their point of view. Smart chiefs have learned to say "interesting" and "hmmm" a lot during these exchanges. They often avoid choosing sides and promising a particular response until they confirm what they are hearing for themselves and know a lot more. It is a measured response that you would be wise to copy.

Show interest. Show empathy. Agree with things that are clearly agreeable. ("Justice *is* a good thing!") But save the big pronouncements until you have the whole story. Most reasonable people will not be stunned by your very practical and fair response.

YOU DON'T HAVE TO FIX EVERYTHING

It is highly doubtful that any leader has ever solved every problem delivered to him or satisfied everyone who ever brought him a complaint. That just is not likely in the real world that you and your community members inhabit. Reality doesn't work like that.

Too often, pleasing one individual or group in the community means ticking off another one who wanted you to do just the opposite. The latter citizens now see themselves as losers in the contest, and at least some of them are not particularly happy about it. The examples are as numerous as they are varied. An instance may be found in your crackdown on noisy vehicles. One part of the community–almost certainly the far bigger part–will thank you for addressing a quality of life problem. Another, smaller group–the obnoxiously noisy vehicle owners and their parents and supporters–will damn you for "fixing" a problem that did not exist, at least not in their minds.

Noisy vehicles will seem like a minor manner compared to some of the challenges you will face. Regardless of the problems you are facing, it is important to realize that you will not be able to solve every one of them, at least not to everyone's satisfaction. Virtually no chief is able to do that. The last one didn't. The one who follows you will be unlikely to do it, either.

The fact is that you do not have to fix everything that anyone ever complains about. You cannot do it for your own employees. You can't do it for your community, either. Do the best you can. Make an honest effort at problem-solving. But realize in the end that the world you live and work in is an imperfect place. It always will be. Do what you can and then leave a few things for the person who one day assumes your position. After all, you don't want the next chief to get bored.

DON'T PLAY FAVORITES

You can't help liking some people more than others. That is simply an ingrained trait of the human animal. What you can do, however, is keep that tendency from rearing its head in your relations with the individuals and groups that make up your community.

You are ethically obliged to spend just as much time addressing the issues of those who say they don't like you as you do helping the people who are in your corner. You are just as obligated to appear in front of a group of critics as you are the local mothers of police officers club. You are the local law enforcement boss. It is your job to provide an open ear for both groups.

Be as opinionated and judgmental as you want, but do not permit either your opinions or your judgments to interfere with your ability to interact with others impartially. Do not place yourself at the beck and call of one group while ignoring others. Those you attempt to freeze out will resent it and may retaliate later. That is not a basis for open communication among yourself, your organization and the community you serve.

As in your relationships with the people inside your own organization, it is alright to have friends. It's *healthy* to have friends, especially friends from outside of law enforcement. Just don't grant them special breaks and privileges that you would not offer the average guy on the street. If you do that and it gets out, it could harm your friend as well as you and your organization. Do not play favorites in your relations with members of the community. No good can come from it.

MAINTAIN A HIGH PROFILE–APPROPRIATELY

Whether you like it or not, you are a public figure. Many in your community will recognize you on sight. Even more will recognize your name. Hopefully you gave that reality some thought before you took the chief's job in the first place. As the chief law enforcement officer you can expect to get asked for your opinion a lot. You also can expect to be invited to a lot of meetings and events. In sum, a lot of people will know who you are and want to hear what you have to say.

That does not need to be a problem for you. All of these things you likely expected when you elected to pursue the job. As the leader of a very important and very visible arm of government, your employees and your public expect you to be visible. They expect you to act like you are in charge and have the confidence that goes with knowing what you are doing. They expect you to speak out on matters of import for both your department and the community as a whole. That's what being a leader is about. People don't expect you to vanish from public view, particularly when times are tough. No one really wants an invisible law enforcement leader. They want the comfort of knowing that someone is firmly in charge and that things will be OK.

It is alright, then, for you to be a public figure in your town or city. The key for your reputation, however, is where you are seen and what you are doing when observed. You *do* want to be sighted at school, civic and other community events. You *don't* want to be glimpsed hanging out in rowdy bars or other disreputable places. You *do* want to be seen participating in charitable affairs; you *don't* want to be observed driving drunk down the town's main drag. You *do* want the local newspaper's subscribers to read about the recognition you just received from a professional association; you *don't* want them to read about your public brawl with your spouse. You *do* get it, right?

A few ill-advised chiefs have attempted to keep themselves totally out of the media and away from the public eye at all times and for all occasions. This policy is neither practical nor appropriate. Within reason, your citizens have a right to know what the person they are paying to be their top law enforcer is up to. What you are saying and doing relevant to your leadership role is legitimate news. Accept that fact along with the obligation to be as open and transparent as possible. Surely you are doing some really good things as a leader. There are plenty of things for you to be proud of. Let the members of your community know that their faith and their money are well-invested.

ANSWER MOST PHONE CALLS AND E-MAILS YOURSELF

There is absolutely no doubt that you are one very busy individual. Unless you practice some excellent time management skills, you almost certainly will be overwhelmed. For that reason you must ration the time you spend responding to telephone calls and e-mail messages. At the same time, you can cause yourself needless damage by isolating yourself *too* much.

It almost goes without saying that you should always respond personally when the call or message needing returned comes from one of the movers and shakers of the community. That's just good career survival. Who these people are will vary from one place to the next, but they often will include elected and appointed officials, representatives of the news media, leaders of ethnic and racial minority groups and other recognized civic and community leaders. Most of these people will *expect* that you will grant them a piece of your time and will badmouth you if they don't get it. That doesn't mean you must spend hours on each contact. Neither should you ignore the communication or have it returned by a member of your staff. You can make a lot of points simply by connecting with someone who talks to a lot of others in your town or city every day. Your reputation for good or ill develops through such interactions.

You also will receive plenty of calls, letters and e-mail messages from people who are not necessarily "somebody" but who also want your time and attention. Once more, how you handle these people can contribute towards your reputation as an approachable leader or a snotty, standoffish jerk.

Answer personally as many calls and messages as you can, even if the contact is from a stranger. Learn the person's issue as early as possible in the exchange so that you can refer them to someone else, if necessary, to help them. That will save time, too. If their particular concern is best handled by someone else in your organization, get the citizen's contact information and relay it to the person you have delegated to handle the situation. (You already should have made your subordinates aware that you expect these assignments to be handled with dispatch.) Thank the individual for his or her message and let them know that a follow-up contact will occur soon.

Handled in this manner, a caller or writer can tell his pals that he had the chief's personal attention as well as the chief's promise that follow-up would take place. For many people, that will amount to at least a small gold star for you. They got to pitch their gripe to a chief who took the time to listen to them, even though they may not have gotten exactly what they wanted. That was worth something, to you *and* them.

As the song says, little things can mean a lot. Returning calls and messages is one of those little things that can help you more than you perhaps realize. On top of that, it's the *right* thing to do.

LET THEM SEE YOU'RE NOT AN OGRE

If you are the kind of police chief that you should be, you will benefit from having as many people as possible meet you "in the flesh." Far from hiding, you want them to see and report to others that you are approachable and personable. You likewise want your citizens to witness firsthand that you have neither horns nor a tail.

By the very nature of your job you are going to make some people mad at you. It simply cannot be helped if you are doing your job correctly. (You don't *want* the bad ones to like you, you know.) As they go about their jobs, your people are going to anger even more who ultimately will shift the blame to you if you fail to address their beef to suit them. In addition, you probably will have at least a few disgruntled and/or terminated police employees actively engaged in poisoning the public image waters for you. For those reasons it is important that as many people as possible see you as the decent, "normal" person that you really are.

For your citizens to know that you are really an OK person, they need to hear you, see you and meet you. They can only do that if you are out there and accessible, mixing it up in the community. Some of this contact you can achieve by attending various, formal community functions and events. Doing so is, after all, part of your job description. You also can contribute to your own image as a pretty nice person by taking the time to share greetings and some brief conversation with people who recognize you when they encounter you in the restaurant or grocery store. Just a little time spent in pleasantly conversing with these people can earn you a lot of "currency" in the public relations department.

Some people will take pride in saying that they spoke with the chief and shared their opinions with him. Just that brief contact may serve to gain you their support now that they have seen you as a "nice guy" who is not all that different from themselves.

Continue to meet your citizen-customers throughout your career. Doing so will buy you a lot more than it will cost you in time and effort. The proverbial "bottom line" will end up very much in your favor.

STAY AS INVOLVED IN COMMUNITY ACTIVITIES AS YOU CAN

Taking care of your personal physical and emotional health must be Job One for you. You owe that to your loved ones and yourself. You cannot help anyone else if you don't take care of yourself first. And that means that you must jealously guard your downtime.

At the same time, you knew (or quickly learned) the all-encompassing nature of the chief's job when you took the reins of the agency. One of the keys to success for you as the chief is to stay in front of your community in a positive light. This you must balance with your need for some personal time.

The taxpayers need to know what you are doing to lead your people in an effort to keep the community safe. They need to see you not as a faceless bureaucrat but as a real leader who does good things. They need to believe that they are better off having you as their chief of police as opposed to someone else. They won't know any of these things unless they see you in action and hear what you have to say.

Your citizens won't see you as a leader if they don't see you at all. That means you must get out there even when you would much prefer to be reading a book at home or spending some quiet time with the family or a significant other. "Getting out there" is staying involved in community activities as much as possible.

To be a successful chief you must meet the public–a lot. You do not have to love it, although many chiefs do. But you have to do it, regardless. Not every popular, successful chief is an extrovert. Some are just the opposite. But the best ones can put on their extrovert personality when they need to, which is pretty often.

Whether you are a new chief or a veteran, stay involved in your community to the maximum extent that you can and still preserve your own life away from work. It will bring you benefits that outweigh the considerable physical and emotional energy you expend.

LIVE WHERE YOU WORK

If your town or city is one that requires its chief to live within its geographic borders, where to reside won't be a question you have to answer. Many jurisdictions do require just that.

If you can choose whether or not to live within the boundaries of the jurisdiction you police, things are a bit more complicated. Many police CEOs elect to live within the jurisdiction they are responsible for protecting. For one thing, it's just more convenient for someone who is eternally on-call and in attendance at events taking place at all hours, seven days a week.

Living among the people who are paying your salary also says something about your support for and ownership in the place that employs you. What your boss and your citizens expect (or have a right to expect) about where you live is another factor to consider. Particularly in a metropolitan area with many suburbs and just as many police departments, no one may care all that much where you reside. In another city–especially one that stands alone without close, neighboring jurisdictions–some people may be seriously troubled that their chief lives two jurisdictions away. Reasonably or not, they may expect their chief to live literally within shouting distance.

One small city went through two police chiefs in two years. Although there were other factors involved in each chief getting his "walking papers," one of the beefs in the "indictment" of each man was that "he thought he was too good to move to our town." True or not, this perception led to ill feelings which, compounded by other complaints, resulted in each chief's quick exit.

Absent a residency mandate, you will have to decide for yourself where you will live. Some city and town managers will want you to reside locally, even if they can't officially require it. Others, probably fewer in number, really don't care one way or the other. Home prices in your chosen jurisdiction will have something to do with it, too. Some chiefs have found themselves literally unable to afford to live in the jurisdiction employing them. Your family's wishes also will weigh in the decision.

Living in the jurisdiction where you are a leader has more benefits than downsides for you. Live there if you can.

SUMMARY

To succeed as chief of police, you will need to have the support of the majority of the community and its influential individuals and groups. At the very least, you will need to avoid active opposition by significant segments of the community.

Fortunately, there are a number of things you can do to manage your relations with the community in a positive way. Appear in front of local groups as often as possible and let them hear your plans for the department and community. Put together a chief's advisory group of influential locals. Listen to just about everyone, and don't be quick to choose sides on controversial issues. Consider staying out of arguments that don't really involve policing or criminal justice. Avoid allying yourself with extremist groups of any stripe. Do not isolate yourself. Personally answer as many calls and messages as you can. Stay visible and in touch.

Remain active in your community but realize that you'll never solve all of the problems or please everyone. You do not have to. Just get out in public and let your citizens see for themselves that you are a pretty nice person, after all. Remember that you can best manage your relations with your community by favorably managing your relations with its people, one at a time.

POINTS TO REMEMBER

- Appoint a chief's advisory committee of influential local citizens.
- Particularly when you are new to the job, accept any reasonable opportunity to appear before the public.
- As your tenure grows, don't mistake public apathy for continuing support. Don't get lazy.
- Be visible when controversy involving your department develops in the community.
- Don't overdo it in limiting public access to you; stay in touch with all parts of the community.
- Listen to everyone, but do not ally yourself with a fringe group known for its extremist views.
- Don't rush to make a public pronouncement until you know the whole story.
- Realize that you cannot solve every problem and make everyone happy.
- Don't have "pets" among the community's leaders; treat everyone with equal respect.
- Maintain a high profile in the community by doing the right thing, not

by messing up.

- Be yourself in public. It will be good enough for most people.
- Get involved in as many community activities as you can while still leaving time for you and yours.
- Try to live in the community you work in.

Chapter 8

MAINTAINING A HEALTHY RELATIONSHIP WITH YOUR BOSS

You can be declared a hero by your employees, be worshipped by your community and take a serious bite out of crime and still fail to hang onto your job as police chief. You can accomplish that dubious feat by failing to maintain a good working relationship with your boss. That unfortunate reality of life holds true whether you work for a mayor, town administrator, city manager or a board of elected officials. That's bad news for the ethical leader who has, in his own mind and perhaps the minds of others, done a good job as a law enforcement CEO.

The good news is that there are some pragmatic, common sense things you can do to work effectively with your boss without sacrificing either your ethics or your sanity in the process. By doing them you can increase the likelihood that the relationship you nurture with your boss will enable you to survive your position long enough to be a force for positive change in your department and community. This chapter is all about some of those practical, common sense things.

WILL A CONTRACT HELP?

Less than one-third of America's police chiefs have a contract with their employer. For many chiefs, it may never have occurred to them to ask for one. If they had, they might have been rebuffed by an employer who didn't see the need for one because "we've never done that before." Other bosses and their HR directors may have wanted to avoid putting their obligations to their chief law enforcer in writing. Of course, it is likely that at least some of these same bosses opposed to putting their relationship with their police chief in writing had a contract themselves.

Should you seek a contract with the town, city or county employing you?

Will having one really improve your working relationship with your boss? The truth is that an employment contract or agreement will not turn a bad boss-subordinate relationship into a good one or guarantee that your work life will be always pleasant. A contract does, however, bring certain advantages for both you and your employer.

First, you will benefit by having some basic job security and the psychological pluses that go with it. Some financial comfort will result from the fact that you know exactly how much you will be earning and how your salary and benefits will change. In addition, a several year contract will give you the time you need to implement some departmental changes and programs that will not have to be completed overnight in order to be deemed successful. It's difficult to concentrate on what you are doing when you must glance frequently over your shoulder to see if the ax is about to fall.

You will have a greater opportunity to develop into a successful leader, as a contract will tell your boss, your employees and potential "opponents" that getting rid of you is unlikely to be done on a whim. If you are wise enough to get a severance package as part of your contract (and you should) that will grant you several months pay if you are involuntarily terminated, your hiring/firing authority is more likely to think twice before sending you packing.

An employment contract with his chief of police also has benefits for your employer. When he's hiring a chief, letting the prospective candidates know that a contract is offered may bring in a greater number of good applicants. The potential for a nasty, highly-publicized dispute also will be reduced when the termination and severance process is carefully spelled out.

Your boss additionally should like the fact that the formal agreement defines your duties and working relationship with him and eliminates at least some of the areas where misunderstandings might arise. Finally, giving you a contract may help assure both you and your boss of a better working relationship between the police chief and the other department heads if those individuals know that the chief is unlikely to be fired just because an interdepartmental dispute arises.

The fact that your boss (or boss to be) has never had a contract with his chief of police before is not a good reason to turn down your request for one. Stress to him the contract's benefits for the boss and the organization. Note the advantage of having "everything on the table" to foster a good working relationship between the two of you. Whether you get a contract sometimes will depend upon just how badly the hiring authority wants to get you onboard. If he or she simply will not grant you one, you are left to decide if you want the job badly enough to sign up without the relative "protection" a contract can bring.

It must be said that many chiefs have enjoyed long careers and a terrific relationship with their boss without ever having a contract. On the other hand, chiefs with a contract have sometimes fought with their boss like cats and dogs. A contract will not guarantee you eternal bliss or turn a whack-job boss into a saint. It will, however, improve your job security to some degree. It likely will contribute favorably to the overall working relationship you enjoy with your supervisor.

This is not a book about employment contracts. Such texts are readily available. Publications from the Police Executive Research Forum cover the topic well and even offer some sample contracts to copy. (You should offer to provide a draft agreement if your hiring authority professes to be unfamiliar with them.)

Contracts can vary a great deal in their content and attention to detail, but many include the following sections:

DUTIES: What you are expected to do will be spelled out here.

TERM: How long will the contract run? Will it be open-ended?

SALARY: What will you be paid and how will the amount be adjusted in the future? Will there be provisions for "merit pay" or bonuses? What process will have to be followed to effect a reduction in pay?

TERMINATION AND SEVERANCE: How and why can your employer fire you? Most important, what will he owe you if you are discharged against your will? (Seek at least six months of pay at time of severance. Some chiefs have sought to include continuing health and other benefits for the same time period.)

DISCIPLINE AND APPEAL PROCESS: How can your employer discipline you and what is the process for contesting such discipline?

DISABILITY: If you become physically or mentally unable to do your job, what compensation will you receive? What is the process involved?

HOURS OF WORK AND TIME OFF: Your boss's expectations for your time on and off the job should be spelled out here. Compensation for long hours worked beyond "business" hours should be spelled out, as should arrangements for sick, vacation and holiday leave time.

PERFORMANCE REVIEW: How will your job performance be evaluated? What are the consequences of an "unsatisfactory" review?

RELOCATION EXPENSES: If you have had to relocate to accept the job, what will your employer provide to help defray those costs? Think about things besides the cost of the physical move of your "stuff." Some police CEOs have gotten the expenses of realtors' commissions and temporary lodging covered here, too.

OUTSIDE WORK: If you want to teach, consult or do some other work away from your chief's job, document your right to do so.

VEHICLE: Be sure that your right to the use of a city-owned vehicle or mileage expenses for your personal vehicle is covered in the agreement.

If you are allowed a city car, be sure that you document the right to use it for "personal business," including the transport of members of your family. Gas, maintenance and insurance should be covered by your employer regardless of whether you use a city-owned vehicle or your own. Document this, too.

BENEFITS: Be certain that your retirement, health, dental, life and related benefits are covered in sufficient detail to protect you and your loved ones. Pay attention to family benefits if they apply in your situation.

INDEMNIFICATION: Your employer should insure you against the lawsuits and legal assaults almost certain to be levied against you as the police chief. You are seeking to be as legally bullet-proof as possible so long as you are doing your job properly and lawfully.

OTHER TERMS AND CONDITIONS: This catch-all section might include such details as guaranteeing you funds for memberships, dues, subscriptions, uniform allowances and other expenses.

When you are discussing a contract with the hiring authority you do not want to come across as greedy, but the old saying about "you don't ask, you don't get" applies in contract negotiations. If you want the job, be willing to negotiate and compromise. If you cannot get something included that you feel you absolutely must have (example: severance pay), be prepared to walk away and mean it. There will be other opportunities.

Contracts can be complicated. Consider having at attorney look at and interpret yours before you sign it. Afterwards it's what you will have to live with.

If you are newly chosen as the police chief, ask for a contract. But there is nothing prohibiting you from requesting a written agreement even if you have served as the police department's boss for years without one. It won't take too long to find out if your boss is receptive to the idea. It will depend at least partially on how badly he wants to keep you and if he believes you really will look elsewhere without one. If he likes what you have been doing he just might be willing to grant you a contract in order to keep you around. Hiring a new chief is, after all, an exhausting process.

Do not assume that refusal means a lack of faith or trust in you on his part. Your local elected board may have tied your boss's hands on the subject. They may not want to start a precedent of police chiefs with contracts. Try not to worry over it. Just continue to do an excellent job. Sometimes things change as the roster of elected officials changes. You may get another shot at it one day.

Some chiefs who have not succeeded in getting a contract have instead obtained a letter or memorandum of understanding with the employing authority. While neither is as satisfactory or legally binding as a contract, such a document can improve the working relationship by specifying what you and your boss expect of each other. Such documents are generally shorter and much less-detailed than a contract.

Finally, be willing to stand up (courteously!) for your right to an employment contract. This holds true even if the boss indicates by words or body language that you've just asked for his first-born. (He may be just as good an actor as you are!) After all, there's a decent chance that *he* has one. Allow your powers of observation, best judgment and good common sense to tell you how hard to push.

WHAT YOUR BOSS WANTS FROM YOU

One veteran city manager put it thusly: "What I want from my police chief is that my telephone doesn't ring about the police department."

While what that manager wanted may have been beyond the realm of the likely (and he probably knew it), his wish should not be lost on you. While some city managers, town administrators and mayors are fascinated by law enforcement and want to know the tiniest details about what is going on in the Cop Shop, many more have other, pressing interests (like economic development, for instance) keeping their focus elsewhere. They expect you to keep all but the most "exceptional" issues and decision-making regarding police matters on your plate, not theirs.

Asked why they appointed a particular individual as chief, more than a few town and city leaders have furnished a brief and direct response: to make my police problems go away. If you happen to be the appointed problem-solver, the Big Boss's problems have just become yours. He expects you to fix them, preferably with as little intervention as possible from him. That does not mean he won't offer you direction or that he won't answer your questions. It simply means that he expects you to carry most of the load in solving the community's public safety issues and the police department's internal problems, ranging from personnel to resources to finances.

Your boss hired you to make his life better. If he inherited you from his predecessor, he will be examining you closely to assure himself that you will serve his needs without him having to go to the trouble of finding a replacement. That's why a change in the mayor or city or town manager almost always creates at least a minor pang of discomfort in the serving chief. It is why you want plenty of community members around who can tell the new guy what a great job you have been doing. It's why you want the majority of your police employees to say the same thing. If you have done a good, honest and effective job over time you should have little to worry about when the community's top leadership changes. Your new boss should soon learn what the prior one knew: the incumbent chief of police is an ethical professional who takes care of business–and his supervisor.

New or old, your boss needs several things from you. He needs to be able to believe and trust you. He needs to know that you are loyal to him, the organization and the community. He needs to know that you are technically competent. He needs to be sure that you can lead people and manage personnel. In sum, he needs to be comfortable that having you at the helm of his most important department will be better for him than having someone else in charge of it.

Give your boss all of these separate but related assurances and your position likely will be secure for as long as he holds office. When and if he leaves his position, it will be your task to start the "education" and familiarization process all over again.

WHAT ROLE IN ORGANIZATIONAL POLITICS SHOULD THE CHIEF PLAY?

As more than a few chiefs have learned to their dismay, local politics can be as nasty as any political intrigues that exist at the national or international level. In small- and medium-sized municipalities across the country bare-knuckles politics have ended the tenure of numerous chiefs. In a few cases, local law enforcement CEOs have found themselves dragged into civil or even criminal court after siding with one political faction or another and engaging actively in "dirty politics." One Southern chief, for example, found himself doing time in a state prison after convincing himself that it was OK to help his mayor by engaging in electronic eavesdropping of the mayor's political foe.

As a chief of police you cannot be oblivious to politics in a world full of politicians. For your own survival you must know who is politically related to whom and what their goals are. You also need to have that knowledge regarding the internal workings of the city, county or town organization you are a part of. You likewise require a working knowledge of the political workings of the community as a whole.

By talking and listening to others in the larger organization you can get a feel for who communicates with whom, who is trusted, who is distrusted or otherwise disliked and who you can count on when you need help and advice. You especially need to know who your boss trusts and talks to a lot. Much of this background information you can learn over time via your own observations as well as through a few, well-placed questions. Your staff should be able to help you learn these things as a result of their own organizational contacts.

One new chief was surprised to learn that everything one of his fellow department heads knew about the police department's most-sensitive personnel issues was soon known to the city manager, too. He discovered that the pair had worked together for a long time and enjoyed sharing gossip with one another. Another law enforcement boss found to his dismay that his boss knew about every minor hiccup in the police department's budgetary process. He quickly realized that the town's manager and its finance director were old high school chums who still enjoyed playing together. The finance guy took particular delight in sharing with his boss what he knew about the various department heads' wrangling with budget woes during tough financial times. It could be argued that this was part of his job. It was also something that the chief needed to be aware of. As in any other organization, information is power in a municipal government. Whoever has it is powerful.

You cannot change who your boss talks to and associates with. But by better understanding the relationships you can better prepare for your own dealings with him or her. That way you can have at least some idea of what your boss may hear about your operation from others. You can even put information out there that you want your boss to hear from someone besides you. Knowing who talks to who is a good thing to know.

In the end, the best advice you can follow about the games that organization members play is to participate in them as little as possible. Protect yourself and your organization, but avoid the very human temptation to plot and choose sides. You naturally will like some of your department head colleagues better than others. But resist the urge to talk badly about peers or participate in feuds.

Strive to treat everyone equally. You of course will want to shield yourself by watching carefully those you have learned from solid evidence not to trust. Work with them anyway. Carry out without rancor whatever interaction is required to get your own job done well. Just stay alert while you are doing so.

Do your job. Do it honestly and ethically. Do not become entangled in political game-playing or organizational intrigue. That way you will sleep better and like yourself more. You just might increase your job effectiveness and security at the same time.

SURVIVING THE BOSS FROM HELL

If you truthfully can say that you never have worked for a truly bad boss you should consider yourself fortunate. Most people have at one time or another in their work lives. Poor bosses are far too common, it seems. City and county governments, unfortunately, have drawn their share.

Bad bosses come in a wide variety of types, shapes, sizes, ages and genders. They range in malevolence from the only slightly irritating to the mentally unstable. Their bad behavior can be manifested in almost endless ways. Some bad bosses are bullies who enjoy belittling their employees. Some will pick out a "goat" while leaving other underlings virtually untouched. Some bad bosses are quick to criticize but never award praise for well-done work. Others take the credit for the good work done by others and allow their staff's efforts to go unrecognized.

Some bad leaders lie routinely. They kiss up to their own bosses while criticizing their people. Some lack the courage to do the right thing, or show no sign of knowing what the right thing is. Some lack the ability to grant even the most basic of common courtesies to their employees. These characters seem unable to utter the words "please" or "thank you." Other bad bosses routinely permit or commit sexual discrimination or harassment. They lace their language and actions with obscenities. Some are just plain dishonest and may even engage in criminal behavior.

Some bad bosses may exhibit only one or two of these bad behaviors and to varying degrees of severity. Others display all of these poisonous tendencies with additional bad behaviors added to their toxic personalities and practices.

A few bad bosses eventually see the light and change their behavior for the better, at least to a degree. If that happens to your boss, you are blessed, indeed. It is more likely, however, that you will have to compensate for a poor leader by altering your own practices to some extent.

As you do in so many other areas of your leader's responsibilities, confronting the issue of a bad boss is probably the most reliable means for mitigating the problem. This does not mean you have to instigate a shouting match with your supervisor. Bringing up a problem issue gently and privately is your best option for dealing with a difficult boss. The meeting should not start with accusations. While it hardly seems possible, some bad bosses actually do not realize that they are bad bosses. By making your point in a non-threatening manner, you may be able to get through to your boss without bringing down lightning on your head.

With adjustments made for whatever the boss problem you are facing happens to be, your approach might go thusly: "Boss, I know you don't intend to embarrass me in front of other people. You're too good a person for that. But when you treat me that way it makes me feel pretty worthless. I know you don't mean to do that."

Your boss is thereby left a way out if he wants to take it. He didn't *mean* to be a jerk. It was all a misunderstanding. He may try to change his behavior, at least somewhat. If he repeats the offense, you can repeat your reasonable, restrained objection, in private, of course. It is unlikely to work every time. But it won't fail every time, either. A problem not confronted is unlikely to get solved.

You won't feel very good about yourself if you don't at least try to right a wrong. Not confronted, the difficulties may only multiply and grow in severity. You owe yourself the attempt at making things better.

You may be able to affect some positive changes in a bad boss. If not, by realizing what his shortcomings are you may be able to mitigate their effects on you and your organization. You may learn when to avoid him and which hot buttons to refrain from hitting. You may be able to compensate for some of his weaknesses by the way in which you do your own job.

If your boss is a bad leader, chances are that you are not the only one who has noticed. By doing your own job ethically and well you just may outlast him.

There's a final lesson for you here. You know what a bad boss acts and feels like. Resolve never to do your own job in a manner that will leave your subordinates grumbling about *their* bad boss.

THE DANGERS OF GETTING TOO COZY

You know about the hazards of getting too firmly in the camp of one political faction or another in the community. You could well find yourself out the door when the political control of the local government changes. Better, then, that you work to get along with all factions and treat each one with impartiality. You are, after all, a professional law enforcement leader, not a professional politician.

To perhaps a lesser extent, the same advice holds true for your relationship with your boss. Naturally, it is absolutely vital that you show your supervisor your absolute loyalty and support in every aspect of your professional relationship. As your boss and the leader of the organization you both work for he has the right to expect that of you. You expect no less from your own managers.

You will have to rely upon your good common sense and your grasp of the local political situation to tell you how close to your boss you should be away from the job. If you and your supervisor truly have a liking for one another and enjoy some of the same things off-duty, then by all means enjoy that social relationship. Realize, however, that the closer you appear to your supervisor the more likely it becomes that you will be seen as a member of his inner circle. If he is a good and ethical guy and remains secure in his post throughout your career there, all should be well. Your visible, close relationship to the Big Boss could even prove beneficial to you.

If your boss gets in trouble and/or departs under less-than-favorable circumstances, his pals and close associates may come under close scrutiny by those hiring the next head of the organization. The departed boss's internal enemies may get their licks in, too. The new Big Boss may feel compelled to remove anyone seen as "tainted" by the former leader. That could mean big trouble for you.

Count on your good judgment in determining the kind of personal relationship you want with your supervisor. Obviously, his wishes will have a lot to say about it, too. Many police chiefs have enjoyed long careers in which they worked for a whole series of different town or city administrators. In many cases they have survived because it was obvious to the New Boss that the incumbent chief was competent, ethical, capable and well-accepted by police employees and the community. It was obvious to the new guy that he could turn his attention to other, pressing matters without having to invest time and energy in finding a new chief. By continuing to do a top-notch job you thereby control your own future, at least to a reasonable degree.

In the end, it will be up to you to decide how close you want to try and be with your boss, especially away from work. Hopefully, you will like and respect him enough for the question to arise in the first place. By calling on your ample common sense and good judgment applied to your knowledge of the local situation your decision should be a sound one.

THE YOUNG BOSS VS. THE OLD LION

Every boss you have ever had was at least a little different from the previous one. Your subordinates doubtlessly have compared you to the person you replaced. They have had to learn what you expect and how to work with you with as little conflict as possible. You will have to do the same with your own supervisor. It is all part of survival in the work world.

Most likely you already have sized up your boss's eccentricities and wants and adjusted your performance accordingly. (At least, if you're wise you have.) You also should expect to see some differences in the style and expectations of your boss based upon his or her age and amount of experience on the job.

An older, more experienced leader is often more sure of himself and set in his ways as to what he expects of his subordinates. He often does not want to know the details of what is going on in your department. He does want to know about the things that are big enough to bring publicity to the larger organization–and him. Otherwise, he expects you to handle the day-to-day crises of law enforcement leadership on your own and not call on him for help too often.

The young and/or less experienced Big Boss often will require more of your attention and effort. Particularly if it's his first Top Dog posting, he may worry a lot that a crisis or disaster will cost him his job almost instantly. He will want to know more about the goings on in a department (yours!) that holds great potential for things to go very wrong. He probably will require regular reassurance from you that it's going to be alright and that you have things under control.

You may have to watch yourself lest you overreact to what appears to be micromanagement by your nervous boss. Try to remember that he's likely very uneasy and needs your help, not your derision. You almost certainly have felt at one time or another the way he is feeling now. Try to help him out.

You can strengthen your boss-subordinate relationship considerably by letting your supervisor know that you are going to take care of him and that things are going to be OK. But take care not to sound like you are talking down to him in the process. Like you, he has his pride to defend.

Of course, relationships between human beings are never simple or cut and dried. Everyone is different. Your "old lion" boss could have less self-confidence than a rookie town manager. Or a first-time manager could want to know very little about your department's daily operations, assuming that things are under control unless you tell him otherwise.

The "old lion" could turn out to be a nervous pussycat; the "kid" could prove himself to be an unexpectedly calm and mature leader. By getting to know your boss well you will be able to gauge his strengths and weaknesses. You should then be able to provide the assistance he needs to do his job comfortably and confidently. A comfortable, confident boss is an easier boss to work with, and that's good for you!

NEVER EMBARRASS OR SURPRISE YOUR BOSS

No matter how good you are at taking care of your boss, it is still going to happen: your supervisor is embarrassed, surprised or both by something that was within your ability to control. That's just life in the real world. The important thing is that such happenings remain rare.

If you are to get along well with your supervisor and maintain his trust in you, you must adhere to the two cardinal rules inherent in every good superior-subordinate relationship: don't fail to tell your boss something important, and don't make him look bad. You expect that same degree of respect from your employees; it is reasonable for your boss to expect the same of you.

Bad things are going to happen and bad news is going to flow from those bad things from time to time. This is especially true in the law enforcement business. It cannot be helped. It is up to a good law enforcement leader to keep those things to a minimum. When they do happen, it is your job to assure that your boss is advised in advance that bad tidings are on the way.

If the bad happenings are the fault of you or your organization, it's up to you to say so. You should not expect your boss to take responsibility for a foulup that was not his. The foul up might not have been the result of your personal doing, either. But it's your department and you should expect to answer publicly for it.

You also are responsible for minimizing the number of instances in which your boss must make public explanations for your actions, apologize for them and thereby be embarrassed by them. Mistakes are going to happen from time to time, and you are almost certain to make some of them. Your boss knows that. Your obligation to him is not to have to call for forgiveness too often. Once again, he has the right to expect the same from you that you ask of your own subordinates: don't make a habit of making us all look bad.

No intelligent leader believes that his people will *never* disappoint him or cause discomfort. You are smart enough as a leader to know that. Assume that the leader you work for is bright enough to know it, too. As long as the bad surprises and embarrassments are kept to an absolute minimum, the working relationship between the two of you will remain a good one. That should *not* come as a surprise.

SHARE YOUR GLORIES WITH YOUR LEADER

It is amazing how much can be accomplished when no one involved is concerned about who gets the credit. You have heard that before, and it's true.

If you are wise, you will attribute the credit for the good work done by your department to the police personnel involved. You also will share credit, as appropriate, with the elected officials who support your department. You already appreciate the importance of doing that. But there is someone else who merits mention when the credits roll: your boss.

There will be any number of occasions when you and your agency receive accolades from groups or individuals for the good work being done. From time to time, it is a good idea to slip in an acknowledgment for your boss's role even as you express your gratitude for the praise. The credit you allot to your boss should be legitimate and not contrived. It would be rather ridiculous, for example, to include your supervisor in your acknowledgment of the good police work done in the capture of an armed robber, assuming your boss didn't nab the crook himself. Your cops did that and deserve full credit.

On the other hand, if you are being congratulated for your city's marked decrease in stickups and you plan to attribute the decline to the creation of the new robbery squad, it is only fair to mention your boss's name as the one who authorized the extra funding for the new team, if that is, in fact, the case.

If your elected, governing body had a hand in the creation of the new unit, credit its members, too. Extend kudos to everybody but yourself. Trust your citizens (and your boss) to have enough intelligence to grasp that you had a role in it, too.

As chief, you will have a lot of opportunities to talk to civic clubs and other gatherings about what the police department is doing in the community. You doubtlessly will use these opportunities to praise the good work being done by your people. On occasion, toss in a complimentary comment about your boss by mentioning something he or she has done in support of the department. You do not have to go on and on about it or make it seem a bigger deal that it really is. That would look insincere and trumped up. But the legitimate, brief praise you accord your boss likely will get back to him or her, sooner or later. That's good for you and your organization.

YOUR RELATIONSHIP WITH YOUR BOSS WILL HELP DETERMINE WHETHER YOU SUCCEED OR FAIL

There are many aspects of your difficult job that will help make your reputation for good or ill and play a role in determining whether you succeed or fail as a police chief. Most of them are within your control and influence to one extent or another.

How well you lead your department, handle your personnel, interact with the local citizens and elected officials and serve as a role model in the community all will impact on how successful you are. All are important tasks that must be done well by a successful leader. None of that, however, overshadows the importance of getting along well with your supervisor and being highly-regarded by him.

If you have established a close personal relationship with every supervisor you have ever worked for, your experience almost certainly would be described as unique. That kind of track record does not happen all that often. Fortunately, it probably has not been necessary for you to have a close, personal relationship with each of your past bosses to earn their respect and support. The same should hold true with your current boss, also. But having him respect your abilities as a leader certainly will make your success more likely. If he likes you as well, so much the better.

You will have to define "success" in your own way. For many chiefs, success could well mean remaining employed at their agency for as long as they choose to be there while accomplishing the goals they have set out for themselves and their department. You may have something similar in mind. Certainly, you should set your sights higher than continued employment alone. As a leader, you should seek to leave the organization and the community much better off than you found either upon assuming your post.

Do what you reasonably can to get along with your boss and assure his continued support. Take the time to listen to his worries. Consider his opinions of what you should be doing in your department, even though you may not agree with him. Never belittle his ideas or suggestions. Take him to lunch or coffee on occasion and talk about something (anything!) besides work. Let him know that you are going to look out for him as well as the bigger organization beyond your own department. Don't suck-up, but do make an honest effort to get along.

Try your dead-level best to get along well with your supervisor, even if he would not be your choice for Boss of the Year. It's just easier to work for someone you can relate to and honestly like. Chances are your chances for success as police chief will be enhanced by that kind of relationship.

YOUR BOSS IS UNLIKELY TO CHANGE TO SUIT YOU, SO . . .

When law enforcement leaders get together, often the talk eventually gets around to the topic of their supervisors. Inevitably, horror stories are shared and humorous episodes passed around. An informal "world's worst boss" contest may even ensue, as each new storyteller strives to better the last. It may surprise you to learn that *your* name gets bandied about when *your* subordinate supervisors and managers engage in such free-for-all discussions.

Everyone has eccentricities. Some have at least a few personal oddities that are, well, downright *odd.* Almost everyone does something that aggravates, irritates or frustrates somebody else. Probably even *you* do! It is just human nature.

You likely have a large degree of control of the people who report to you. If your secretary's gum-popping makes you crazy, you can require her to knock it off. If one of your staffers is notorious about appearing late for your staff meetings, you probably can bring that behavior to a halt, also.

But things get a lot tougher when it's your boss's character, habits, tendencies or traits that are driving *you* to distraction. You certainly can bring the issue up with your boss, if it is bothering you to the extent that you can no longer stand it. (You probably should not, however, imply that you are going to shoot him if he doesn't stop cracking his knuckles.) Tact is the byword here. Your efforts at changing your boss's behavior may or may not succeed if you elect to confront the issue, whatever it is, in the first place.

Adjusting to your boss's particular eccentricities may, in the end, be your best bet, assuming that what he is doing to irritate you is neither illegal nor unethical. It may be the least painful and most successful route for you both. If, for instance, you know from experience that your boss never reads the written background material you have prepared for him ahead of the Big Meeting, you may want to give him a brief oral accounting of the key points before the session begins. If you know he has a habit of losing the work you have produced for him, be sure you always have a spare copy close at hand.

Adapt, adjust, overcome. It's a tried and true way of circumventing a boss's very human frailties. He doesn't have to change. And you don't have to go crazy. It *can* work for everybody.

PANDERING TO YOUR EMPLOYEES WILL COST YOUR BOSS'S SUPPORT

Everyone who is at least marginally normal wants to be liked. You do, too. There is nothing wrong with that. If most of your employees like you–if at least the majority of them don't hate you–your job as leader of the organization will be easier. The challenge for you, then, is to get most of them to like you without giving away the farm in the process.

One chief who came into a troubled department learned that his forced-out predecessor had, to the frustration of the management staff, conceded to the employees almost every request they had made over a period of years. Unsure of just how secure his position was, the chief worked hard in an effort to "buy" the support of his front-line employees, often contrary to the desires of his command staff. The chief's supervisor also noted where the law enforcement boss's apparent loyalties lay. That same boss eventually sacked the chief for a variety of reasons. When that happened, none of the employees whose loyalties the chief had attempted to buy lifted a finger to help him. They had readily accepted his gifts and then figuratively waved as he was shown the door. So much for trying to buy loyalty and support.

There are plenty of other, real-life examples to reinforce the truth of the preceding story of a chief's career demise. You cannot purchase job survival by pandering to those who work for you. Your employees probably will not respect you if you do. Your boss most certainly won't. Fairness and loyalty to your people is mandatory. Trying to buy their favor does not work.

As in so many aspects of your job, there is a common sense balance to be struck. One of your most important tasks is to take care of your employees and secure for them the support and resources they need to do their jobs safely and well. The support and resources that they really *need,* that is. It is not unusual for people to *ask* for a lot more than they really require in order to obtain via compromise what they believe they actually need. You may have played that game yourself. You probably expected your boss to say "no" on occasion. Your people and your boss may be expecting *you* to be the naysayer now. Sometimes that is your job as a responsible leader who sees the big picture that exists well beyond the walls of your own organization.

As you know, it is unreasonable for anyone to expect to receive everything that they ask for 100% of the time. Even kids at Christmas soon grasp this harsh fact of life. Chances are, your people know it, too.

Do stand up for what your people really need, not necessarily what they want to have. They will respect you for it more than if you cave in to every whim that comes down the road. When you must say "no," be willing to explain why. But say it clearly and forcefully when needed.

One kind of "pandering" is a crime in the criminal statutes book. Chances are the other kind is at least equally contemptible in your boss's book. Don't be guilty of it.

DON'T FRET EXCESSIVELY ABOUT WHAT YOUR BOSS IS THINKING

It *is* important to know what your boss is thinking. That's more than a career survival skill. Knowing your boss's take on things also can help you run your organization well. It can help you craft the proposals and plans you put before him. Likewise, it can help you in creating the plans for the organization that you need his help to implement.

Knowing what your boss is thinking is a good thing. You can accomplish that by maintaining good communication with your supervisor. The more you talk with him, the more likely it is that you will know how he views you, your department, your personnel and what it is that you are trying to accomplish. By knowing his prejudices and understanding his attitudes concerning your agency you can better prepare your arguments and responses for getting what you need. Knowing these things can aid you in defending your positions, when necessary. Hopefully, a real friendship or at least some mutual respect will develop along the way. That, too, will make your job as a leader easier.

Keeping track of your boss's thoughts and attitudes is important for all of these reasons. It is something that a savvy leader does. At the same time, it would be counterproductive for you to worry *too* much about what is in your boss's thoughts. The energy can be better spent elsewhere on the countless other duties you face.

For one thing, it is virtually impossible for you to know your boss's mind on every conceivable subject. It is doubtful that *he* knows it, either. And, like you, his thoughts and opinions on a given topic are subject to change without notice. That's one of the consequences of being a conscious life-form with a brain. Like you, he may not react exactly the same way to one set of facts or circumstances today as he did yesterday, or will tomorrow. How he is feeling physically and mentally from one day to the next can help account for the changes. So can new information (or misinformation) to which he has been exposed since the last time he thought about the matter.

Gathering intelligence to do your job well while protecting your job security should include knowing what your boss is thinking where it is feasible. Worrying yourself sick over it makes no sense at all. Know what you reasonably can and go forward. It is the most effective and reliable means for working with the person you call "boss."

PROVE THAT YOU CAN BE BELIEVED AND TRUSTED

In a tough spot, in the middle of a big crisis, it is vital that your boss as well as your subordinates have absolute faith in your credibility and integrity, not to mention your competency as a leader. You know that.

But the day that the Big One hits is much too late to establish your reputation for trust. That is something you begin working on from your first day with the organization. If you are wise, you have established your reputation for honesty and truthfulness in many, many actions and decisions you have taken since your first day as the leader of the organization. If you came up through the ranks of the agency, you began to construct that reputation long before you became chief.

Your reputation for character is built from incidents large and small that have accumulated and built one upon the other over time. Over that time your boss hopefully has seen the integrity and impartiality with which you have handled personnel matters and disciplinary decisions. He or she has observed how you have dealt with bumps and bruises in your own career when things have not gone as desired. Perhaps you have stumbled in your own adherence to the rules. In other words, your boss probably has seen you mess up. More importantly, he has seen how you responded when the missteps came to light.

If you have lied or attempted unfairly to shift the blame when trouble has called in the past, you will be hard-pressed to get your supervisor to believe you now. That's why the way you have responded to minor crises will help determine how you are perceived when a really big one arrives. Your boss may rely upon the same guideline you do in predicting human behavior: With rare exceptions, what a person has done in the past is a good indicator of what he will do in the future.

It is up to you to assure that all you have done in the past and will do in the future practically drips with integrity and credibility. Your reputation for trust is, after all, established one promise, one statement, one act at a time.

Strive to keep your missteps to an absolute minimum. Tell the truth. Be an excellent role model for your people and even for your boss. In doing so you will prove that you can be both believed and followed.

NEVER SHOW FEAR OR SELF-DOUBT

There is an old deodorant commercial that fronted the expression "Never let them see you sweat!" The same advice is applicable to your role as the police chief.

Both your employees and your boss expect you to be in control of yourself and your organization at all times. Unfortunately, you are not really allowed time for even normal human weaknesses. They expect that you will show neither fear nor indecisiveness. They want and need you to exhibit calm in the face of danger and uncertainty, whether the turmoil exists because of a "bad" police shooting or a tornado that devastated the community. They expect you to demonstrate confidence and leadership in tough budget times when layoffs are in the offing.

None of this means that you cannot harbor privately your own worries, fears and doubts. None of it requires that you cannot bare these things to a really close confidante whom you know will keep your secret. None of it says that you cannot be a normal person with fears and foibles. *You just cannot exhibit those things to those below and above you.*

Particularly if your boss is inexperienced in his leadership role, it is important that he can count on you as a safe place in a storm. The HR director may be able to waver, the water and sewer guy can shake and the Big Boss probably won't think any less of them for it. The chief of police must remain strong when the wolves are at the door. Even beyond that, he must be capable of leading the way in turning those predators into fur coats, if necessary.

You must, in a word, *lead.* Your boss is counting on it. You will be diminished in his eyes if you fail this acid test. That will not bode well for your future, whether your boss is a nervous rookie or a grizzled veteran. A big hole in his protective armor has just been revealed and he will not be happy about it.

Stay visibly strong when adversity of any kind hits, even if doing so requires your finest acting skills. Your organization needs to feel that strength. So does your boss.

LET YOUR BOSS KNOW YOU WILL TAKE CARE OF HIM

As noted, your supervisor needs to see and know that you are a strong and competent leader. He needs to feel comfortable that you will take care of business under the most trying of circumstances. Just as important, he needs to know that you will take care of *him*.

Mayors, town administrators and city managers face a lot of threats to their tenure. Some of those threats are very political in nature. Some of them you cannot do a lot about. (You probably cannot repair the aging infrastructure all by yourself.) But there are other things that you can and should do.

Law and order issues are big in any community. Public safety is one of the primary reasons for government's existence, and your citizens have high expectations for both you and your boss. If you are not perceived as doing a good job of keeping your constituents safe, they may blame your boss almost as much as they do you. That could have serious repercussions for you both.

Reassuring your leader that taking care of him is a responsibility you take VERY seriously may be something you have to do more frequently with a novice manager than an experienced one. Regardless, it is a good idea to let your boss know from time to time that you have got the situation under control, or will have shortly. The smoke looks worse than the actual blaze happens to be, or something like that. The point is to reassure your supervisor that you are there to take care of his interests.

You will have to be the judge of how often and how strongly you let your boss know that it is going to be alright and that you are there for him. With a veteran manager who is not prone to panicky behavior you may need to convey the message once and then simply reinforce it through your actions. With a less-experienced and visibly-nervous leader you may need to repeat the message on a fairly regular basis, especially when you sense through his words or actions that he is stressed, uneasy, even frightened. One veteran chief made a point of sending such a supervisor e-mails in times of crisis: Your staff is behind you. We will take care of you. The timely reminders appeared to help the uneasy boss stay in control. That was good for everyone.

Let your boss know that you will take care of him in every way legally and ethically appropriate. Show by your actions that you mean what you say and say what you mean. Do not surprise him and do not embarrass him. Support his decisions, even if you did not initially concur with them. Never quarrel with him in the public eye. Then, don't be surprised if he supports you in the same way.

DETERMINE WHAT YOUR BOSS KNOWS ABOUT POLICING AND EDUCATE HIM

Police chiefs sometimes make the mistake of assuming that their supervisor knows either a lot more or a lot less about police and policing than he actually does. It is an error you will wish to avoid.

Once again, by spending some time with your boss you should have the opportunity to discuss a good many things with him. While you should not endeavor to talk only "shop," discussing police matters with him will give you some idea of what he really knows on the topic. It also will give you insight into his opinions on some topics relevant to what you and your employees do for a living. All of that could prove very useful to you in your future interactions with your boss.

A few city and town managers have little interest in things that smack of police work. They hope that by having you on board the problems inherent in maintaining a force of uniforms with guns will be kept at a distance from them. They may not particularly like cops or the political liabilities they bring with them. They do not know a huge amount about policing, nor do they necessarily want to. They see police issues as *your* responsibility.

If that is the case with your boss, you may be wasting your time if you invest a huge amount of effort into his education on matters of law enforcement. You may be well-advised to keep him briefed on major matters but screen him from the smaller issues. He may simply not care about them unless it appears they will impact him by becoming noisy public affairs.

Other elected and appointed city and town leaders have a lot of interest in policing, a few to the point of practically becoming badge buffs. You may be able to make points with these individuals and gain their support by sharing police news with them when you are not betraying an ongoing operation by doing so.

A leader of this sort *wants* to have timely notification of big cases and good arrests. He *wants* you to talk about your department and its issues. He likely won't be slow to proffer his opinions on police matters, whether you ask for them or not. Be patient and indulge him. You may gain considerable good will for your department by doing so. You soon will be able to measure his relative knowledge of your profession. Teach and gently correct misconceptions as necessary. He will be a stronger advocate for you and your organization with correct information as opposed to misconceptions.

Talk to your boss. Listen well to what he has to say. Do not hoard the interesting information you have about what you do for a living. Share it with your leader. Take him out to the firearms range or on patrol. The backing you may generate from the effort will be worth far more than the energy you expend.

With the boss who is not as interested in policing, answer his questions and seek to increase his understanding of what you do and why. Do not bore him with details if he does not appear that interested. Give him the condensed version. Let him know that you will handle the law enforcement issues for him. Do your best to keep those pesky carnivores away from his door.

IT'S OK TO VOLUNTEER

That old, military-based saw about never volunteering for anything will not serve you well as a successful police chief. Adhering to it may, in fact, cause you serious problems with your supervisor. You are better than that, anyhow.

You have talents other than being your jurisdiction's top cop. You can do a lot more than investigate a crime or referee a drunken dispute. You can do things besides lead police people, as important as that skill is for the chief of police.

In other words, you can do other things that could be of assistance to the man or woman you work for. You also may be able to help your colleagues who run the other departments in your town or city organization. But all of the people you might help are unlikely to know of your abilities and willingness to apply them unless you speak up.

Your boss probably looks at his department heads as a team of which he is the captain. He probably expects his team members to help each other out, as required. He probably expects them to offer *him* their assistance and expertise, as well. It is up to you to meet your boss's expectations in this regard. He cannot read your mind, so let him know that you are ready to help.

Virtually everyone has some special strengths or talents. You do, too. Whether yours are of the technical variety or are more in the realm of "people skills," as a leader you are obliged to share them for the good of the group.

Some chiefs have proven to be very good at math and accounting and have helped out with the city's budget work. Others have demonstrated talent in personnel matters and have volunteered their help in creating employee policies and regulations to help an HR colleague. One chief who was a good writer constructed news releases and public service announcements for the entire town government. Another police CEO with more than a little creativity turned out to be an excellent speechwriter for his boss.

There are a lot of things you can do outside of police work that can help make your boss's life a little easier. By seeking out where you can help and filling that niche on occasion you can help yourself even as you benefit the other person and the bigger organization. All of that starts when you volunteer to help. Don't be stingy with your skills.

YOUR GOAL: MAKE YOUR BOSS'S LIFE BETTER

Almost certainly, your boss hired you for the very same reason you hire people. He did not hire you to make your life better. He hired you to make *his* life better. When the police organization is functioning smoothly and your boss's telephone isn't constantly ringing with complaints about the police department, his life *is* better.

Making your boss's day as good as possible should be one of your paramount goals. Your personal objective is an obvious one: by keeping your boss reasonably content you improve the chances for your own success. That's good for you. But by remaining in place you also help the organization you lead. You cannot make the department better if you are no longer there. It is important to the agency, then, that your boss allows you to finish the job you started.

Your goal of making your leader's life better leaves no room for ethical lapses. You do not make things better for either him or the organization if you cheat for him or bend the rules on his behalf. He doesn't get his traffic ticket "fixed" any more than Joe the bartender does. He isn't given access to statute-protected information such as national or state criminal record databases. Nor is a relative of his given a break on a criminal charge.

That's not what taking care of your boss is all about. Instead, you will make your boss's life better by telling him the truth, even when it is unpleasant. You will demonstrate your loyalty by not gossiping about him or criticizing his decisions behind his back. You will carry out the assignments he gives you in a timely manner and be sure they are done correctly and thoroughly the first time. You will be as disappointed as he is when he has to return an assignment to you for repair.

You will keep your boss advised of not only law enforcement developments but potentially troubling political ones that you become aware of so that he is not ambushed by events of which you had knowledge. You will defend your boss appropriately in discussions or debates with others who are armed with incorrect or incomplete tales.

Perhaps the most important of all, you will run your department capably and ethically with as little intervention as possible required of your supervisor. You will take charge of the key department your boss has entrusted to you and run it effectively, efficiently and ethically. You will be the leader that your boss believed he or she hired to do an incredibly difficult job–well.

SUMMARY

There are many reasons why chiefs fail, but being unable to work well with one's boss remains at or near the top of the list. Understanding what your boss wants from you is vital to your success and survival as police chief. It is equally important that you build a relationship of mutual trust and excellent communication between the two of you. Learning your supervisor's style and way of doing business is vital, as you will need to adjust to both.

There are cardinal rules to remember in working with your boss. They include avoiding surprises, never embarrassing or blaming him and sharing with your supervisor the credit for good things you have accomplished. You also must prove to your boss that you can be believed and trusted in all things. Your leader needs to know that you will protect him and just generally make his life better. He needs to know that you are the experienced, competent law enforcement leader who will take care of him. For that reason you must never exhibit fear or uncertainty in his presence.

There are countless ways to get in trouble with your boss and thereby shorten your tenure as chief. Lying to him, appearing to pander to your employees to the detriment of the rest of the organization and showing disloyalty to your employer are among them. Being on the losing side in organizational political games and intrigues can do it, too.

There are bad bosses out there, and if you are unfortunate enough to have drawn one it will be up to you to make the relationship a tolerable one or start submitting your resume. Honest, open communication can mitigate some boss problems. Patience and tolerance can help solve others. In the end, the burden will fall primarily on you to turn a less-than-desirable boss situation into a workable, survivable one. It also will be up to you to decide if it is worth the effort.

You must have a good working relationship with your boss to succeed as police chief. Achieving that relationship won't always be easy, but reaching it is one of the most important tasks you will encounter as a law enforcement CEO. Getting it done is critical. Fortunately, you are up to the task.

POINTS TO REMEMBER

- If it is possible, getting a contract can help define the relationship with your boss.
- It is important to understand what your supervisor expects from you.
- Engaging in organizational politics is a dangerous game to play.
- Learn some techniques for surviving a difficult boss.
- Your boss's behavior may be related to his depth of experience and knowledge of policing.
- Be prepared to educate your boss about law enforcement issues and operations.
- Do not surprise or embarrass your supervisor.
- Share your credits and accolades with your boss.
- Realize that you will have to adjust to your boss's style; he is unlikely to change to suit you.

- To succeed you must have the support of your boss; work honestly and ethically to obtain it.
- Proving your credibility to your supervisor is vital.
- Never show fear, uncertainty or a lack of self-confidence in front of your leader.
- Let your boss know that you will take care of him.

Chapter 9

HANDLING DISCIPLINE WELL IS VITAL

Most normal people do not enjoy doing things to other people–particularly people they know–that will make those people unhappy. That is why many supervisors and managers dread having to administer discipline to the employees under them. That is why some of them quibble and delay disciplinary discussions and decision-making for as long as possible. Some delay even more before administering the corrective action itself. In such an atmosphere of delay and dread no one's interests are well-served.

Discipline is important in an effective, efficient law enforcement organization. While self-discipline is the best discipline of all, corrective measures must be taken when performance falls short, particularly when the poor performance was intentional.

Handling all aspects of discipline well is required of you, a leader who serves as a positive role model for his or her people. Your people will expect you to face this vital task in a timely and impartial manner. They will expect you to know the difference between mistakes of the head and mistakes of the heart and address improper behavior accordingly. They will be watching to see if you mean what you say and actually will carry out the corrective action you announced. You also will be observed for your reaction when the discipline you ordained is reversed by the disciplinary appeal process–or your boss. You will be watched even more closely when you are the recipient of disciplinary action yourself.

Good discipline is too important to a successful law enforcement organization to be left to chance. It requires your full engagement and your best efforts. It may require you to educate your subordinate managers in the intricacies of doing discipline the right way. But all of it has got to be done. Discipline is that important. Doing it right is what this chapter is about.

THE BEST DISCIPLINE IS SELF-DISCIPLINE

Management course instructors sometimes speak of positive vs. negative discipline. They offer training or re-training as an example of *positive* discipline for an employee misstep. *Negative* discipline is what they call corrective action or punishment for serious infractions of the rules. Negative discipline can run the gamut from a letter of reprimand to a suspension without pay to termination.

Beyond the positives and negatives of discipline the undisputed fact remains that self-discipline–the personal, internal rules and codes of conduct that you impose and follow yourself–is the noblest and perhaps most effective discipline of all. This self-discipline is something you routinely display as the leader of your organization. Self-discipline is also something you expect of those who would be the leaders under you. Self-discipline is vital to a healthy law enforcement organization.

Because you are a powerful advocate for self-discipline your boss should have little need to impose sanctions on you on the rare occasions on which you inadvertently foul-up. (He may do it anyway to show that everyone is treated equally.) With your intense focus on always doing it the right way, you have already punished yourself more than he could. That's worth keeping in mind when one of your people whom you know has the heart for doing it right makes a rare mistake. You are smart enough to know that over-disciplining in such a case could well turn a good employee into an embittered one. Your knowledge of the real value of self-discipline means that when you must impose corrective action it is very thoughtfully done.

You also are well aware that organizations populated by employees with a lot of self-discipline seldom have to rely on more coercive disciplinary measures. So-called negative discipline still will happen. But it will not happen as often as it will in organizations with less emphasis on the expectation of employee self-control.

Self-discipline can be bolstered by strong religious beliefs, personal moral values, strict adherence to a professional code of ethics or all of the above. The point is that people who make a point of scrupulously following the rules, whatever their reason or reasons, almost universally display the self-discipline that transforms them into good law enforcement officers and leaders. That's why self-discipline is so important to you, the man or woman who must lead the leaders. Self-discipline is a major component of the ethical, effective leader's character. It's what you are all about.

BE A ROLE MODEL HERE, TOO

You are already a role model for the positive traits you want to see in your subordinates. You also must serve as a good example of the self-control and internally-driven discipline you want to see in your people.

Resist the temptation to take an active role in determining the need for discipline and its scope when these are decisions that should be made by your subordinate managers and first-line supervisors. While your desire to "get it right" may be pure, by taking over a task that should be handled by others you remove the opportunity for them to grow as leaders with backbones. You can still review their final decisions and weigh in if it is evident that a clear error or miscarriage of justice is in the offing. Otherwise, allow your subordinates to learn how to handle discipline and its repercussions. Some of their decisions will not be perfect by your standards, but neither are most destined to be disasters.

When you must be personally involved in disciplinary decision-making, model for your people the thought processes and skills you would like to see them demonstrate in your absence. Get all the facts before you decide. Weigh opposing views and statements carefully and objectively. Truly listen to what is said. Place your prejudices towards the involved actors out of your mind. Be willing to change your mind if the evidence demands it. Temper with mercy your earnest desire to make a point. Be certain that disciplinary decisions and actions are taken in a timely manner and without procrastination. Say what you mean, mean what you say and stick by your guns in the face of hostile opposition by the discipline's recipient.

All of these things you expect of your subordinates in matters regarding discipline. Role-modeling them yourself will make it easier for your people to understand what you expect of them. Living by them yourself will deny others the opportunity to depict you as a hypocrite.

On occasion, discipline can take a nasty turn. You may find discipline you have imposed overturned by an appeal process. You may even find yourself the subject of discipline assessed for some infraction or another. (After all, even chiefs of police occasionally have car wrecks, experience accidental firearms discharges or otherwise sin against the rule book.) Whatever the case, you must continue to display a positive, business-as-usual demeanor. If you are to expect your subordinates to carry on without a hiccup in the face of adversity you must set the example for them. Stay focused, don't pout, do not get visibly angry. Remain on task and do not permit your attitude to sag. This is where your ample supply of self-discipline takes charge.

A REPUTATION FOR FAIRNESS IS YOUR GOAL

Try as you might, not everyone is going to love you. A very few might even hate you, for one reason or another. You know that and have prepared yourself to live with it as the chief of police. You know not to let it distract you from doing your job. But that's a little easier said than done when you know that a few of your own employees are likely among those who wish you ill.

That can't be helped. You cannot promise happiness for each of your employees. What you can and must guarantee them is that they will be treated fairly by you and the organization you command. In no aspect of your job is that more important than in the realm of discipline. Your sworn and civilian employees must be able to assume that when it comes to determining the need for sanctions for substandard or improper performance the requirement for justice will outrank all other considerations.

What you have to say is very important to your people. Even more vital to your reputation for integrity and fairness is what you *do,* most especially in matters concerning discipline. For you to maintain your reputation for integrity, there must never be legitimate cause for someone to believe that discipline happened a certain way because of the involved employee's relationship with the chief, good or bad. It must be evident that discipline issued or approved by the chief is based on proven fact, not on bias or half-truths. Your people must know that you will defend them when they are falsely accused just as vigorously as you will administer corrective action following deliberate malpractice.

Likewise, the members of your organization must know that their boss always will look at extenuating circumstances and mitigating factors before negative sanctions are imposed. They must know that when you sit in the role of disciplinary review or appeal authority you will make your decision based on the facts alone, not preordained beliefs and prejudices. In sum, they must know that you will be *just.*

A reputation for fairness in matters involving discipline does not develop overnight. It accumulates and is strengthened by many different actions and decisions, big and small, that you take over time. This cumulative record for fairness (or the lack thereof) is what your people will know you by.

Always do your best to be just. Realize that virtually never will *everyone* concur that you were fair. Accept that as fair enough and move ahead.

NOT DEALING WITH THE BAD WILL COST YOU THE GOOD

It is very, very hard for most of your employees to commend you for the good you do, at least publicly. They do not want to be seen by their peers as "boss's pets." As a result, you probably will not receive all that many "attaboys" from your people when they know that you have done the right thing. As a leader, you accept that.

You also should be aware that it is even harder for your people to let you know that you have done the right thing when you discipline a wayward member of the organization, even though they recognize that it was the proper thing to do. Many of them probably hoped you would do it. Many of them are glad that you did. But few if any will say so in front of their peers. You likely will have to be content with silent support.

Although your people may not commend you in public for the good disciplinary decisions you make, you safely can assume that they are watching what you and your subordinate leaders are doing. Some of them will be quick to criticize if they feel you are allowing the slugs and misfits to slide while the responsible employees are working their tails off to do things the right way.

While it probably will never be easy for many cops to call publicly for serious discipline for their misbehaving colleagues, many nevertheless expect you to punish inappropriate behavior accordingly. They will expect you to hold your subordinate managers accountable for doing the right thing, as well. If you or your subordinate bosses fail to hold the mischief-makers accountable, an increasing number of your good employees will question why they are investing energy and emotion in doing the right thing. Some of them may lapse into less-than-desirable behavior themselves if it looks like the department doesn't reward good deeds and punish bad ones. By not dealing effectively with improper behavior you may thus encourage more of it. And that you truly do not need.

Your good employees deserve your earnest support. So do your non-stars, who simply do the right thing, day in and day out. Even your rare problem children need your support, which well may include disciplinary action. Do not show all of them disrespect by tolerating substandard work or unethical, illegal or otherwise improper behavior.

MISTAKES OF THE HEAD VS. MISTAKES OF THE HEART

Everyone makes mistakes. Even you. If you are as active as you should be in decision-making in your agency, you probably make them on an almost daily basis. Unless your boss is an idiot, he knows and understands that, as he makes them, too.

Most mistakes are both forgivable and recoverable. You learn from making them. Indeed, more than a few effective leaders will confess that they have learned more from painful errors than from any other kind. That's just how the human animal functions. Mistakes are inevitable. You are going to make some.

You also know from both life experience and your role as a leader that there are two kinds of mistakes. The first category includes the "innocent" kind that people make simply because they forgot, misinterpreted or accidentally erred in one way or another. There was no intent to do wrong on the police employee's part. But regardless of his intent, he nonetheless messed up and there were bad results of one sort or another. Mistakes of the head committed by cops can include accidentally missing a scheduled court appearance, improperly booking a piece of evidence, using the wrong charge on a summons or forgetting to return an important phone call. In the busy, complex world that your people work in, mistakes of the head are going to happen.

Mistakes of the heart are a very different story. They are committed on purpose by people who know better, or should. They are committed by those who know the pertinent rule or expectation, but consciously elect to do something else anyway. Mistakes of the heart are not accidental or incidental happenings. Sometimes they require plotting and scheming before they are perpetrated. Frequently they involve actions that cannot be tolerated in an ethics-driven organization. Mistakes of the heart sometimes made by police personnel include lying to supervisors about misconduct, theft of prisoners' property, lying under oath and abuse of authority. Less-serious but nonetheless intolerable improper behavior might include regularly sleeping on duty or repeatedly operating a police vehicle in an illegal manner. Like mistakes of the head, mistakes of the heart are going to happen in even the best law enforcement organization. Your law enforcement organization. When they do happen, prompt and effective measures to correct them are necessary.

As a general rule of thumb, mistakes of the heart, being intentional misdeeds, should be more heavily disciplined than "honest" errors. Where a mistake of the head may merit no more than an oral warning and/or additional training in the right way to do something, intentional errors may require sanctions ranging from a letter of reprimand to a termination from employment. In an extreme case involving illegal conduct, the filing of criminal charges may be appropriate. Training or other "positive" discipline can still be a response to a mistake of the heart. But punishment is often a part of the official response, as well.

You must remain aware of the big differences in the kinds of mistakes that can be made by your people and treat each appropriately. Discipline different kinds of errors differently. Match the sanction to the offense. Then be willing to forgive and proceed with your duty of leading an effective, ethical law enforcement agency.

DISCIPLINE AS A TEACHER

You can learn a lot from doing wrong. Sometimes the learning is even painful. You learned that as a child and doubtlessly have had the lesson reinforced many times in the intervening years.

Correction for misconduct is important for the perpetrator of the misconduct. Knowing that there will be consequences for misbehavior is necessary for the culprit to learn to avoid committing the same misdeed in the future. But the benefits of discipline extend far beyond the individual who is sanctioned for his transgression.

One of the primary purposes of corrective action is education of all members of your organization. Through discipline administered to a single member of the group everyone learns which actions will and will not be tolerated by the organization. Everyone also learns what the consequences are likely to be for someone else who elects to repeat the misconduct. The advantage for all your other people is that they learn at the transgressor's expense.

Every disciplinary measure you implement should be taken with the knowledge that the rest of the organization is watching. Its members will make judgments about the fairness of what you are doing. They likely will measure the mistake against the assessed penalty. That is one more reason why it is vital that discipline is both appropriate and just. Your employees also will note and record what they should expect if they engage in the same intentional misconduct. That's educational for them, but it also requires that you pay attention to what you are doing to assure balance and consistency in your agency's disciplinary decision-making.

It is unlikely that you will be personally involved in every disciplinary decision or action taken within your organization. For that reason you must be sure that your philosophy and guidance regarding fair, consistent discipline is well-known throughout your department's leadership structure, beginning with your top management personnel and extending down through your cadre of first-line supervisors. If employees are to learn good things (like fairness) rather than bad ones (like favoritism) from the organization's disciplinary machinery, the department's bosses must speak with a single voice. Your subordinate leaders must know what you value and expect from them. They must understand the difference between mistakes of the head and mistakes of the heart and the appropriate responses to each.

All discipline has a powerful ability to teach. You are responsible for assuring that what it teaches is what you want your employees to learn.

GET IT DONE

People tend to put off what they do not enjoy doing. People tend not to want to do things that they think other people they like are going to find unpleasant. Thereby, people, yours included, tend to avoid making discipli-nary decisions and (especially) taking disciplinary actions. You likely would confess to such a tendency yourself.

The truth is, however, that disciplinary decisions delayed are beneficial to no one. The same holds true for the implementation of disciplinary meas-ures. The old saw about "justice delayed, justice denied" comes to mind here.

In fairness, your employees deserve to know without unnecessary delay whether or not their department will find that they did wrong. If they already know that they erred, it is not unreasonable for them to want to know as soon as possible what the consequences for their foul-up will be. Particularly if the alleged miscue was one that drew considerable attention within the organi-zation, your other employees will be curious to learn the outcome of the affair. Everyone will expect that the situation will not drag on endlessly. For the employee anxiously waiting to learn his or her fate, the phrase "cruel and unusual punishment" may come to mind if disciplinary decisions and actions are delayed too long.

It is not your fault if your organization's formal employee rights and dis-ciplinary appeals procedures slow everything down. It is appropriate to let your people know what is causing the delay, if that is the case. But do not use that as an explanation unless it is the whole truth.

Basic human psychology says that you don't give junior a time-out today for pulling his sister's hair six weeks ago. Understandably, he is unlikely to make a connection between his misdeed and the penalty assessed for it. The same principle holds true for the adults that make up your organization. An individual's recollection about what he did or didn't do also can change over time. Get the discipline done promptly for maximum effectiveness. Its use-fulness will diminish with the passage of time. Get it done as quickly as your agency's policies and procedures will allow.

BOUNCE TOUGH CALLS OFF OF YOUR PEERS

Making decisions in situations that involve major discipline can be among the most difficult tasks you will face as a CEO. The job gets even harder when your decision-making literally will decide someone's future livelihood. It is not unusual to feel very, very alone at such a moment.

The good news is that you are really not alone. There are plenty of other law enforcement agency heads out there who have at one time or another encountered the dilemma that you are facing now. Collectively these leaders share a lot of knowledge and experience. Most if not all of them will share their experiences if you just ask. And ask you should when you feel stymied about what to do next.

You realize the importance of maintaining a close circle of perhaps half a dozen fellow law enforcement chief executives that you can call on for advice on all kinds of things. Do not hesitate to call on this same corps of leaders when disciplinary decisions weigh heavily on your mind. If they have not experienced a situation identical to yours, one or more of them likely has faced one similar enough to offer you relevant advice. But you won't know that if you don't ask. Do not hesitate to make the contact. You can return the favor one day.

People you know who are in leadership positions outside of law enforcement also may be able to give you good advice. They may offer a different but helpful perspective from someone who isn't a cop. They probably have encountered some of the same behavior and misbehavior from employees who *don't* carry guns. With or without a badge, people and their foibles are similar across the broad spectrum of humanity.

People–police chiefs included–sometimes exhibit a proclivity to agree and tell their friends what they think they want to hear, sometimes at the expense of the absolute truth. For that reason you will want to be cautious about how you tell your colleague about the disciplinary situation you want his opinion on. It is only human to tell the story in the light most favorable to your own position or decision. It is easy to leave out mitigating or complicating circumstances that might lead your listener to reach a conclusion different from your own. Relate the whole, unbiased story.

It is also very easy to give away inadvertently what *you* feel is the right response to the situation you are describing. Given that tip-off, your peer may find the temptation to agree with you strong indeed, even if internally he harbors doubts.

To get the most value from your consultations with your colleagues, present your "story" as neutrally as you can. Listen to his advice and show your gratitude for his contribution. Let him know that you stand ready to reciprocate. Then, consider all that you have heard in reaching a decision that you and you alone will be accountable for. In spite of all the help that you can and should get, that is your job as the ultimate disciplinary decision-maker.

MEAN WHAT YOU SAY

You have been there before. In a moment of exasperation or anger, you have said something you regretted. Regrets or no, your perhaps ill-advised statement, promise or threat was now out there for the whole world to witness.

As the leader of a law enforcement organization you no longer have the questionable luxury of spouting forth whatever might come to mind in a moment of pique, anger or even jest. All too often what the boss says is seen by those both inside and outside your organization as the "official" word or judgment from on high. While something outrageous said by a front-line employee might easily be dismissed, what you say has authority behind it, whether you meant it that way or not. It's hard for you as the chief to make a flippant comment!

In other words, as chief you have to be as careful in what you say as you are in what you do, on the job and away from it. What you have to say is under virtually constant surveillance. The need to be verbally cautious is particularly critical when you are speaking about matters involving employee discipline. Naturally, personnel matters are confidential in the first place, so *where* you speak up is critical. Think before you unleash your tongue.

One Western U.S. chief had a well-known penchant for spouting off concerning the guilt or innocence of his employees accused of misconduct long before he knew the results of an inquiry into the allegations. The chief appeared to be relying solely on his knowledge, real or imagined, of the accused employee's reputation. Unfortunately, the chief also had the nasty habit of announcing what he was going to do to the assumed "guilty" employee long before he knew that the individual was actually in the wrong. The chief's bad habit of exploding before all the facts were in resulted in more than one embarrassing situation in which his premature pronouncements of guilt turned out to be in error. His promises of disciplinary mayhem had to be withdrawn, with resulting bad feelings all around.

Know the facts before you make a pronouncement regarding discipline. But when you do announce your intent to administer corrective action, mean what you say. Barring the discovery of previously-unknown facts, stick with the disciplinary plans you made. Your employees may come to doubt your sincerity if you back down and abandon your plans to discipline because you feared the reaction of the involved employee or his peers.

Once you have determined that you are doing the right thing, neither threats nor pleas nor tears should cause you to veer from your planned course of action. Backing down may win you temporary gratitude. It won't earn you affection and/or respect in the long run. Expect your subordinate leaders to show the same backbone that you do.

If the facts truly have changed, be prepared to alter your disciplinary plans accordingly. Otherwise, mean what you say and take care of your disciplinary business without apology.

DISCIPLINING "OUTSIDE THE BOX"

Lots of people, many cops included, appreciate structure. They like to know that B will follow A much as night follows day. When it comes to discipline, they feel some degree of comfort in knowing that a certain type of malpractice will draw a specific disciplinary response, or at least a predictable reaction within a given disciplinary range. Predictability is good, at least in some things.

There is nothing wrong with any of this. Predictability and fairness often are allies when it comes to discipline. It is a good thing that your employees can expect a certain and predictable range of discipline in response to a specific infraction, whether the act was committed by the department goat or the chief's fishing buddy. That is where the element of fairness comes in.

Standard, predictable disciplinary practices are good. It is good that your employees know approximately what to expect from you when someone clearly does wrong. At the same time, you should have the courage to try something new and perhaps untried previously when it may have value for both the involved employee(s) and the organization. Perhaps the standard penalty when Patrolman X backs his police vehicle into Mrs. Brown's car door has always been a letter of reprimand. Perhaps it still should be. But there is nothing sacred that says a driver safety school for Patrolman X cannot replace or accompany the letter. The class actually might do more good in preventing future driving errors by that same officer than would a piece of paper stuck in his file.

It is not unusual for an officer to be the recipient of a supervisory counseling session after being the subject of complaints of discourtesy by one or more citizens. The counseling may be helpful, but it might be even more useful if accompanied by a class on customer service.

Another officer may get into a disciplinary bind by losing his temper in a trying situation. Negative discipline may be appropriate. But a class on anger management may help to prevent the problem from arising again. If it does, much more serious discipline is indicated. The organization has at least tried to help the angry employee before lowering the disciplinary boom. The heavier discipline is more likely to be judged as just when preceded by a preventative effort.

Some agencies involve the "offending" employee in writing a revised order, policy or procedure when doing so might prevent a similar problem from arising in the future. An employee who violates an existing guideline that, if followed, would have prevented the problem from occurring might be assigned to do roll call briefing training on the proper procedure. The goal here should never be to embarrass but rather to prevent a recurrence of the mistake by anyone.

You think "out of the box" in a number of areas as you go about handling your challenging role as leader. Discipline should be one more of those areas.

WHAT TO DO WHEN YOUR DISCIPLINE GETS UNDONE

No matter how carefully thought-out your disciplinary decisions and actions may be, occasionally one will be reversed or modified after it leaves your desk. The change may be made by your boss, a formal appeal or grievance process or even a civil court ruling. The point is that the carefully considered correction you had a hand in formulating has been undone. Much or all of the benefit that you felt could have been gained from the discipline has been wiped out. Now what?

It is easy to become embittered by such a turn of events. At such moments it is too easy to pout, plan retribution or even give up in your key role as a disciplinarian. A little time for reflection should expose all of those thoughts as poor, bankrupt responses to not having things go your way. Your intentions in disciplining were pure, or at least they should have been. Now it's time to get past the derailment of your good intentions and continue to march.

Your boss, your staff and your employees most likely are watching you at such moments. They will not be favorably impressed by temper tantrums or wide-reaching condemnation for the processes or individuals involved. If you say or do anything that even sounds like you are contemplating retribution against the now-undisciplined employee (or anyone else) you can count on an employee complaint alleging retaliation. Only this time *you* may be the one on the receiving end of organizational or civil suit punishment.

When your disciplinary decisions are changed or overturned you must show the same maturity and professionalism that you demonstrate in other trying moments of your job. Reasoned, calm responses and reactions–not ones based on emotion–must be your means for handling disciplinary disappointment. As always, you will be on the lookout for lessons to be learned from the experience.

One of the first things to be considered is whether or not you erred in your disciplinary decision-making. Did you miss something that mitigated the misconduct in another's eyes? Did you overlook a particular piece of evidence? Did you misapply the department's disciplinary machinery in reacting to the perceived misconduct? In other words, did you make a mistake that was properly reversed after the discipline left your hands? Everything, including a mistake on your part, is an opportunity to learn.

It is also possible that an appeal authority agreed with your determination of misconduct, but felt that the penalty was too harsh. That, too, offers an opportunity to learn. It does not mean that you have to water-down your standards or lower your expectations. Do what you think is right, as always. Just be aware that your decision may get undone again if you decide exactly the same way in an identical, future set of circumstances.

The intended recipient of the now-revised discipline probably wants to know that he will not face repercussions from you or anyone else as a result of the altered decision. It is a good idea to let him know that you consider the matter closed and a part of the past. The employee should not have to work while looking over his shoulder to see if you are dogging him, hoping he'll mess up. You are bigger than that.

Undone or modified discipline is old news. Learn from what it has to teach and prepare yourself for the next time you must deal with discipline. It is very likely just around the corner.

HANDLING YOUR OWN NEGATIVE DISCIPLINE

You didn't intend to do it. You really didn't. Nevertheless, you *did* run over that shopping cart with your police car. You *did* fail to go to the firearms range when you were supposed to. Or you *did* commit one of a hundred other policy or procedural violations that would bring a negative sanction down on the head of one of your employees. Now you are facing your own encounter with negative discipline.

Your employees, your boss and the community will be looking for any clue that you received a special dispensation from corrective action when you clearly have fouled-up. Your position as a positive role model will be critically undermined if you accept lesser consequences for a miscue than one of your employees could expect. Rank definitely must *not* have its privileges when it comes to receiving discipline for serious mistakes made. Indeed, as a leader you might expect to find yourself more heavily disciplined than the rookie who made the same mistake. You should, after all, know the rules that you may have helped write. If you didn't write them, you almost certainly have cited them in disciplining others. You should expect the same outcome from the same actions. Or worse.

Whether it is self-imposed or comes from your boss, discipline for the chief should be both swift and known throughout the law enforcement organization. The truth about it almost certainly will get out anyway, so it is better that your people hear the correct account from you rather than picking a garbled version off of the department grapevine. This is not the time to make excuses or change the rules to benefit yourself. Just state what happened, what the consequences were, and go on.

If you have committed a public transgression that has brought embarrassment to your boss and your employees, a public apology may be in order. Briefly state why you were disciplined, apologize and let the matter drop. Don't carry on like a chastened TV evangelist caught with his hand in the piggy bank or the honey pot. Say what you have to say in as few words as possible. Then shut up and start putting it behind you. Maintain an attitude of normalcy and don't hide. Carry on with business. Let it go. If you can do that, most others will, too.

One more thing: Don't repeat whatever it was that got you disciplined in the first place!

SUMMARY

A leader who displays any semblance of being a normal human being does not relish the prospect of having to impose negative discipline on his personnel. At the same time, that leader recognizes the value to the organization of discipline that is decisively, promptly and fairly administered. You are that leader.

You realize that the most effective discipline is self-discipline, but you also recognize that not every individual is capable of that level of self-control. When you must instead deliver corrective action, you assure that you provide a good role model for your people in administering discipline that is effective as well as fair. You are able to differentiate between mistakes of the head and mistakes of the heart and respond to each appropriately. You are well aware that by failing to deal promptly and effectively with misbehaving employees you run the risk of losing the support of the ones who follow the rules.

As you make disciplinary decisions you must not forget that your peers are there to help you with advice on the tough calls. Do not hesitate to call on them. Likewise you must fight the very natural impulses to put off the administration of corrective action or water-down your first disciplinary decision in order to appease an offending subordinate or his colleagues. Staying the course is as important in disciplinary matters as it is in the many other difficult challenges you face.

Finally, you must be ready to handle the repercussions when discipline you impose is reversed by an appeal process. You must keep up a public face that transmits self-confidence and control. That attitude also is a must when you must handle discipline administered to *you* for some transgression or another. And that brings you full-circle to the absolute requirement for strong self-discipline.

You have the vital, internal discipline needed to get it done. By serving as an excellent role model in this area as in so many others you will guarantee that your organization is a strong one. That by itself will help minimize the frequency with which you must take corrective action.

POINTS TO REMEMBER

- How you handle discipline will have much to do with establishing your reputation for impartiality and credibility.
- The most effective discipline is that which is self-imposed.
- You must be a role model for your subordinate leaders in the way you handle discipline.
- Not dealing promptly and effectively with problem employees will cost you the support of the good ones.
- Mistakes of the head are honest errors that often can be corrected without punishment.
- Mistakes of the heart are often intentional violations that merit a more severe response.
- Discipline for one member of the organization is intended to alert all members concerning expectations.
- In order to be fair to everyone involved discipline must not be delayed unnecessarily.
- Call on your fellow chiefs for advice on tough disciplinary decisions.
- When you set out to discipline, do not back off or apologize for your actions.
- Realize that there are disciplinary options besides the "traditional" ones.
- Be prepared to handle the aftermath when discipline that you approved is undone by the appeal process.
- You will be watched intently for how you handle your own discipline.

Chapter 10

WHEN THINGS GO WRONG

You have heard it before and you probably have said it yourself. When all is well, anybody could run this place.

As you know, times of disaster, tragedy and crisis are the moments in which men and women are confirmed as true leaders, or fall short and lose stature. These are the tough times that will test your abilities to continue to lead your organization while events are detonating around you.

The reasons for a crisis involving your organization are almost limitless. The flap could have developed over a very public legal, moral or ethical lapse by one or more of your personnel. It could have arisen over the police-involved accidental death or serious injury of a citizen, as in a car wreck or in-custody casualty. The crisis could have been caused by a questionable or clearly in error killing of an individual by one of your officers. It could even have erupted from something you personally did or didn't do.

In one of the most emotionally devastating scenarios of all, one or more of your personnel may have been killed in the line of duty. An accidental death is devastating; death from a criminal act may be virtually off the scale for the emotional turmoil it will have on your department and community. The death of one of its serving peace officers is by common consent of police CEOs the single, most devastating event that can befall a law enforcement agency.

Your courage, empathy and decisiveness as a leader will be tested to the maximum when a major blowup occurs. External forces of nature, such as floods and earthquakes, can wreak havoc enough to try you sorely as a leader. When the tragedy touches personally the members of your organization, as when an officer dies in the line of duty, the emotional impact can be almost overwhelming. It is in this terrible atmosphere that you must excel as a comforting and reassuring yet dynamic and in-control leader. Leading effectively now will require you to apply everything you have learned. You will be tested. Neither you nor your organization can afford to have you come up short. By applying what you have learned and *will* learn, you won't.

OFFICER-INVOLVED SHOOTINGS

Anytime one of your officers discharges a firearm at a suspect it is a big event for the news media in your area. Even if he doesn't hit anyone, media and public interest is likely to be intense. If someone dies as a result of the gunfire, the intensity of the attention your agency will receive will be magnified greatly. If there is even a hint of controversy about the shooting, the focus on you and your agency will be even stronger.

Following an officer-involved shooting, your people, your boss and the community's leaders will be keenly interested in learning as quickly as possible exactly what happened. Once they have learned the fate of the involved police personnel, the next most urgent thing on their minds will be the "legitimacy" of the shooting. Was the incident properly handled or not? You can bet that the rumors already will be flying. If it wasn't handled perfectly, what are the consequences to be? What are you, the chief, going to do to fix the problem? What will be the fate of the employee(s) involved? And is what you have elected to do the *right* thing in the opinions of the members of your diverse audiences? All of these things will, in reality, take time to determine. But some people will be clamoring for quick answers. You will have to deal with them in a firm but courteous manner while maintaining your own, appropriate timetable.

Naturally, you will want to be informed immediately anytime there is a discharge of a firearm by one of your people outside of a training environment. You will need to know the details and consequences of the shooting, once again as quickly as possible. The buck will stop with you to assure that the incident is thoroughly and impartially investigated. If the firearms discharge was outside the bounds of the law or your department's policies and procedures you will be responsible for determining what is to be done about the transgression, and what can be done to make it less likely to happen again.

You likely also will want to confer with the local district attorney or prosecutor before announcing a course of action. At the most extreme, the proper response could be a grand jury indictment and/or the filing of criminal charges on your employee. If that happens, you can expect to respond to a lot more emotional disruption in the department and the community. You will need to get out front quickly with an explanation.

It is not enough that you do all the right things following a police-involved shooting or a similar critical incident involving serious injury or loss of life. You also must assure that your employees and the public at large know as many of the details about what happened as you possibly can give them. Rumor fills in the blanks when the facts are missing. The last thing you need right now is to have either your employees or your citizens reacting to incorrect information. Get the facts out as quickly and totally as time (and the lawyers) will permit. Stay in close touch with both the investigators and the legal authorities who ultimately will determine whether criminal charges are appropriate. Correct any false tales you become aware of. Inform your people (don't forget your non-sworn employees) via roll call briefings and any other means at your disposal, including all-hands meetings. Get the true facts out. If you have a chief's advisory group of local citizens, get them together for a special meeting and let them know what happened. They can help you spread the truth. Answer every question as completely as you can.

Do the same in front of the media and the rest of the community. Even if everything did not go exactly right, demonstrate that you are not trying to hide something. After you have briefed your boss, get his permission to update the elected officials, unless he wants to do it for you. Don't forget to update either these people or your advisory board members as additional information becomes available. All of these influential individuals can do a lot to support you and spread accurate information throughout the community.

Remain accessible to your own people as well as the news media during trying times. You do not want to look like you are hunkering down into a bunker mentality. Now is when everyone needs to see and hear you, so do not disappoint them. Many of those both inside and outside your organization realize that times like these reveal what a leader is really made of. This is your opportunity to show them.

THE DEATH OF AN OFFICER

There is little doubt that the death of one of your officers will be one of the most stressful, traumatic occurrences that you and your organization ever will face. Deaths of retired officers can prove traumatic. The death of a serving officer from natural or accidental causes will be terribly trying and disruptive. But for sheer emotional impact nothing will approach the personal and organizational upheaval brought about by the murder of a sworn member of the department.

Many law enforcement agencies experience the loss of an officer to a criminal act every year. For the largest agencies, the tragedy may be an almost annual event. Other big departments lose an officer to murder at least once every few years. But for many small- and medium-sized law enforcement agencies the killing of a serving peace officer is an absolutely devastating, first-time occurrence. If you are the leader of one of those agencies, your employees and your community will look to you now more than ever for guidance and reassurance in getting through a localized disaster of huge emotional proportions.

As in any other great crisis, you will be expected to be highly visible and seemingly everywhere at once. Your civilian as well as your sworn employees will expect you to tell them quickly what happened and reassure them that they will be alright even if not whole following the loss of a comrade. Your own boss, your elected officials and the news media will expect to hear the same from a very accessible chief. You may find that if people do not hear and see you a lot now, they may not want to hear and see you at all afterwards. Personal leadership displayed in the face of a major crisis is that critical.

While the disaster that surrounded the landfall of Hurricane Katrina did not involve the murder of a peace officer, the lack of visible, in-control leadership by certain key officials remains the gist of leadership courses to this day. When people are frightened and confused, they want to see and hear that their calm, confident leaders are on the job and in control. While some leaders in the storm-ravaged areas performed in a superb fashion, citizens of the region still remember badly the ones who hid or simply vanished. There is a valuable lesson in this for you.

Fortunately, you will not be alone in the aftermath of a police death, whether accidentally or intentionally caused. National organizations such as Concerns of Police Survivors can offer sound, experience-proven advice in everything from organizing memorial services and funerals to post-event emotional fallout. The advice comes from people who have been there before. The organization's web site likely can help you find a COPS representative in your own area.

You also should not hesitate to reach out to the agency heads in your own vicinity who have been through the tragedy you are experiencing now. These CEOs can offer you valuable, practical advice in coping with the day-to-day practicalities of responding to the death of an officer. If you ask, one of your peers likely will be willing to appoint a knowledgeable representative of his own agency as a liaison to yours in helping carry out the myriad details to be attended to in the wake of a tragedy.

Unless your organization is small enough that you elect to handle the details yourself, you probably will want to appoint a supervisory-level member of the department to coordinate all post-death activities involving the agency. Unless you choose to do it yourself, you should appoint still another member of the department to provide direct assistance and information to the deceased officer's loved ones and, eventually, help them apply for whatever financial and other benefits are applicable.

Naturally, you also will want to spend some time with the officer's family. Every family is different. You will have to rely upon your skills of observation and common sense to tell you how much they want you around. They almost certainly will desire time for private, personal grieving, even though they may hesitate to tell you so. Try not to intrude or permit others to do so.

For example, the family may not want to see members of the press or public officials just now. Be courteous but firm in helping shield your officer's loved ones from well-meaning but nevertheless unwanted intrusions.

THE CHIEF'S RESPONSIBILITIES

In the time immediately following the death of an officer it will feel like you have a million things to do. If the death was a result of a criminal act, the list will grow. As important as it is for you to be seen everywhere, you must not try to do everything yourself. If you do, you only will succeed in making yourself sick to the point of collapse.

You probably will find that there are a number of people anxious to help you. Where you feel it is appropriate, avail yourself of their assistance. Rely on your staff for help. Times such as these often bring out the best in people. Give your staff the opportunity to serve by providing them with meaningful things to do. Staying fully occupied following a tragedy will help them, too.

Your colleagues from other agencies likely will offer their help, as well. Accept their generous offers if there is something they can do. Be sure to acknowledge their offers with your personal thanks even if you do not presently require their assistance. You may need it later.

Courteously acknowledge offers of help from the community. Many people want to help at such times but often are not quite sure what they can do. Personally answer as many calls and contacts as you can. Assign someone to track food, flowers, cards and similar acknowledgments so that you can respond personally to the sender once things quiet down somewhat. Try hard not to miss responding to any act of goodwill.

Your boss may offer to assist you following the death of an officer. He also wants to express grief and take part in the healing process. Don't fence him out. He likely wants to feel a part of the police family at such a moment. Accept him into it and allow him to help in some significant way. He may want to visit with the family of the fallen officer and may want to have some role in a memorial or funeral service. If you sense that he seeks such involvement, try to facilitate a role for him unless the family is clearly opposed. He might, for instance, be asked to make a brief comment at the service.

You will have at least three major areas of responsibility following the death of an officer. First of all, you must assure that a competent, thorough investigation is conducted into the circumstances leading to the death. If criminal action was involved, you will have the added responsibility of assuring that the pursuit and arrest of the party or parties responsible is conducted in a lawful and ethical manner. The suspect's rights and personal safety must be scrupulously guarded. This does not mean that you must personally investigate the death or lead the search for the offender. There are doubtlessly competent others who can do that. But you must retain overall leadership of the operation and be briefed regularly on developments. You must not lose track of something that you will be held accountable for, because ultimately you will be.

Along with overseeing the investigation it is your responsibility first to determine who will do it. If your agency is large enough to have a solid homicide unit your decision may be a relatively easy one. If not you may need to request the assistance of your sheriff's office, state police or a nearby, larger agency. Realize that you may unintentionally insult some of your own people if you reach "outside" for your investigators. But do not burden your willing but emotionally-involved people with a case that they are not prepared to handle. You can explain your logic to them and work to smooth any ruffled feelings. Ultimately, however, you will be responsible for how this critical investigation is handled. Justice for the victim demands that the case gets the most expert handling you can secure. In the end, the decision is yours.

Regardless of whom you call on to pursue the investigation, be sure that you have the concurrence and involvement of the district attorney or prosecutor who eventually will have to take the case to trial. Touch base with him or her often. After all, if there is a still-living suspect (as you know, cop killers often commit suicide before capture) you very much want him to receive full justice for his evil acts.

Your second big responsibility is to the family and close associates of the deceased officer. You must tell them in person how you feel and offer them all the resources of your organization to aid and comfort them. Do not make promises that are beyond your authority or ability to keep, but do everything you can to meet their wishes at such a time. Give them a telephone number at which they can reach you 24 hours a day. But give them breathing and grieving room, too, and do not try to be constantly in their presence. Do appoint a member of your leadership staff as your liaison to the family and make that individual responsible for keeping you updated on problems, concerns and requests involving the family. Act where you feel there is clearly a need for your personal intervention, but do not try to force yourself or your organization on the family at times and places where the close attention is not really wanted.

Your third major responsibility is to keep all of the members of your organization informed about what has happened and what is going to take place next. Your people will want to know how and why the officer died. It is best that as many of them as possible get the word directly from you. That will mean a shortage of sleep for you as you visit a lot of shift briefings and specially-called employee meetings, but the task is a vital one that many of your people will expect you to carry out in person. Additional meetings will need to be held as additional information becomes available.

Get in front of your people and be prepared to answer hard questions. Be honest in your responses. Your people will want to know if a policy, procedure or piece of equipment may have contributed to the tragedy. If you don't have an answer, admit it. Get back to your people when you do. Do not repeat rumors or report possibilities as facts. Your people are looking to you as the "absolute final authority" for the truth.

Do not overlook civilian employees and spouses groups following an employee death. They, too, are parts of the organization and want to know how the tragedy happened and what might be done to prevent a similar occurrence in the future. Be accessible and honest with them. They want and need to help you grieve. They likely will want to have a role in a funeral or memorial service. Keep them involved and reliably informed.

Be open, be sensitive, be available, be visible following an organizational tragedy. It is what your people need and expect from a leader.

RECOVERING FROM A TRAGEDY

When very bad things have befallen your agency, your people will need time to recover from the blows. There is shock to overcome, grief to share and comfort to be expressed among the members of the police family.

At the same time, the sooner your people and your organization can return to a sense of normalcy the better it will be for everyone. Most people take comfort in experiencing the predictable, the normal. That is why employees who may be living through critical illness or even the death of a family member may be in a hurry to get back to work. There is at least some degree of security in being among supportive co-workers while carrying out familiar duties. Even in police work, it is possible to predict much of what is going to happen in a day at work. For an employee who has encountered anything but normalcy lately, that sense of the *normal* can feel quite good.

Trying to return to a sense of normalcy does not indicate a lack of concern for someone who has died, or sympathy for the loved ones of the deceased who still are in mourning. It simply recognizes that it is important for human beings to feel better as soon as they reasonably can. They need that in order to stay emotionally healthy. No disrespect for those emotionally torn is intended. Life has to go on. So does organizational life.

Once again, you have a key role to play in helping your people recover from a disaster. Stay visible. Make a point of being seen all over the organization. Engage in the activities you normally would do, ranging from meetings to appearing at public and employee functions. It is perfectly alright to acknowledge the recent tragedy and accept condolences for it if they are offered. Be appreciative. Then, move on to the planned topic.

If you normally exercise or engage in some other activity at a particular time of the day, resume doing so. To the extent possible, *act normally.* You can do that while still being considerate towards any members of your organization who were touched especially closely by tragedy. Be sensitive, but steadily move yourself and your organization back to the normal. You owe that to *all* of your people as well as the community you all serve.

WHEN YOUR PEOPLE MAKE TRAGIC ERRORS

Sometimes a tragedy will have occurred because of something your own employees did or failed to do. A child is hit by a patrol car. A high-speed pursuit results in the injury or death of innocents. A "bad" shooting ends in the death of a citizen or police officer. Or one or more of your officers are involved in committing criminal acts. Whatever the nature of the mistake, your organization, and by implication, you, have caused or contributed to the problem. Now what?

The "prime directive" that requires you to always tell the truth comes into play here. First of all, telling the truth is morally and ethically the right thing to do. Second, telling lies is practically guaranteed to make things worse. Once you are found out as a liar, a relatively minor event will be blown up into a major one. Regardless of who made the initial mistake, once you are exposed as a liar *you* will become the focus of the whole affair. That does not make for good career survival.

When something goes badly wrong, take the initiative by responding quickly, openly and honestly about what happened. First, clear your announcements concerning major controversy with your boss and your legal advisor, but do get out there as quickly as possible. Otherwise you will be playing catch-up endlessly.

Give an accurate summation of events. Answer questions truthfully. When you don't know the answer, say so. When you can't answer because of the nature or status of an ongoing investigation, say that, too. But don't play word games or get angry with a questioner. By doing so you'll only succeed in looking silly, or worse.

In addition to owning up to what happened, try to find something positive in the occurrence that you can emphasize even as you relay the bad news. For instance, as a result of the problem related to evidence-handling the department has reviewed its evidence policies and procedures and placed new guidelines into effect that should prevent future difficulties. Or because of the vehicle pursuit that ended badly the agency has increased its officers' training in emergency vehicle operation and updated its policies to offer more guidance to personnel facing a pursuit scenario.

Personally get out front when bad news erupts over something your people did or didn't do. This is not the time to rely on a spokesperson. Those inside and outside your department want to see and hear the boss. This is a job for the person in charge. That's you.

WHEN YOU PLAYED A ROLE IN THE DISASTER

It is always important to admit it when your organization has done something wrong. It is even more important to concede that an error was made when you had a role in it. That does not mean that you have to resign or fall on your sword. It does mean that you should acknowledge your role in the miscue.

Being honest about the role you played in a foul-up is absolutely mandatory if you want to maintain credibility with your employees. They are not dummies. They will know before anyone else if a decision, policy or statement attributable to you contributed to the current problem. They also will know–and intensely resent it–if you make any effort to deny your connection to the debacle or lay the blame elsewhere. Engaging in conduct like this could well begin your slide to losing the support of your people. With that support evaporated you will find it difficult to survive as an effective leader in the organization.

As the head of the agency you are ultimately accountable for good things and bad done by yourself and your employees. Your boss as well as the community at large is aware of that. None of that means, however, that you should cry, tear your hair and apologize profusely when you have done nothing wrong. Yes, your employee beat-up his spouse while he was off-duty. Yes, your people have appropriately arrested and charged him for the offense. But nothing in his past on- or off-duty behavior gave evidence that he was going to do that. It is not your fault that he did. Do not accept blame that does not rightfully belong to you. *That* also is part of maintaining your reputation for earned credibility.

It is really not all that difficult. Responding honestly and appropriately when you have contributed personally to a major mess is simply in keeping with the sincere posture you maintain in your day-to-day duties as the leader of a professional law enforcement organization. You tell the truth. You get to the bottom of a problem in an effort to keep it from recurring. You accept accountability for your actions. You never blame others for poor choices that you have made. You always question yourself before you act as to what an ethical leader would do. Then, you do it.

Sometimes you are going to be wrong. Very occasionally there are going to be very serious repercussions from your mistake. How well and how quickly you recover from a bad situation will help define who you are as a leader. You must not be found wanting.

HANDLING PERSONAL REVERSALS

As a veteran supervisor you probably have said it numerous times: how an employee recovers from a bad happening will help determine just what kind of individual he or she really is. It should come as no surprise to you, then, that the same rule of thumb applies to the Big Boss: you.

Personal reversals can, of course, come in endless varieties and degrees of seriousness. Yours could arrive in the form of the loss of a loved one, a divorce or a major financial loss. It could be work-related and result from a very bad decision you made and/or disciplinary action taken against you by your boss.

When personal disaster strikes, you will be watched by many different interests for how you respond to the crisis. Your employees will be monitoring you carefully, as will your boss. Since even very private disasters seldom stay private, it is safe to assume that at least part of the community and the local political structure will have heard about the situation and will be watching you, too. Some people who don't like you will be among the spectators, and it's likely that they will be hoping to enjoy the show. That is simply life in the real world you live in.

Your employees and your supervisor probably will be the most riveted onlookers in the crowd. They all want to see if you can handle the added stress without folding-up. Most of them are hoping that you can. If you respond badly by engaging in self-destructive behavior (like drinking to excess, for example) or striking out unfairly at others you will lose face immeasurably and potentially shorten your tenure by leaps and bounds.

Most people will not expect you to display superhuman self-control. They do not expect to see you giggle in the presence of calamity. But most of them *will* expect you to treat others civilly and continue to lead. They do not want to see you go into hibernation or foist off your responsibilities onto your subordinates. They won't like it if they detect what appears to be a long-term change in your normally outgoing, positive demeanor. In sum, they won't be happy with a new chief. They want to see *you.*

Acting "normal" when you feel anything but will not be an easy task to perform. It will require a large dose of your inner strength and resolve. It is nonetheless what others want to see in a leader. They want to know that the individual they depend on to lead them in the face of adversity is still there for them even during personal hard times. They need to see that leader and be comforted by his or her strength.

The leader is still *you,* even when personal disasters temporarily have sucked much of the pleasure out of a job you usually enjoy. Remaining a leader even when you really crave a break from the responsibility is part of the deal you signed on for when you accepted the chief's badge. You've got to hang on through the bad times to get back to the good ones. They really *are* around the corner.

BE HIGHLY VISIBLE WHEN THINGS GO BAD

Time and time again you have heard emphasized the value of visibility for the chief both within his own organization and throughout the community. Visibility is indeed required of a successful leader, regardless of the profession he or she has chosen to follow.

But visibility is never more vital for you than during times of tragedy and great stress. It is now that your people and your community need to see and hear an in-charge leader. It is now that they need to see you take charge. It is now that they need to hear that, while things may be rough for a while, it is going to be OK again. People need to be comforted by a figure they trust telling them that normalcy will return. That trusted figure has to be *you.*

It is very human to want to steal away to grieve and cry and lick one's wounds when things have gone terribly bad. You can reserve yourself some private time to do just that if you need to. But the time in which you drop out of sight to nurse your personal hurts must be very brief if you are to fulfill your role as a leader. Indeed, it may have to be limited to the personal time that you allow yourself for resting if you are to succeed in leading a stressed organization back onto its feet. The comforting yet determined face that you show to your people is that important in assuring that they recover as rapidly and completely as possible.

When things have gone badly, appear in front of your people and your community as often as possible to let them know that someone is in control and things will return to normal. They all want to know that. Answer questions and give honest assurances. Tell the truth. Do not sugarcoat bad news. But always return to your main theme of reassurance: *It will be alright again. We will get through this by helping one other. We will prevail.* It is a message you will need to repeat again and again.

Do not overlook your own needs and those of your loved ones during a time in which you must be eternally "on" in response to a crisis. Be sure that you eat, rest and sleep, even if you don't feel that you are interested in any of those things. You cannot help anyone if you have collapsed from illness or exhaustion.

Take care of your family, too. Find time to spend with those who love you. Realize that your stress is contagious to those who are closest to you. Tell them what is going on and what you have to do in response. You likely will find that these people will be one of your greatest sources of strength in the presence of adversity. Allow them to help you.

KNOW THE FACTS BEFORE YOU RESPOND

Law enforcement leaders are action-oriented people. Confronted with a difficult situation, their first impulse often is to act decisively to resolve it. When it comes to taking action to solve a problem, your natural tendency to attack the challenge head-on can prove helpful and often is exactly the right thing to do. That's one of the strengths of an effective leader.

On the other hand, it is sometimes true that what appeared to be a cut-and-dried set of circumstances turns out to be something else entirely once all the facts are in. If you detect even a hint that you don't have the whole story, resist the impulse to speak out and react before you know more. You thereby could forestall some embarrassment for yourself and your agency by taking a figurative deep breath before sounding off.

Law enforcement is rife with examples of "look before you leap" (or talk) situations that you can learn from. In a classic case, a well-respected chief of police responded to a media question about why an arrested burglar had a broken jaw by proclaiming "those things are sometimes the wages of being a criminal." Shortly thereafter the chief learned that the burglar received the injury from being kicked in the face by an officer while lying handcuffed and unresisting on the floor of the crime scene. The chief appropriately fired and filed criminal charges on the offending policeman. But that did not cancel out the bad publicity that he and his organization had to endure from his initial speaking without knowing.

Especially when your people are accused of misconduct of which you believe they are innocent, it is natural for you to want to come promptly to their defense. That's a good thing and your people have a right to expect it. But be cautious in how you frame your response. It is perfectly alright to say something like "From what we know at this point it appears the officers handled the situation appropriately. The investigation is continuing." That makes a lot more sense than saying something like "That's impossible" when you don't know for a fact that it is.

Accusations of police misconduct are not, of course, the only area in which premature verbal barrages can get you in trouble. Making proclamations about the details or legitimacy of a critical incident such as a high-speed pursuit or police-involved shooting before you know the whole story also can result in your having to eat your words later. Say only what you know to be solid fact and save the rest for subsequent statements after things have become clear. You could save yourself, your organization and your boss some real grief in the process.

KEEP EVERYONE CURRENT IN A DEVELOPING CRISIS

When people are very interested in an ongoing situation yet lack accurate information about what is happening, some of them will make up the missing details to suit themselves. Many others will not originate the misinformation but will pass along rumor they have heard from others. As you know from your observations of human nature, the story will grow and become increasingly distorted with each, subsequent telling. That helps no one, particularly when the "story" results from a real crisis of some kind.

You already know that you need to utilize every means at your disposal to keep your employees advised of what is going on during and following a critical incident. That includes frequent and authoritative e-mails from the chief to all employees. It also includes personal contact with you via team meetings and special all-employee gatherings.

But there are others that you must keep informed during and after an emotion-evoking crisis or other critical occurrence, such as the loss of an officer or a natural disaster. You must keep your boss fully briefed on what has occurred and what is expected to happen next. He or she can help take some pressure off of you by in turn briefing others in the ranks of elected and appointed officials.

The political landscape is different in every community. If you know that yours requires personal contact between the chief and the elected officials in times of crisis, make time for these people. Be sure that your boss knows what you are doing. The effort you expend now, as busy as you are, could pay big dividends later. Help these shakers and movers feel that they have "inside information" and are in the know because the chief took them into his confidence. From a practical standpoint, by their position in the community they can help circulate accurate information, thereby reducing the number of individual inquiries you may receive from concerned others. (Realize that you will receive some calls and e-mails from "concerned" others anyway. Handle as many as you can personally.)

The members of the news media will be the last but certainly not the least important group that you will need to keep informed about the major event. Resist the temptation to label these people as interfering pests. They can provide you with a lot of help in disseminating accurate information about what is going on. They are going to do their stories anyway, so it is to your advantage that the information they spread is helpful to your citizens and paints your organization in a positive light to the extent feasible. More about that in the next chapter.

BE CAREFUL WITH THE BLAME GAME

When a bad thing has happened it is just human nature for many people to blame someone else for what went wrong. Elected and appointed officials can be especially susceptible to this practice. As the police chief, you cannot afford to be susceptible.

You already know the importance of knowing all the facts before you climb atop a stump and start issuing pronouncements. That guideline for your personal behavior includes a prohibition on publicly assessing blame, particularly when your first temptation is to blame somebody else for something you or your agency is suspected of doing wrong.

Once more it will be incumbent upon you to get all the facts before you start assigning accountability for what went right and what did not. Your assessment may change dramatically as more information becomes available. What at first blush seemed clear may become less so as more facts emerge. In other words, the facts of a given event may become less as opposed to more certain as additional voices are heard and additional evidence is gathered. You do not want to find yourself in the position of having blamed an individual or organization for something they did not do.

You want to be especially careful not to criticize publicly another law enforcement agency or official. This rule remains true even if that person or organization may have handled a situation less than ideally and perhaps in the process exposed your own agency to unjust criticism. Speak publicly only for your organization and what it did or didn't do. Permit the other CEOs to speak for their people and their actions.

It is unseemly, unprofessional and counterproductive to get into a public debate with the head of another organization. If there were indeed problems with the other agency's handling of the event, iron out your differences in a private, civil discussion. Highly-publicized interagency squabbling makes everyone look bad. Do not participate in it.

Even if you are certain that an action or decision of your own boss contributed to the debacle, whatever it was, remember the cardinal rule about never speaking ill of your supervisor in public. Doing so amounts to a shortcut to the unemployment line. The same rule holds true where your jurisdiction's elected leaders are concerned. You can privately let your boss or bosses know that you are unhappy and why. Tell them what they did that you object to. But keep the discussion courteous and respectful. Odds are, your job performance isn't perfect, either. You probably would not appreciate being blamed in front of the whole world for your mistake. Grant these people the same forgiveness that you would like to see extended to you.

Blame can be a bitter thing. Use it *very* sparingly.

SUMMARY

Nothing will stress a law enforcement agency like the unexpected death of one of its members. The stress will be magnified if the death was the result of a criminal act. Such a critical incident also will focus the intense interest of the entire community on you and your law enforcement organization. Employees within and without the agency will be watching you and listening to what you have to say. Consciously or not, people will be assessing your ability as a leader when such an event strikes.

Other critical incidents can focus an almost equally-intense spotlight on you and your agency. Tragic accidents or mistakes involving your people will result in harsh scrutiny. At such times you will be expected to lead your employees and keep morale elevated while simultaneously responding effectively to harsh questions and even blatant attacks on your department. Depending upon your perceived role in the situation, the unwelcome attention even could include attacks on your character.

Remaining in firm control of your organization during such tough times will require all of your skills as a leader. You must tell the truth while communicating effectively to those inside and outside the organization. You will have to remain highly visible and accessible for the duration of the emotional upheaval. You will have to share accurate information in a timely manner. You will have to assure that things get done right even when everyone is tired and stressed out. You will have to be, in a word, a *leader.*

As a successful chief of police you routinely handle the administrative, procedural and political challenges of the job. You efficiently direct the crime fighters and thoughtfully work through the personnel issues that every CEO must face. But it is when crisis occurs and things go very wrong that you will be the most severely tested. It is now that your effectiveness as a caring but decisive leader will be established–or not.

Your employees and your community need you now more than ever before. Because of who and what you are, you will not fail them.

POINTS TO REMEMBER

- An officer-involved shooting or a similar critical incident will focus an incredible amount of attention on you and your organization.

- The death of a serving police officer likely will be the biggest single stressor your organization will face.
- You absolutely must carry out each of your vital responsibilities following the death of one of your officers.
- It is up to you to lead your department to recovery following the death of an employee.
- Critical incidents also can result from mistakes made by your people.
- If you contributed to a major error, you must own up to your role and lead in responding to the aftermath.
- You must capably handle personal disasters in your own life in order to continue as an effective leader.
- As chief you must be everywhere when things have gone very badly.
- Have a firm grasp of accurate information before you make a public statement regarding a critical incident.
- When a major crisis is unfolding, make sure your people are kept advised of the latest, accurate information.
- Do not assess blame unfairly when things go terribly wrong.
- Look to your own emotional and physical health and that of your loved ones during a crisis.
- Remember that your people and the community are looking to you to lead them through a tragedy and beyond it.

Chapter 11

MANAGING NEWS MEDIA RELATIONS

As a street cop, you probably would have preferred searching a darkened building for an armed offender over answering the questions of a fresh-faced young man or woman armed only with a pad, camera or microphone. For a street cop, that attitude was acceptable. Now that you are the leader of a law enforcement organization you can no longer afford to be so shy.

As a police leader, your ability to communicate effectively is a necessity. Communicating well with the public via the news media is an *absolute* necessity for you. The media represent one of your most useful tools for getting your message out to the taxpayers who pay the bills so that you can run your agency. These people need to know what you are doing and how they can help you. The media can help you tell them.

Managing your news media relations for maximum benefit does not mean that you must "kiss up" to reporters and their bosses. It does not mean that you have to like every media rep you meet. But you do owe yourself and your organization your best effort to work constructively with the media and require the other members of your agency to do the same.

You already know that your reputation for credibility is vital if you are to be effective inside your organization. Earning a reputation for truthfulness is your first and most important step in establishing a positive working relationship with the news media, too. You will not succeed in earning their trust without it. Your life certainly will be more pleasant *with* it.

This chapter will offer you assistance in working successfully with the media in order to obtain the greatest value possible for your organization and yourself. It deals with the news releases, media interviews, press conferences, bad news and other things you will encounter in forging a mutually beneficial (or at least mutually tolerable) relationship with the press. It also provides a set of personal rules you will need for working effectively and honorably with the people of the media.

It's time for the police chief to meet the press.

THE VALUE OF CREDIBILITY

You already know how important it is to possess an earned reputation for truthfulness within your organization and your community. The same holds true in spades when you are standing in the bright light of media scrutiny. If you are caught lying to the press, good luck in re-establishing a reputation for integrity. With a lot of hard work, you may be able to do it. But it won't be easy.

It just makes good sense to *keep* something valuable rather than labor to regain it later. For that reason you must spare no effort in establishing with your media contacts that you are a person to be trusted and believed without exception. There is a very simple way to earn that reputation. Don't lie. Period. Not by intent. Not by omission.

Say nothing at all as opposed to saying something you know not to be true. Veteran network newsman Mike Wallace put it this way: "We'll forgive you for not knowing. We won't forgive *or* forget if you lie to us." That is advice worth remembering.

You probably have built an increasingly trusting relationship with your peers, subordinates and superiors based upon your interactions with them over time. During those interactions you doubtlessly have noted the truthfulness (or lack of same) displayed by those people. Their reputations for good or ill in your mind are based largely on the evidence you have amassed of their perceived truthfulness. You safely can assume that news people will be observing and evaluating *you* in the same way.

A reputation for credibility can be established from a major incident or a series of them. Just as often it is built over time as a consequence of numerous "minor" or routine interactions. From a news reporter's standpoint if he has seen you tell the truth (or not) over the course of time in things of minor importance he probably has already formed an opinion of your reputation for credibility. You want to be sure that the reputation you establish with him is a positive one.

You will need to do more than assure that you personally tell the truth in your dealings with the press. As in so many aspects of your personal and professional life, your conduct will be observed and copied by your people. It is important that you make clear to the members of your organization that you expect no monkey business in their interactions with the media. You speak the truth, and you expect them to do the same. If they cannot talk to a reporter or respond to a specific question, that's fine. They need only give a courteous response as to why they can't. But if they *do* speak, they are obliged to tell the truth.

In the end, the news media will hold you responsible for the behavior of both yourself and your subordinates in matters of truthfulness. It is your job to see that the image they have of you all is a good one.

YOUR PERSONAL RELATIONSHIP WITH THE PRESS

You will find that your day-to-day relations with the representatives of news-gathering organizations will be both more effective and more cordial if you adhere to a set of experience-proven personal guidelines for working with the press. These guideposts are from a survival kit of sorts for maintaining your effectiveness and your sanity while working with the press. These time-proven tips are based upon little more than common sense and basic courtesy, but they work. Here is a sampling:

TELL THE TRUTH: It is worth saying again because everything else depends on it. With a reporter, your word is your bond. Your proven credibility is your greatest asset.

STAY HUMBLE: It isn't about you. Keep things in perspective no matter how many cameras and microphones are thrust in your face. It is the job title they are focused on, not you. When you're gone, the next guy or gal will get the same attention.

BE COURTEOUS AND TACTFUL: Once more, you *are* your organization. Be nice, even when you don't feel like it. You are building a reputation and an image. Make both good ones.

KEEP YOUR PROMISES: If you pledge to get back to a reporter, do it. Once again, you have a reputation for believability to uphold.

DON'T USE THE MEDIA FOR FEUDING: If you are mad at some other individual or agency, do not use your media access to attack them. You will only encourage a response in kind. Remember that reporters love to highlight controversy. Settle your disputes out of the spotlight.

BE CAREFUL ABOUT GOING "OFF THE RECORD:" Reporters sometimes refer to this as "going on background," and either way the idea is that they won't attribute anything you have said to you. You are playing a dangerous game when you elect to do this, as the reporter is under no legal obligation not to use what you have told him AND give away his source. If you choose to go "off the record," first be sure you know the reporter well and trust him thoroughly. Closely limit the number of people with whom you will risk an "off the record" comment.

GET TO KNOW YOUR FREQUENT MEDIA CONTACTS: Have coffee or lunch with a reporter or editor when there is nothing of consequence to talk about. Get better acquainted with the media people you work with the most often. It is important that you each see that the other does not have horns and a tail. The familiarity can help both of you in moments of crisis or controversy.

SET A GOOD EXAMPLE: If you are nasty to newspersons you cannot expect your employees to treat them nicely. Set a good example for courtesy and professionalism in all your interactions with the media. Do not disparage reporters in front of your troops.

KNOW THAT GIVING "EXCLUSIVES" IS DANGEROUS: It is very risky business to give information to a favored reporter while denying it to his competitors. He may appreciate it. But by doing so you may turn his colleagues into your sworn enemies. Try hard to treat your media contacts impartially, even though you naturally will like some of them better than others. At the same time, do not penalize a reporter whose initiative has turned up a story his peers do not have. You are not obliged to notify them of his "scoop."

TALK OUT YOUR DIFFERENCES: Sulking won't help. If you truly feel you have been wronged by a reporter, talk show host or editor, discuss it with him in a straightforward but courteous manner. (No name calling!) Talk to his or her boss if you need to. But pick your fights well. Every little snide remark is not worth an all-out battle. Don't even think about trying to "get even" with a journalist who has wronged you.

KNOW THAT BAD NEWS WILL PASS: All news has a shelf life. A really negative, hurtful story or broadcast from Monday often is largely forgotten by Friday. Repair what needs repairing, but try hard not to become obsessed with bad news. Odds are you and your organization will outlast it.

ASK FOR HELP: Don't be shy about asking the media for publicity assistance when you need aid with a case, cause or program. That help is one of the benefits of nurturing good relations with the news organizations. You generally will find them willing to help, as "cop news" is very much of interest to their audience.

KNOW THAT YOU'LL GET BURNED OCCASIONALLY: Realize that even when you have maintained a great working relationship with the media, a reporter's job is to ferret out the news. If that news casts you in a bad light, it is ethically still his job to report it. Try not to get mad because he does. The good news is that by maintaining a good relationship with the press you are more likely to get a fair chance to respond. A pre-existing good relationship and your reputation for credibility also may take some sting out of the story.

TRY TO ENJOY YOURSELF: That may sound strange. Thanks to the media, you are going to be the focus of public attention. If you are doing your job well, most of the time it should be in a *good* way. People, maybe a lot of them, will hear and see you. Stay modest, but enjoy the attention.

When you are not the chief anymore, it's quite possible no one will care what you think or say about *anything*. Enjoy today to the extent that you can!

WHAT NOT TO DO

There is a saying in the medical profession: "At least do no harm." In other words, don't make it worse than it was before you got involved. You would do well to follow the same advice where your agency's media relations are concerned.

There are actually a number of ways in which you *could* make things worse. Probably the most serious "crime" you could commit is intentionally providing to the media information you know to be false. *Lying* is the word for that. Do not do it. If you do and are found out, you will become the focus of the story instead of whatever the reporters were initially pursuing. Do not allow your staff or public information officer to lie to the press, either. Eventually, lying will catch up to you with predictably bad consequences.

You can makes things worse by blatantly playing favorites among reporters and media outlets. Giving a good story to everyone except the guy you are mad at could feel nice at the moment. But there's just a chance you could fall the victim of payback later. You don't need that. Play fair.

And speaking of payback: do not make plans to retaliate against a newsperson you suspect of treating you unfairly. Complain to his boss if you want, but clumsy attempts at revenge (such as ticketing the offender's vehicle) are almost certain to blow up in your face. On top of that, it is not an ethical thing to do.

As noted previously, do not carry on a war of words in the media with an individual or organization you are mad at. Back and forth arguments in print or over the airways keep the dispute in front of the public and, in many cases, make everybody involved look bad. Say what you have to say once, if you must, and then shut up. Someone has to be the more mature and responsible leader in ending such a public exchange of differences. It is best that it is you.

Don't fail to accord credit where it is due. In your public utterances highlight the good work done by your officers, not yourself. Show appreciation for contributions made by other agencies or citizens. You look big when you contribute to others looking bigger.

Enjoy your "positive" news clippings but do not allow praise for yourself or your organization to go to your head. The news is fickle and can change drastically overnight. Sometimes today's hero is tomorrow's goat. Take pleasure in the fruits of your hard work but remain alert for challenges that tomorrow may bring.

Finally, do not forget your bosses when it comes time to hand out credit. The harsh truth is that some Top Dogs do not like for their little dogs to upstage them. That is simply human nature. Where you can do so honestly, share the praise for work well done with your employees AND your boss. Accept little public credit for yourself. The good news is that more people than you think will know about your contributions to the success of the team. You are, after all, the team's leader. You just don't need to shout out that fact. Help others enjoy the glory.

HANDLING BAD NEWS

Bad news is going to happen. It is inevitable. Whether it comes from a "bad" police-involved shooting or climbing crime rates, sooner or later you will have to respond to news that does not make you or your organization look great. How you react to the media during trying times can either hurt or help you. At such a moment your goal must be to minimize the lasting damage while presenting your people and your agency in the best possible (but honest) light. How well you do that will help establish your reputation as an effective leader–or something else entirely.

There are a number of things you can do to mitigate the effects of bad tidings and help your organization recover from the assault as quickly and completely as possible. None of them are complicated; all of them work:

MAINTAIN YOUR CREDIBILITY: There it is again. Always tell the truth. If you cannot answer, say so and why. But don't make things worse by lying.

NEVER SAY "NO COMMENT:" Doing so makes you sound like a gangster in front of a Congressional committee. There are better ways of saying essentially the same thing: "Bob, I can't answer that question right now because. . . ."

KEEP YOUR MEDIA RULES CONSISTENT: You should not change horses mid-stream. Neither should you change your agency's rules for working with the media right in the middle of a smelly situation. If, for instance, you always have permitted any member of the organization to talk to the press, you should not muzzle your employees now. Doing that looks suspiciously like you are trying to conceal something.

DO NOT HIDE OR SHOVE SOMEONE ELSE OUT FRONT: Like your employees, the press and the public deserve to see the Big Boss when all is not rosy. It's fine to use a Public Information Officer (PIO) for the routine, daily news that a law enforcement agency generates. When the news is bad or the department is under attack, it is *you* who should speak for the organization, however uncomfortable that may feel. Your people, the media and your citizens will expect it.

CONVEY A SENSE OF NORMALCY: Regardless of how bad the bad news may be, your department will in the meantime continue to answer calls for service and help people in need. Your organization should be seen as engaging in business as usual even as you respond to negative happenings. Keep up your own, normal activities to the extent possible. Do not cancel public engagements if you can avoid it. The last thing anyone needs to believe is that the chief has gone into hiding.

STAY CALM AND IN CONTROL: It is easier said than done, but it is no less a requirement for a good leader. Your media contacts need to see that you are rattled by neither events nor reporters. Don't get testy or rude–reporters will sense blood in the water if you do. Be your usual, self-assured yet courteous self. Do your crying on your own time!

DON'T TRY TO SHIFT BLAME: Do not publicly blame other people or agencies when things have gone badly and the reporters are at the door for an explanation. Resist the temptation to lash out at others. If somebody else truly was responsible for a foul-up, that fact probably will surface eventually. Speak for (and about) your own organization.

IT WILL GET BETTER: Many times bad news gets brief if intensive coverage by the media. Then the media reps are off to chase the next story. It's sort of like having a really bad cold. Although you may not feel like it at the moment, you know that it *will* pass and you'll feel good again. The same holds true for bad news.

LEADING A SUCCESSFUL NEWS CONFERENCE

The first thing you need to determine concerning a news conference is whether or not you need to do one in the first place. Nothing falls flatter than a party without guests, so try to ascertain if what you have to say is really exciting or interesting enough to draw a lot of media attention. If not, you or an appropriate member of your staff can deliver the word on a one-to-one basis with your media contacts. Or you can publish a printed news release and send it to potentially interested media outlets as well as post it on your department's web site.

A news conference (or press conference) should be called when the information to be covered, such as a new program or high-profile crime or arrest, is apt to draw so much media interest that responding to a crowd of news people one at a time is impractical. But don't overdo it. An agency that calls news conferences promiscuously for minor happenings or non-events may soon find no one showing up for future sessions. It's a version of the old "cried wolf too often" syndrome.

Once you have decided to have a news conference, notify your agency's media contacts of the date, time, and place for the event. One of your staff can do this by telephone as well as e-mail or text messages. Tell the media what it is to be about. That way, each news organization has some idea about whether or not they want to cover it. It is the courteous thing for you to do. Do not leave out anyone who even *might* be interested in covering the conference.

Be sure that you have enough chairs and plenty of room in a comfortable, quiet, well-lighted environment. Avoid locations that have loud background noise, such as roaring air conditioning systems. Leave space at the back of the room for the television people to set up their cameras. Someone–like your press officer, if you have one–needs to get there early and stay late to help sort out the little problems and surprises than can arise. There also may be additional questions. That is why it's advisable for someone (not you) with knowledge of the subject matter to be tagged for this duty. If you are fortunate enough to have a Public Information Officer, this is a good job for him or her.

Once the conference is underway, keep your opening statement brief. Two to three minutes is plenty. Your audience almost certainly wants to ask questions and will get antsy if you go on and on. Determine before the session begins how much time you want to spend there. Then, stick to your plan. Twenty to thirty minutes for the whole affair is probably sufficient. You don't want to wear out your audience or yourself. Get it done without wasting *anyone's* time.

Open up to questions as soon as you finish your statement. Because not everyone can hear everything that is said in the room, it is a good idea to repeat each question you were asked before answering it. Your audience will appreciate the courtesy. By doing so you also will give yourself a little time to formulate an answer.

Expect "surprise" questions that may be off the topic you are there to talk about. Answer if you want, but it is also acceptable to tell the questioner that you'll instead be happy to talk with him one-on-one later, since his new subject is not why the group was called together. Obviously this advice won't apply if you follow the practice of periodically calling a conference where reporters can question you about anything at all. A few chiefs do that.

There's an old television deodorant commercial that advises "never let them see you sweat." This advice is pertinent for you in front of a news conference crowd. Do not get rattled or visibly angry. Remain calm, courteous and in control even if you are being treated unfairly by a questioner. By keeping to the high ground you'll win both sympathy and points. Your goal is to demonstrate that you are a professional and a leader. You do that by *act-*

ing like one.

Try to have some "visuals" for your press conference guests. They want pictures. Whether it is seized drugs, money, weapons or something else, try to have something of interest there for the picture-taking. That may increase the amount of time or space devoted to the story you have to tell. If you have nothing else, even still photos may help. One department's news conference on the solution of a decade-old murder was accompanied by an enlarged color portrait of the victim in life placed on an easel. (The permission of the dead woman's family had been secured in advance, of course.)

Consider providing your media audience with copies of a printed handout, especially if your opening statement is lengthy or if there are a number of names, addresses and criminal charges involved. You want to help the media get it right. Everybody looks bad if the drug raid is reported as taking place at 401 Elm Street when in fact it happened at 104 Elm. And it's not good if reported child abuser Henry Smythe gets misidentified as Henry Smith, local big shot.

If another organization assisted in the operation you are reporting on, be sure that the agency gets appropriate credit. Have the head of that organization join you at the podium, if he is so inclined. More than one long-running feud between law enforcement leaders owes its origin to someone getting left out of a news conference where kudos were distributed. If the news is good, allow as many people as possible to bask in the favorable publicity. You will make friends by doing so.

When the questions taper off or cease entirely, it is time to bring the conference to a close, even if the amount of time you allowed for it has not elapsed. Don't forget to thank the participants for attending. That may make it more likely that they'll show up the next time. It is also the polite thing to do.

Even if you have put on a very thorough and detailed press briefing, expect follow-up calls and requests for one-on-one interviews. Every good newsperson wants to report something that no one else has, thus the need for your individualized attention. Grant those requests for additional coverage if you possibly can. Doing that will aid you in getting out the story you wanted told. It also may earn you a reporter friend for the future. That is worth the additional effort.

News conferences are very useful when you need to reach a lot of news media outlets without having a lot of time to do it. While conferences should not be overused or called for insignificant events, they are valuable tools for you. Using them effectively can bring big benefits to your department.

THE VALUE OF NEWS RELEASES

A news release can provide a brief, accurate recounting of a crime, arrest or other significant event involving your organization and its personnel. Picked up and used by a media outlet, a good news release can keep your public up to date about what their law enforcement officers are doing.

There are a number of ways of disseminating a news release. You can snail-mail them, e-mail them, fax them or even read them aloud over the telephone. One of the most effective means used today is posting them on your agency's web site where not only journalists but just about anybody can have a look. Your citizens want to know what their police are doing, and a good news release can help them satisfy that hunger.

Handling the release itself is a different but not complicated matter. First, be sure you really need to do one. Routine or minor happenings do not merit news release treatment. (You will have to determine for yourself what is "routine" or "minor" in your locale.) Once again, "the boy who cried wolf" effect can apply here. The small to medium-sized agency that issues several releases daily may soon find them all ignored by the press. When you do issue a release, be certain that it contains the same, vital "Five Ws and an H" (who, what, when, where, why and how) that go into a good police report. The difference is that a news release should be much shorter than a report and not contain the rigid, formulaic language that many law enforcement offense reports contain. Basics, not details, are required. A news release should take its audience into account and should read like a newspaper story, not a legal document. As one veteran journalism instructor told his class of police Public Information Officers: "Be concise, be correct, be gone. Don't turn a pretty simple event into a novel."

Like a good police report, a news release is accurate. Double- and triple-check your facts for accuracy. Check spelling and grammar. Your agency's name is going on the release. You do not want your people depicted as a bunch of illiterates. Your reputation and that of your organization is riding upon every release, so make the picture a good one.

Your news release should speak plain English and avoid law enforcement jargon. There is no place for "perps" and "pinches" in a professional organization's news release. Use civilian–not military–format for writing dates and times. You do not want the reporter who is trying to build a story from your release getting aggravated from trying to decipher it. Make his task a little easier.

Be sure to cite a source or "authority" for the news release. Whether it is you or someone else in your organization, someone will have to be identified as the source for the information contained. The reporter needs to cite this source as the provider of the facts. He wants to cover his tail if the information turns out to be wrong. That's why his story says things like "according to Chief Jones. . . ." That's the way it works in journalism.

At the close of your news release be sure to provide a name, telephone number and/or e-mail address for the use of a reporter seeking more information or clarification of what he already has. This does not have to be you unless you want it to be. The department's PIO, assigned investigator or other staff member might be listed here.

The idea is to write a news release that gets used. To that end consider having a trusted reporter or editor friend critique some of your agency's releases for you. How could they be made more useful to a reader? Ask questions and get better.

Realize, however, that ultimately you do not have control of whether or not a given release or announcement gets published or broadcast. Its use may depend upon what other news is going on at the time or even the personal whims and interests of the reporter or editor. All you really can do is be certain that a professional-looking product is prepared and made available in a timely manner. (Reporters are generally not interested in stale news.) The rest is out of your hands.

Do not give up if today's well-crafted release never sees the light of day. Or tomorrow's. Keep posting them on your web site and sending them out to any media outlet that even *might* be interested. Eventually your efforts will pay off.

SOME MEDIA PITFALLS TO AVOID

Most reporters are, like you, likeable, ethical human beings simply trying to do a difficult job well. That does not mean there are not a few rascals out there, unethical hacks who will lie or misrepresent what you had to say. You will need to be on your guard to protect yourself against these people, just as you remain on alert to protect yourself against the other threats that show up from time to time in a police chief's life.

The best way to keep from stepping into a media trap is to know what the most frequently-encountered ones look and sound like. Here are some of the more common ones:

THE INTERRUPTOR: This fellow may simply be discourteous or clumsy as opposed to evil. Rather than give you a chance to respond to his queries, he continuously interrupts you with more questions or comments of his own. While it may sound equally impolite, your best response is to keep talking until you have finished what you have to say, even if it means raising your voice and talking over him. You can hope he catches on and knocks off the rude behavior eventually.

THE MISINTERPRETER: This guy takes what you have said and spouts it back incorrectly, accidentally or not. ("So, Chief, what you're really saying is. . . .") No, that actually *wasn't* what you were saying. Whether he is misrepresenting you accidentally or on purpose, you must correct him immediately. That rule holds true even if you are doing a "live" interview. What you have to say is too important to be distorted in front of the public.

THE CONVOLUTED QUESTIONER: This individual's questions are so long and complex that even *he* may be confused as to what he is asking. He may ask you so many questions at once that you lose track of which one you are answering, and that's bad for you. Whether he is trying to trick you or is simply a poor interviewer, you must set the record straight. Just as you would do if the tactic were tried on you by a tricky defense attorney, answer one question at a time. Ask for clarifications and repeats of whatever else he has to say. Take your time. If you effectively deflect his multi-part queries he may cease the practice. By your delays and counter-questions you already have spoiled his routine.

THE MACHINE GUN QUESTIONER: He may be emulating the lawyer who tries the same tactic with a witness. Like the attorney, he may be trying to speed your responses to the point that you become rattled or confused. Don't play that game. Avoid hurrying your normal rate of speaking. Slow things down by asking him to repeat, if necessary. That's likely to ruin his little game.

THE "DEAD AIR" PLOY: You may have tried this trick on a suspect, and now a newshound is trying to use it on you. The idea is to say nothing and stare expectantly at your interviewee when he has finished answering a question. The hope is that the person will say more than he intended in order to fill the uncomfortable silence. You must not fall prey to this device. Simply stop talking when you have said what you intended to say and stare right back at your questioner, even if it's a live interview. After a volley or two of this match he may back off.

THE AMBUSH INTERVIEWER: The perpetrator of this routine shows up when and where he's least expected, perhaps on the street or in the parking lot, and shoves a camera and microphone at this prey. The idea is to surprise and upset the "victim," who may react in an unprofessional manner. While your chances of encountering this tactic are not great, maintaining a calm and professional demeanor is the antidote for it. Say as much or as little as you wish to say in a courteous, matter-of-fact manner. Remain calm and be nice. When you're done, excuse yourself and walk quietly away. (Never, ever try to put your hand over a camera lens or shove a microphone away. Doing so makes you look as guilty as sin.) An ambush interview is nonproductive if the intended victim refuses to overreact.

And remember, just like guns are always loaded, cameras and microphones are always "on." Be on your best behavior anytime either is present. This is not the place for inappropriate or off-color comments, jokes, gestures or other unprofessional behavior. If you do not want to see or hear it on the evening news, then don't do or say it. Once it is out there in the public domain you can never call it back. Careers have been damaged or ended by a camera or microphone that was supposed to be "off." You do not want yours to be one more of them.

ALL YOUR EMPLOYEES MUST UNDERSTAND

As your organization's leader, you naturally will want to maintain excellent personal relations with the local media reps, at least to the extent possible. You will have learned from experience the good things that can flow from that relationship.

But it is not enough that you get along well with the press. It is not enough that you understand the benefits that can be secured for your organization through maintaining mutually-useful, decent working arrangements. Your management staff and your first-line employees also must grasp the importance of a police-press relationship that at the very least does not involve open hostilities.

While it is probably unreasonable for you to expect your people to invest the same amount of energy into the relationship as you do, it is vital that they at least realize how important it is to you that "bad blood" be avoided to the extent possible.

Your best opportunity for demonstrating to your employees the value of a positive relationship with the media may be found in the behavior you model in front of your people. If you curse the reporters out of their presence and ridicule them in front of your officers, you should not be surprised when your people do the same. If you lie to the media reps and perhaps even brag about doing so, you can expect your cops to emulate your bad behavior. Positive example-setting is important for you in everything you do. Your relationship with the members of the media is no exception.

Let your employees know via your policies, procedures and actions that being honest with the press is expected in your organization. Let them know that it is absolutely correct not to give out requested information when there is a valid reason not to, but that you see it as important to be tactful and courteous in that denial. In the end, it all gets down to playing nice and having a good reason for what you do, or decline to do.

Help your people with their media-related decisions by providing them with a clear, current set of news media policies, procedures or orders. Back them to the hilt when they get it right; provide them with additional training when they don't. But don't kill any of them over a media-related gaffe. Doing so likely will only succeed in making the punished employee and his peers truly despise the news people. That's not good for you or your agency.

When the opportunity presents itself, use the media to get your people needed help for a tough case. Use the press to get one or more of your employees deserved accolades for work well done. Stay out of the light yourself and let them enjoy the attention. Over time you just might see your peoples' opinion of the news media get better and better. And that will be a good thing for all of you.

TAKING A REPORTER INTO YOUR CONFIDENCE

Sharing secrets is always risky business. Sharing confidences with someone who has an audience of thousands via his access to the paper or electronic media represents an especially hazardous undertaking. Both elected and appointed officials have seen their public service careers seriously damaged or ended by information that wasn't supposed to be spread by the media, but was.

As police chief, it is likely that you are going to meet a number of representatives of the news media. You probably will find at least one or two of them to be likeable people with whom you enjoy conversing. That's good; it is normal human behavior. Most people are sociable creatures who enjoy at least some interaction with other human beings. A part of that interaction is conversation, and nothing spices up conversation and builds one's own sense of importance like sharing information that the other person does not have. The spicier or more exclusive the information, the better it is.

You certainly have information of interest to a good reporter. Even stuff that may seem pretty tame to you may be of major interest to a journalist sniffing for inside tidbits from the cop shop. As a result, what you shared in confidence or even mentioned as a toss-off remark could end up as a headline in the local news.

Sooner or later almost all law enforcement CEOs tell trusted reporters about an in-progress investigation or planned bust that will mean big news and (hopefully) numerous accolades for the department. That is practically destined to happen in a political world that tempts you to display the good work your people do in order to continue as their leader. Sharing secrets is sometimes seen as a good way to keep a reporter on your side, or at least help assure that he treats you fairly in a pinch.

But it remains a hazardous practice. You should remember this: No matter how good a pal your reporter friend may be, he is under no legal obligation not to publish or broadcast something you gave him in confidence. Doing so may violate his professional ethics and it may end your personal friendship, but there is nothing legally binding to keep him from doing it. Know that when you talk with a journalist buddy. He may indeed be your friend. In the end, however, he has a job to do, just as you do. But he has a different person signing *his* paycheck. If he is put on the spot of choosing between getting "The Big Story" and preserving his relationship with you, he has a big ethical dilemma to face. His decision may not go in your favor.

Regardless of what you may have learned in kindergarten, sharing isn't always a good thing. Share when you feel you must. Just realize that when you have done so you have put it out there for the whole world to get at, even though that may not be your intention. The decision as to whether or not it actually gets widely disseminated is no longer in your hands. If you are alright with losing that control in order to share something with a friend, whatever your motive for doing so, go ahead. If not, resist the powerful temptation to share sensitive information. Talk about something else, instead. Such as what interesting tidbits *he* knows!

DON'T SPOUT OFF BEFORE YOU KNOW THE FACTS

Your agency and its people are always going to be a big source of local news. You know that. On occasion, the news being reported (or about to be) may not display your department in the best possible light. When that happens, it is quite normal for you to want to place a version of events in front of the public that presents what you feel to be a more accurate and favorable perspective of the happenings. Doing that is one of your jobs as the organization's leader.

The not-unreasonable tendency, then, is to want to respond publicly as quickly and forcefully as possible. A rapid and forceful response is not a bad idea, but with a significant caution attached. Before you make big pronouncements, *know* that what you are putting out is accurate information. Otherwise you could be guilty of the same false data distribution that some cop-haters practice on a regular basis.

Resist the powerful temptation to sound off before you know that what you are about to say is 100 percent accurate. In doing that you can avoid having your words fed back to you by a less-than-sympathetic newsperson later. You may likewise save yourself some very uncomfortable moments and very public embarrassment.

It is a basic rule of the journalist's craft that he must double- and triple-check his facts for accuracy before he puts a story in the paper, on the air or over the Internet. Not all reporters follow this excellent advice, but you should. Just as a good law enforcement leader expects his officers to confirm as accurate what they put into their reports, you also should expect your people to check carefully for correctness anything they release to the media. You should set a good example for them by doing the same. You also can save yourself a lot of extra work by getting it right the first time.

If you do discover that you have disseminated information that is unclear, misleading or just plain wrong, waste no time in setting the record straight. Fix the problem right away. You may have lost a little credibility by getting it wrong the first time. But you'll lose a whole lot more if you don't correct your error as soon as you learn of it. Don't trust to luck that no one will spot your mistake. If they do and it is evident that you have not moved to fix it, your reputation for believability may be shot.

Check before you blab. That's not a bad policy for life in general.

DON'T HIDE YOUR AGENDA

As its leader, you represent your organization to the public, the people who pay the bills to keep you in business. Even if you have a press officer or department spokesperson, you are the face and the voice of the organization. As the "final authority" for local law enforcement, what you do and say has special meaning.

Both your public and your employees deserve to hear about what the chief is thinking. One of the best ways for communicating that is via the news media interview. Whether live or taped, done on the radio, television, Internet or printed media, the interview is incredibly valuable to you for its built-in ability to spread the word quickly and widely.

You can use some time-proven tactics for winning at the interview game. They have been applied with success by many successful leaders, and they include the following:

FIRST DETERMINE IF YOU SHOULD GIVE AN INTERVIEW: If there is a good reason why you can't talk about the subject that the would-be interviewer wants to discuss, let him know that. But be sure your reason is a valid one and does not emanate from a desire to avoid the sometimes-prickly press. As the chief you have to suppress that particular wish. Or perhaps you can answer the reporter's queries in a simple telephone conversation. Check a little further and decide upon the best way to handle the request.

ARE YOU THE ONE? Are you the right person to do the requested interview? You should know what he wants to talk about because you have asked him (that's legitimate.) If it's a technical or legality-laced subject, he may need to be talking to one of your people who is an expert in that area. You can be there, too, if you want. Political or policy statements should come from the boss, however. And that's you.

EXPECT SURPRISES: It is alright to ask the interviewer what his questions are going to be so you can organize an informative response to them. He knows you need that information to do a good job that will do the both of you credit. But realize you likely will be asked some things he had not warned you about. This does not necessarily mean he is being sneaky. New questions may have arisen from your statements or the interview may have taken an unexpected turn.

GATHER YOUR FACTS: Once you have a general idea of what you are to be asked you should assemble the information you will need to answer accurately. Go to the best source of information on the topic. Double-check to assure that your information is correct, but also be certain you are not revealing things that should be held back regarding an ongoing investigation or operation.

PRACTICE: If you have time, practice aloud the responses you want to give to the questions you anticipate. You can even have a friend or colleague pose the questions and critique your answers. If you are pressed for time, rehearse your responses in your head, instead.

HAVE YOUR OWN OBJECTIVES: Politicians call it *bridging* when they move an interview from what the journalist wanted to *ask* to what they wanted to *say*. If you want to praise your personnel for something they have done, plan in advance as to how you might work your statement into the interview. Do the same for plans or programs you want to plug. You can, for instance, acknowledge that your city has been experiencing an increase in residential burglaries, and move without pausing into what your department is doing to reduce their numbers.

YOUR IMAGE IS SHOWING: Strive for a relaxed yet professional appearance during an interview. Check how you look before you go on. You don't want to look sloppy, but neither do you want to come across on TV as a ramrod-straight storm trooper. Avoid distracting mannerisms, such as rattling the keys in your pocket or gesturing wildly. Your goal is to look like the confident yet very human leader that your citizens want you to be.

SOUND GOOD, TOO: Keep your answers direct, concise and brief. Do not ramble or wander off-subject. This probably isn't the time for war stories. Remember that only 10 or 15 seconds of what you have to say is likely to get used. Speak in a normal, conversational voice and maintain good eye contact with the person asking the questions.

DO IT RIGHT: Correct yourself promptly if you realize that you have just given out inaccurate information. Tell the truth. If you cannot answer a specific query, say so and explain why. Assuming that the interview is not "live," if you realize that you have stumbled and stammered it is perfectly alright to ask for a "do over." The interviewer wants to produce a professional effort just as much as you do. He or she likely will grant your request.

GET BETTER: Critique yourself after each interview experience. You can learn from each one. The idea is to become more relaxed and in control with every one you put behind you.

DON'T PICK A FIGHT WITH THE NEWS MEDIA

No matter how great your relationship with the media becomes, there are still going to be times when you cheerfully could choke a reporter. Resist the temptation. (It is almost certain to be bad for your career!) Complain tactfully and courteously if you feel the need, then try to let it go. An ongoing, long-running battle is unlikely to be beneficial to anyone. A protracted dispute can serve as a distraction from what you are trying to accomplish. It also expends energy and emotion that could be more usefully spent somewhere else, probably for a lot more gain.

In the "bad old days" cops and reporters did not think too highly of one another. Reporters tended to view cops as secretive, lying dummies who were quick to use excessive force on innocent citizens. Police viewed reporters as lying, sob-sister communists who were quick to believe the word of a felon over that of a law enforcement officer. In that atmosphere of mutual mistrust and dislike, not much of a positive nature got accomplished.

The truth is that police officers and news reporters have a lot in common. They both claim a strong sense of justice. They both stand up for the innocent, the underdog. Both are often aggressive, cynical, egotistical. They stick together with others of their kind. They each feel misunderstood and underappreciated by the public. In other words, they are similar in many ways. And they can do a lot to help each other, as well.

You and the reporter each have something that the other needs. He needs you because you have the information he requires to do his job well. You are a great source of quotes, expert opinions and the "inside track" on some great stories. You have the market cornered on the news that people care about and he will lose out if his competition is on better terms with you than he is.

You need him because he can trumpet the good work that your people do. He can help you educate and inform the public and sell your programs. He can give you a public forum to tell your side of a controversy or advocate for something. He can even produce a positive story or editorial that will help you.

You have the information, the newsperson has the access. You *can* work together for mutual benefit. Neither you nor your employees have to kiss a reporter's feet (or any other body part), but it is worth the effort to get along as much of the time as possible. Make it clear to your people that you expect them to do their part, as you will.

Pick your battles well and be sure it's worth it before you get into a donnybrook with the press. It is very doubtful that you can put a media outlet out of business. But a hostile media certainly *can* complicate your life. Incessant, negative media barrages have contributed to police chiefs losing their jobs. It's an extra hassle you do not need when you have many other important things to do.

DON'T FORGET THE VALUE OF THE INTERNET

Many of today's leaders of law enforcement organizations grew up at a time when newspapers were still king and everyone waited to hear Walter Cronkite's pronouncements on the evening's television news. The up-and-coming generation of police leaders recognizes the value of the Internet as a tough rival of the print or TV news. They realize that the members of their generation appreciate the "get it quick and flashy" convenience of the Internet-based news services. The traditional news outlets have, of course, sensed this big new market and now feature abbreviated versions of the news on their own web sites. The face of the news, and how it is delivered, is changing quickly.

Newspapers, television and radio are not going to vanish anytime soon. The police executive who overlooks their power to help or harm does it at his own risk. At the same time, it would be equally unwise for you to miss out on the opportunities the Internet can hold for you and your organization.

You can recruit employees very effectively through your web site on the 'Net. You can disseminate your department's mission statement and goals. You can publicize the agency's programs and operations that your citizens need to know about. You can feature an employee of the month.

Perhaps most important of all, you can utilize the hot, "what's happening now" flavor of the Internet to educate the public and tell them about the stellar work your personnel are doing. (Your citizens *want* to know what their cops are up to!) You can maintain a "chief's page" or message board. You can swap messages with your consumers. You also can have one of your people put the latest department news releases on your web site at the same time you send them out to the media outlets. The 'Net offers a terrific means for keeping your customers up to date on what their law enforcers are doing to protect them.

More and better means of taking the world with you via a device that fits in your palm or pocket or ear are being developed all the time. Doubtlessly new ones only imagined today will be reality in the near future. It is up to you to remain alert to the possibilities new technology may provide for you to reach your many audiences with the many messages that you want them to get.

The Internet and its offspring are only the first pieces in a new media landscape. You will need to be prepared to fit into that ever-changing picture. The opportunities there for benefiting your organization will be legion.

THE VALUE OF A GOOD PUBLIC INFORMATION OFFICER (PIO)

Obviously you as the CEO must be both accomplished and comfortable in working with the media. But only in the smallest of police agencies should the chief be solely responsible for media relations. You will need some help, and often that assistance can be best provided by a Public Information Officer or PIO.

Depending upon the size of your agency, the PIO may have media relations as his sole task or be responsible for other duties, ranging from crime prevention to patrol. He may be a supervisor, but he does not have to be. In some law enforcement organizations, he or she is a civilian employee. In a few, he or she is a member of some other part of the city or county organization and does not report directly to the chief. You, by the way, want your PIO working directly under your supervision, if that's possible. The position is that important.

Having a reliable, talented PIO is important to you in your mission to keep your organization's best face forward. While duties will vary somewhat from one organization to the next, your PIO should expect to handle some core responsibilities:

- Respond to reporters' daily "beat checks" and contacts
- Prepare news releases
- Prepare public service announcements
- Organize news conferences
- Set up media interviews, as required
- Monitor and collect news stories, editorials and media comments concerning the agency
- Respond to reporters' requests for information on crimes, arrests, programs and events
- Maintain or assist in maintaining the department's presence on the Internet.

Choosing the right person to serve as your PIO is vital to the success of your entire public information function. You will want to be involved in conducting interviews for the job, and you should make the final decision on who is to serve. You are not looking for a flannel-mouthed used car salesman or the department BS artist. You are seeking an extrovert who likes people and likes talking to them about law enforcement. This individual should be a self-starter who can work without close supervision. He should not wait to be called by the media when there is positive news to report about the department. He should take a proactive stance and call the media with the word. He or she should be an excellent communicator in both the written and spoken word. He or she must be well-respected in the organization and have a reputation for integrity and credibility.

Your PIO absolutely must be able to write well. His spelling and grammar must be excellent. He must be courteous, patient and tactful, as he will need each of those traits in working well with sometimes-demanding media people. He will have to hold up well under stress and maintain an external appearance of calm control, just like you do.

To succeed at his or her difficult job, your PIO must have your support and the rest of the department must know that. In order to fulfill his mission, the PIO must have the cooperation of the officer, detective or supervisor he approaches for information. You must give him and the rest of the agency a reasonable, workable set of media policies and procedures to work within. You must wholeheartedly support him and the rest of your people in the face of media complaints when it is evident that your personnel have done it right.

Get your PIO the training he needs to do his job well. One good training source can be found in press relations seminars put on by the International Association of Chiefs of Police (IACP). Also encourage him to network with other PIOs and join state and national public safety PIO associations. All of that (plus your organizational backing) will help your PIO excel in representing the police organization well.

Finally, remain conscious of what your press officer is doing and acknowledge his work when he has done well. You, too, succeed when he does.

SUMMARY

Maintaining a generally positive relationship with the news media can mean plenty of good news for you and your law enforcement agency. By using interviews, news conferences, news releases and the Internet to the fullest, you can reach your public to tell your story and get credit for the good work that your people are doing.

You accomplish a lot by not waiting for reporters to contact you for news, but instead reaching out to them when your department has news to report. You also nurture your continuing good relationship with the ladies and gentlemen of the media by telling them the truth at all times, and insisting that your people do the same.

By maintaining decent relations with the media you can call on the press for help when you need assistance with a case or want to tell your side of the story. You likewise can get help in trumpeting the good work that your people have been doing in very difficult circumstances.

Reporters can be troublesome at times. They likely would say the same about police chiefs. The truth is, collaborating works a lot better than fighting for everyone concerned. You and the media have a lot to offer one another. Each can succeed. Each can look good. Together, you often can achieve that rarest of scenarios: a win-win situation. The reporter gets his story. Your department gets representation and credit when credit is due. Meanwhile, your taxpayers–the journalist's audience–benefit from learning how to protect themselves from crime as well as learning what their law enforcement officers are doing to protect them. They win, too.

Cameras, microphones and reporters are going to be parts of your life for as long as you serve as a police chief. Using them honestly but to your advantage is a mark of a savvy, effective law enforcement leader.

That's what you are.

POINTS TO REMEMBER

- A reputation for credibility is your most precious asset in working with the news media.
- Reach out to the media when you have good news to report; don't wait for their call.
- You need a set of personal guidelines for dealing with the media.
- A successful police CEO must learn to handle bad news well.
- Leading a successful news conference is an important skill for a law enforcement leader.
- There are serious pitfalls you must avoid in your relations with news reporters.
- Know the facts well before you sound off to the media.
- Getting along makes much more sense than fighting with the media.
- The Internet has great value for you when you need to spread your message.
- The ability to give a winning interview is vital for an effective police leader.

- Choosing a skilled Public Information Officer can mean a lot of good news for your agency.
- Your department's news releases need to be the ones that get used by the media.
- Never say "no comment" to a newsperson.
- Realize that on occasion you will get "burned" by the media, but that you *will* survive.

Chapter 12

THE ETHICS OF YOUR JOB

You may have first heard about ethics in the police academy and undoubtedly you have been hearing about it ever since. The Law Enforcement Code of Ethics is something every rookie memorizes, or should, if for no other reason than to get through test day. You, on the other hand, were smart enough to realize that "test day" would be every day for the rest of your career. Events you have encountered as chief have doubtlessly proven you correct in that supposition.

A lot of words and ink have been expended in defining ethics. For many pragmatic law enforcement leaders, it simply means doing the right things for the right reasons, and requiring your people to do the same. The challenge, of course, lies in determining in each instance what the *right* thing is. For the street cop, it may translate into what he or she does at 3 a.m. when no one is looking and will ever know exactly what happened. An officer who does the correct thing, the *right* thing, can truly be declared an ethical practitioner of the law enforcement profession.

One senior chief recalled learning a poem in his long-ago academy that dealt with the "jingle of crooked money and the rustle of unholy skirts." Whatever. As a law enforcement chief executive you certainly have to concern yourself with the "traditional" temptations to go astray that are dangled in front of you, your greenest rookie and all hands in between. But as chief you have other worries, as well.

The political environment that you work in constitutes a constant ethical challenge, as does the limelight cast your way through your being a high-profile member of the community. You likewise must face the dangers of having your personal values diluted by the real world in which not everyone in authority walks the high road with you. You may find it particularly challenging if not everyone you work with–including some of your elected and appointed bosses–shares your high standards.

Serving as an ethical role model for your employees and your community means never surrendering your values and accepting "good enough." You are too honorable for that. This chapter will help you win that continuing struggle.

MAINTAIN ENOUGH FINANCIAL INDEPENDENCE TO WALK AWAY

In today's tumultuous financial times that is much easier said than done. The principle nevertheless remains true.

The harsh reality is that if you cannot financially afford to leave a job you may be more inclined to tolerate or even engage in unethical behavior in order to keep drawing a paycheck. The question for you is where your trip wire for reacting to unethical behavior happens to be strung. Will you tolerate lying but not stealing; accept small gratuities but not payoffs? The slope is a slippery one, and hills can grow into mountains. Hopefully, your ethical trip wire comes equipped with a hair trigger that will tolerate zero unethical behavior of *any* variety.

Virtually no one ever has all the financial independence he would wish to have. Old-time pensions have given way to money purchase plans in which the participant is expected to serve as his or her own money manager. A chief law enforcer can be forgiven if he feels much less certain of his financial security than did his predecessors. Today's economy is that unpredictable. That is the environment in which you must apply your personal ethics to the realities of remaining employed–or not.

As always, you have decisions to make. Your preferred option will be to address a less-than-perfect ethical landscape that you face within your agency or the larger organization of which it is a part. By your contagious attitude, character and actions you may be able to make it a better place to be for everyone. Alone or (more likely) with the help of others, you may be able to repair or mitigate any ethical shortcomings. You may see it transformed into the kind of place in which you would like to spend the rest of your working life.

Failing in that effort, you have a tougher choice to make. Remain in place, receiving a salary and endeavoring to avoid being sucked into doing or ignoring unethical conduct, or walk away. The first choice offers at least temporary financial security at the cost of ethical security; the second surrenders financial safety for the moral and ethical high ground.

Maintaining a reasonable amount of "emergency money" will help you make the right decision to depart an organization that is beyond repair. Try to keep enough funds in stocks, bonds or savings to permit you to walk out the door with head held high if the moral environment of your present position becomes intolerable. Draw on your reserves or take a cut in pay at your next job, if you have to. But get out of a situation that will leave you doubting your own integrity and questioning your own ethics. Job security under those conditions is not worth the mental and moral anguish it will bring.

Get out before you are tempted to do something that will, at least in your own mind, damage your reputation irreparably. It is always the *right* thing to do.

NEVER COMPROMISE FOR POLITICAL EXPEDIENCY

Politics is often about compromise. Like it or not, you are a player on the political scene. While you are smart enough not to participate in the bare-knuckles political fights that erupt from time to time in virtually every jurisdiction, you must nonetheless be politically savvy enough to comprehend your own political environment.

Politics involves give and take. Deals are cut and understandings, both public and private, are reached. You may, for instance, support the Water and Sewer director's budget proposal for a new plant manager in order to gain his backing for something you need down the road. Or you may go out of your way to talk publicly about the good things that have happened because the City Council gave you two extra cops last year. You're doing that because you are hoping they'll support giving you two more *this* year. None of that is unethical. It is basic politics perpetrated in the interest of supporting your organization and its employees. It is sometimes what you do as that organization's leader.

On the other hand, breaking the rules or otherwise compromising your ethics and basic beliefs in order to obtain something of value to you is just plain wrong. You must not go there. You must instead devise another, ethical way to obtain what you are seeking or go without for the time being.

You wouldn't make the mayor's drunk driving arrest go away in order to get a pay raise next year. You would not direct your officers to harass someone that Councilman X didn't like in order to get the Councilman's support for a bigger police budget. And you certainly would not approve "special parking privileges" for a downtown merchant in exchange for merchandise price breaks for you or your spouse.

The preceding are the easier, more readily identifiable ethical compromises you must detect and avoid. Not everything in political life is so cut and dried, of course. A politician's request for your public endorsement in exchange for future, unspecified benefits for you and yours is a little less obvious but equally troubling for its negative ethical repercussions.

As a leader, you will make compromises, too. You will make them with labor, with your own staff, with your boss. Making compromises involves recognizing that in the real world you cannot have everything exactly as you want it. Compromise is a part of life.

But compromise for the ethical leader has a stopping point, a bright line that must not be crossed. You cannot compromise on what you know to be the correct moral stand. You do not bargain where principles are concerned. You never reach an agreement of convenience if it means weakening or surrendering your ethical core.

You lose nothing of great importance, for example, when you grant your employees' union or association a minor change in uniform requirements in order to get their support on something important that you want. But there are other times when compromise is out of the question. When your ethics are involved is one of those times. You would not bargain with an elected official if the end product would be something you know to be lacking in integrity. That's where political expediency must always give way to doing the right thing. Doing the right thing is, of course, what ethics are all about.

DON'T BELIEVE YOUR CLIPPINGS

It has been said that everyone gets his or her 15 minutes of fame. As a public figure, for better or worse you will get a lot more than your allotted quarter hour. How well you use all of that attention is up to you. Ethics come into play here, too.

The danger for many public figures is that they can confuse a modest amount of public curiosity for acknowledgment that they are somehow special, stand-outs above the herd. You realize that fame is a fragile thing and can be gone tomorrow. You also are aware that fame and infamy are spelled almost the same. More than a few public officials who made the news in a big (and perhaps bad) way today were gone shortly thereafter. Police chiefs have been among them.

Realize that as chief your sayings and doings are often newsworthy. You will be in the news on a regular basis. You will be quoted and your opinions will be broadcast. Your gaffes and slipups will be disseminated, too.

If you have done a good job (and you will) the news about you should be positive most of the time. Resist the temptation to regard this publicity as some sort of testimonial that you are something special with accompanying permission to bend the ethical rules. You have been granted no such dispensation. Mess up publicly and see how quickly the media worm will turn. The phrase "penthouse to outhouse" could have been coined to describe the freefall of a suddenly out-of-favor police chief.

It's perfectly alright to cut out your news clippings, whether you do it literally or figuratively. You may get a good laugh (or cry) out of looking at them some day in the distant future. Just don't believe that they make you special. You are human. So is the person who one day will replace you and begin collecting his or her own clippings.

It is important to have a good self-image. It is important to like yourself. It is even more important to like and support what you stand for and never lose sight of your ethical priorities. There is nothing more vital.

FOLLOW ETHICAL RULES FOR RELATING TO OTHER OFFICIALS

Your agency may have a set of written guidelines governing the working relationships between elected officials and appointed staff. If it does, be sure you know what the rules say and adhere to them scrupulously. Doing that could keep you out of a nasty ethical dilemma later.

Sometimes, however, the guidelines for relating ethically to the other members of your larger organization as well as to the members of other entities are not written down. In those instances you will be called upon to exercise your own judgment and common sense in deciding what to do and avoid doing. It is in those relationships that the tiger traps can be the deepest and hardest to detect.

The same internal, ethical compass that guides you in many of your other interactions as an exceptional law enforcement leader will serve you well here, too. Rely on your good sense and focus on always doing the right thing. Don't cheat and don't lie. Treat everyone with impartiality and steer clear of political alliances that require you to attack or undermine someone. Play fair and keep your promises to others. Mean what you say and say what you mean. Treat others as you would like to be treated in return.

If all of this sounds like an attempt to turn you into some sort of Boy Scout, that's probably not necessary. You likely are already there, and from an ethics standpoint that's not a bad thing. You already know what to do. What remains is for you to stay out of the back-biting and dirty tricks that public officials sometimes direct at one another. You as the police chief are a relatively powerful public figure, and the temptation for another official may be strong to try and get you involved in a plot or political strategy of his or her making. Remain courteous and professional towards all, but diplomatically stay out of the game-playing. Not only is it wrong, it also could bite you when things take a sudden turn, as they often do.

Remember: You are everybody's police chief. You do not belong to just the Democrats, just the Republicans, just the liberals or just the conservatives. You serve everyone equally. And you don't cheat or grant inappropriate favors for anyone.

The same holds true for *all* of the officials you work with and for. You will try to serve every one of them in every way ethically permissible. Your personal moral compass will be your guide. By always functioning in that fashion you will never form a relationship that you need to hide from public scrutiny.

PICK CAREFULLY THE HILLS WORTH DYING ON

As a police chief, you will never lack for controversies to join or battles to fight. There will always be something going on within the agency or in the local criminal justice system that will give you grounds to get involved in an argument, if indeed an argument is what you want. Such is the nature of the chief's job. Such is the makeup of the political and organizational environments that you work in.

Your ethics are extremely important to you, and should be. Through your personal role modeling you have set the ethical standards that you expect your employees to follow. You have a right as well as a duty to intervene if you discover that any of your people have committed a serious misstep and are not living up to your ethical expectations. Beyond that, you have a right to be downright irritated. You have the same "permission" to be disappointed and more than a little disgruntled if you learn that one of the officials you must work with is operating in a manner that shows a lack of ethics that match your own.

At the same time, it will not do anything good for your health if you get wrought up over every tiny infraction that you learn about. If the chief is seen to get really upset about virtually *everything,* his getting testy starts to lose its impact on his observant people. Even though you take everything very seriously, your employees may read it as another version of "crying wolf" too often.

"Serious" ethical violations will, of course, depend upon the eye of the beholder. You may find a very minor lapse requires correction while your colleague in the law enforcement agency next door feels it does not merit his official notice. Chief Jones feels that an officer accepting a free cup of coffee from a local merchant has earned a reminder from his sergeant regarding the department policy on gratuities; you feel it deserves a written reprimand. Chief Smith thinks that a detective getting in over his head financially is none of the department's business; you feel you need to counsel the man about embarrassing his employer while he's being pursued by a posse of bill collectors. Every leader's ethical trip wire is strung at a little different height.

Intervene when and where you must. Your ethics are that important. But first give thought as to whether or not a very minor "offense" by someone either inside or outside your agency truly deserves your action. Perhaps the situation just needs watched for further developments. Jump in where the situation calls for the full weight of the chief of police. Restrain yourself where it does not.

You have heard before that you should not make disciplinary decisions when you are really upset. That's good advice. Allow yourself some cooling-off time before you decide what to do about an ethical lapse by one of your people or one of the officials with whom you work. With a little time to think about it, you may decide that the "sin" was not as grave as you initially believed. If it's one of your employees, you may not have to drag him behind a speeding police car, after all. If it's a peer or some other official you work with, perhaps you will not have to cut off your association with him or take some other drastic action.

Ethics are vital in your work. It is equally important to keep things in perspective. Be sure it is worth the blood before you take a stand that requires you to nail any key body parts to the wall. There may be a less dramatic but equally effective way to resolve the issue.

FIND OUT WHAT HAPPENED TO THE LAST GUY

Determining the atmosphere in which your predecessor departed the department could tell you a lot about the expectations you may encounter. If he truly *did* retire, so much the better. Law enforcement CEOs do it all the time. But sometimes a "retirement" is a face-saving screen for something else. The "retirement" may be in lieu of some other kind of departure that would have resulted in controversy and bad publicity for everyone involved. You know that, but you should keep it in mind when you are investigating the circumstances of your predecessor's leaving, which you certainly should do.

Your boss and your staff will be able to give you the true story of how and why the last chief exited. But you'll need to ask in "the right way," and that means privately. The answers you get should tell you if there were past problems now resulting in extra sensitivity that you need to know about. That knowledge could help keep you from blundering into something that has a "history" locally. For instance, if the last chief left because he had a problem with booze, you can expect your boss and probably your people to be especially interested in your imbibing habits. Or if the last guy departed because he displayed the personal morals of an alley cat, expect that people are going to be interested in your dating habits if you're single and your reputation for marital fidelity if you are married. Volunteer the answers to their questions early so you can get on to other issues.

Knowing what befell the last chief could keep you from getting into the same dire straits. One chief candidate learned that the job was open because the last man to hold the position literally had worked himself to death, dying of a massive heart attack. Another learned from the guy he would be replacing that he was quitting because he could no longer tolerate the micro-management of his department by the local elected officials. Yet another chief wannabe found out from the departing chief that he was leaving because he could not stand the strain brought about by an ongoing battle between gay and straight police managers over how the department should be run. In each of the preceding scenarios the chief candidates who wisely did their homework on the local situation each decided to pass on the opportunity to compete. In each instance it just did not seem worth the almost-certain aggravation to come. Interestingly enough, however, in each case *somebody* took the job and had to face the music.

It is an old (and valid) saying in the police chief business that it is much easier to come in behind a devil than a saint. If you have the opportunity to follow a poor and thoroughly disliked leader you will have an initial advantage, as just about anything you are and do will appear an improvement over the last guy. But if you are following a great and charismatic leader who was well-liked both in the department and the community, your job will be a bit harder. You will find yourself compared constantly to the departed, popular leader. You certainly can succeed as your own person, it just may take a little longer for everyone to learn that you *are* a great guy and a terrific leader, too. You can't be anyone else, nor should you try to be. Being youself will work just fine.

DON'T GET COMPLACENT WHEN THINGS ARE QUIET

Occasionally a leader will regard the absence of loud and constant griping as an indication of solid support from his employees and the community. He may be right, but that's a risky assumption to make. Things may not be as they appear. Discontent and active opposition to what the chief is doing may be there, but is being kept out of sight for fear of retribution. If it is present, it likely will surface eventually. If it is noisy enough it could result in serious disruption to the organization's mission. Not addressed, it could even cost the chief his job. It is obviously worth your while to stay alert as to what is going on in your organization.

You are too smart to get complacent about how things are going in your department and in the greater community beyond. You know better than to regard silence as approval. People may indeed be apathetic if things seem to be going well at the moment, but you cannot assume that without first doing some checking of your own. Ask questions, and not just of your command staff.

Employees have been known to get quiet because they have given up hope that the leaders of the organization can solve whatever it is that is bothering them. You don't want that to happen in your organization. Frustrated people who have given up on you because of what they perceive as your inability or unwillingness to help them are likely to go somewhere outside of your organization for help. That's not good for you nor the organization. A feeling of hopelessness is the last thing you need to have prevalent in your agency.

Your best bet for avoiding nasty surprises from unhappy people is to stay tuned in as best you can to what is being said both inside and outside the organization. You do that by listening to as many voices as you can each day. You will not agree with all of them, nor will you consider what each of them has to say important. Out of self-protection you must listen all the same. It is also the *right* thing for a police chief to do. The fewer people you hear each day the greater your chances of being surprised by something you should have seen coming. If that happens, you will be coming from behind to repair the damage when the blowup might have been prevented by paying more attention to your surroundings.

Train yourself to become at least a little uneasy when your agency's or your community's jungle drums are totally silent. Maybe the usual drummers are focused on something else. But just maybe something is about to sneak up on you. Keep your ears open and your finger on the pulse of the local situation. Whether in officer safety or organizational health, complacency is never a good thing. Stay sharp and survive.

NEVER SURRENDER YOUR IDEALS

You came into this law enforcement leadership business with some very clear images of how things should be in an excellent organization. Those ideals may have become even more clear as you have witnessed others fall short, perhaps damaging or ending promising careers in the process. Your high standards–your honorable and ethical ideals–are certainly worth preserving. You probably use them daily in making your organization better. That's how law enforcement as a whole gets better.

Sadly, for too many law enforcement officers a bruising career of 15, 20 or 30 years weighs heavily and causes some to give up on the ideals that may have brought them into the work in the first place. That's tragic. If you are to help some of these folks in your own organization, you must first never allow it to happen to *you.*

A chief of police might be forgiven if he allows the hard knocks and disappointments from his time as head of the agency to wear on him. During a chief's leadership career he may well encounter people in his community who want him to cheat in one way or another–generally for their benefit. He may meet fellow law enforcement officers and even peers whose ethics fall far short of his own. In a worst case scenario he may learn that his boss's personal moral compass is defective in one way or another.

In such a turbulent, troubling atmosphere some chiefs have lowered their expectations and accepted "good enough" for themselves and their people. You might say that they have been beaten down by life until they are willing to settle for something they would never have considered at the start of their leadership career. This is a shame and it's not for you.

You must resist the very human temptation to settle for less when it comes to your ideals. You are what you are because of the things you believe in. You want your employees to see you demonstrating your personal ideals in everything you do, on and off the job. You want them to admire what you do and what you stand for. You want them to try and be like you. That will make them better, and they will make your organization better. Ideals are like that when they are translated into action.

You knew there would be tough days when you took the police chief's position. You probably suspected that there would be times when you would doubt yourself and what you stand for. The good news is that such times will pass. Your way of doing things *is* the right way.

Do not give up what you stand for. Not ever. Don't let it be diluted. The ideals that brought you to your position of leadership will take you all the way through a successful career if you stick with them. After all, good leaders don't surrender.

ONE SLIP DOESN'T MEAN YOU'RE HEADED FOR HELL

You hold high ethical standards, and you should. As the head of your organization it is your duty to set the example for ethical behavior for everyone in the agency. Normally you do that very well.

But you are a human being, too. You are not perfect no matter how hard you try to be. Rare as they may be, you are going to make mistakes. Human beings do that. Very occasionally, one of those inevitable mistakes may be one that qualifies as an ethical slip-up.

There are lots of things that can go wrong out there, so many that to try and guess which one might trip you would be a fruitless exercise. You are aware of your own vulnerabilities better than anyone else. By using that knowledge you can help assure that you are always extra careful around those areas that you already know could result in trouble. If, for example, you know that you shouldn't drink because of what the stuff can do to you, then don't do it. If you know you have a tendency to blame others for your troubles when you are angry, remain aware of that fact and work to control it, even if that means you must seek some private, professional counseling to help you. You are the best judge of what might lead you to an ethical offense one day. Having identified your challenges, you can do a better job of keeping yourself out of an ethical pickle.

Try as you might to walk the straight and narrow path, there is still a real chance you will make that ethical mistake some day. Maybe you've broken a rule in keeping track of your expense account. Maybe you've been stopped by a state trooper after having a couple of drinks. You didn't get busted, but the rumor is rampant that the chief got special treatment when he was caught dead drunk. (You can expect the story to grow as it rolls along.) Or maybe the loud argument you had with your spouse results in the neighbors summoning your own troops to your front door. Wait until the media get hold of that one!

None of these foul-ups has to mean the end of your good reputation as the leader of your organization. None has to mean the end of a good and contributing career.

Face your ethical mistakes in the same way you confront the other challenges of your job: directly and honestly. If you have made a mistake–ethical or otherwise–acknowledge it and move forward. If a private or public apology is required, deliver it and mean it. Say it with dignity and don't blubber like a TV preacher caught with his pants down. Then, go on. Do everything you can to fix a mistake that was of your making. Openly admit your role in causing it. Move ahead from there.

It is OK to acknowledge that you are a less-than-perfect human being. Most people will understand that. They know they're not perfect, either. Most will forgive you if it looks like you mean it when you say you're sorry. Nobody expects you to beat yourself up forever over a mistake. Put it behind you and keep doing your very important job to the best of your ability. That is what real leaders do.

PERFORM AN ETHICS SELF-EXAM FROM TIME TO TIME

There is no doubt that your job as your agency's CEO gives you plenty to do. It's likely that you have more to do than you can fit into a "standard' workday. That's why you come in early, stay late and take work home. You probably do not have a whole lot of time for introspection. You are likely just too busy to take a good look at yourself very often.

Regardless of all the other "stuff" you must handle, it is very important to your ethical good health that you pause long enough to take a look at how you're going about being *you.* You might call it an ethics check-up. And you get to be your own doctor.

It is worth stepping back on occasion to review your associations with others involved in the local political scene. Not only is it important that you do not extend them special favors, it is equally vital that you do not by your words or actions leave the impression that they *could* expect special treatment. Your demeanor here could prevent a problem from ever developing. One veteran chief put it this way: "If you act like you are unlikely to grant special privileges, you are at least somewhat less likely to get asked for them." That prohibition on special treatment includes your personal friends.

You also should examine the financial and business relationships you have with others in your community. You must avoid even the appearance of impropriety. Even though he is your buddy, the owner of the local auto dealership should not give his pal the chief a special deal that he would not extend to Joe Citizen. You should not allow any other businesses to give you or your family members "special deals," either. In the end this special treatment could cost you far more than any possible savings you may have achieved.

Your personal and political friendships need a careful going over from time to time, too. You need to be sure that the company you keep is not going to cause embarrassment for you and your organization one day. If one of your pals has a chronic problem of forgetting to pay his taxes, you probably want to put some distance between him and yourself. If another of your associates wants to fight the world when he's got a snootful, you really cannot afford to have him as a friend anymore, either. The risks are just too great. The same advice applies to your friend the banker, or realtor, or attorney who has a bad habit of getting involved in really shaky deals.

It is just good sense to step back and look at your life and how you lead it every once in a while. You may find something you want to change to preserve your image as an ethical police leader.

Your personal ethics are very important to you. They should be. You are well aware that they are good ones and you want them to stay that way. That is why it is worth the effort to step back and take a look in the mirror every now and then. You always want to be proud of the leader you see looking back at you.

SUMMARY

American law enforcement's history is not a picture of always-correct, ethical behavior. You and many of your contemporaries have done a great deal to overcome the outdated era of sometimes unethical police practices. You have done a good job, but even more remains to be done.

Your personal contributions to ethical leadership behavior are vital to law enforcement and its future. You must maintain your personal ethics and core beliefs in the face of organizational and political challenges. You must not compromise your standards, nor should you be embarrassed to hold them. You cannot ever be perfect, but that does not mean you cannot try to be. You will almost certainly stumble ethically sooner or later, but a minor misstep does not mean you are evil. Fix the problem as best you can and move on.

The example you set for your employees and your community in the area of personal ethics will send a powerful message of what you expect and what you will not tolerate. See to it that the model you display is always a positive one. Poor ethics can be contagious in an organization, but so can good ones. By serving as an excellent ethical role model you will convey what kind of behavior is expected from each member of your agency. Require your managers to do the same. Replace them if they are clearly incapable of meeting your reasonable, ethical expectations.

Never become so focused on the ethics and behavior of others that you neglect your own. Perform an ethical self-exam on occasion and see how you measure up to what you know to be right. That, too, is the mark of a truly ethical leader.

POINTS TO REMEMBER

- Know that retaining your integrity may one day require you to walk away from a job.
- Try to maintain as much financial independence as you can in case you must leave suddenly.
- Never compromise your integrity for political convenience.
- Do not get carried away with your press clippings–you are replaceable.
- Follow the rules in relating to other elected and appointed officials.
- Retain your principles but pick your big battles wisely.
- As a new chief, find out if your predecessor or your organization had a reputation for unethical behavior.
- Do not get complacent when things seem to be going well.
- Don't give up or water-down your standards and ideals.
- A single, minor ethical slip on your part does not mean the end of the world.
- Compare your ethics to your actual behavior on a regular basis and act on what you learn.
- Realize that no one, not even you, is perfect.
- Just do your ethical best, all of the time.

Chapter 13

THE CHIEF AS A PLAYER ON THE POLITICAL SCENE

"I am a professional, not a politician."

You probably have said that with pride on more than one occasion. You have a right to be proud. Sometimes cops do not have the highest regard for some of those who have won their jobs via election or patronage. That's not fair to the many good people who are serving competently and honestly in public office. Regardless, you as the chief will have to learn to move easily and with confidence through the political landscape if you are to serve the interests of your organization and your community.

If you can remember any of your Civics 101 class, you may recall that politics was supposed to be about the science and art of governing for the good of all. A politician was someone who engaged in politics and tried to serve the interests of the public in a statesman-like way. Today that distinction appears to have been lost, as politicians are often regarded in a derogatory manner as people involved in backroom scheming and opportunistic deals intended to help themselves more than their constituents. Again, that is not fair to the principled, civic-minded individuals who labor in government at all levels. But it's the environment you move in when you lead your organization across a very political landscape. You may not be a politician, but you must have an appreciation for things political. You cannot be oblivious to the political things going on around you if you are to successfully represent the interests of your people and your citizen-customers.

It will do little good for you and your cause if you treat the political officials who occupy your world as if they were some sort of unclean beasts. At times you will occupy the same playing field that they do, and it will be to your advantage to get along with them without necessarily agreeing with their politics and political maneuverings. These people may have a lot to say about things that are very important to you. Like your departmental budget, for instance. It is vital for your organization that you are able to handle yourself on this political chessboard.

There is nothing nasty and evil *per se* about politics and politicians. Yes, there have been some unethical crooks and charlatans that on occasion have dirtied the image of the profession. The same thing, of course, has happened in law enforcement. That does not mean that *you* are evil.

The fact is that your world is a political one in many respects. How well you function in that world will have something to say about your success as the leader of your organization. The advice offered in this chapter should prove useful as you navigate the sometimes-rough waters of the political seas. The good news is that you can do that without giving up either your ethics or your effectiveness.

TALK TO EVERYBODY; BELIEVE A SELECT FEW

There are a few jobs where communicating with others is not a big deal. The position of back-country Ranger at a national park comes to mind. But your job is not like that. As police chief, you wisely try to hear from as many different voices as possible each day. That is one way in which you stay abreast of what is happening in your jurisdiction. It is how you learn what is on the minds of your employees and your citizens. It is certainly important that everyone hears what you have to say. But it is even more important that they see and know that you are listening.

Virtually everyone wants what they have to say to be taken seriously. They want to be believed. Often, they want to convince their listener to take some action or decision that will benefit them or their interests. That's natural. You do it, too.

Knowing that, never forget that there often will be agendas, including some hidden ones, in what many people say to you. They may want you to agree with them or do something for them or both. To make it more likely that you will do that, they may shade the facts just a little in favor of their position or version of the story. Again, that's not terrible, it's just human. But as the listener you need to be aware of a possible slant in what you are hearing.

You need reliable information upon which to base your decision-making. For that reason it's wise to take with the proverbial grain of salt much of what you hear from unproven sources each day. That does not mean that you should assume that everything you hear is false or slanted. It does mean you need some proven-reliable sources upon which to call when you must have reliable, accurate information.

You should learn relatively quickly the most dependable sources for information inside your organization. You will need as many of them as possible. The world outside your department will be a little tougher. Experience will help you determine who you can most often depend on to know what is happening and get it right. Your staff can help you identify additional reliable sources. Your own observations will help you locate others.

Many of the players on the political scene are much better at talking than they are at listening. The nature of your job as chief department spokesperson requires that you talk a lot, too. It is something that you must do well. At the same time, your organization's well-being requires that you are an excellent listener, as well.

Listen to everyone. Consider what they are saying. Take their motives into account. Try to separate fact from fiction. Be courteous but be cautious concerning who and what you take as the gospel. Continue to identity your best sources of accurate information and pay close attention to them.

Today the name of the game is information. To be a player, arm yourself with the best information you can get.

REALIZE THE DANGER OF A CLOSE ALLIANCE

Depending on where you serve as a police chief, you were chosen for the job by a group of individuals or a single, appointing authority. You likely were selected by a town board, city council, mayor or city manager. Even if you were chosen by a single individual, it's possible that a group of people such as a town board was involved in the process, perhaps behind the scenes.

Chiefs who actually were selected by a group of people often have the broadest base of support, at least at the outset of their tenure. It is to the benefit of each member of the assemblage that you succeed, thereby confirming his or her judgment that you were the best choice for the job. As the makeup of that group changes by election or other attrition, you will be well-advised to make the acquaintance of each replacement member and let him or her know what you represent and what you are endeavoring to do with the police department. You can best do that, of course, in one-on-one meetings over coffee or lunch. You want to keep your support intact to the extent possible. It's how a police chief retains his position and influence when the makeup of the governing/appointing body changes. While it's unlikely that you will ever have 100 percent support, you want to get as close to that figure as possible.

If you were hired by a single decision-making authority, such as a city manager, you will be obliged to keep him or her briefed on your plans for the department. By doing that you maintain your boss's backing for what you are doing and find out early on if there is something you are planning that he does not like. Then you can decide whether or not you need to change plans or work harder at bringing him around to see the logic of why you want to do whatever it is you're planning. You may elect to do a little of both. Bringing your boss into your planning on occasion can help build a positive working relationship. Don't do it to the extent that you falsely lead him to believe he will be involved in *all* of your planning and decision-making. Leaving that impression is practically guaranteed to lead to trouble.

You want and need an excellent relationship with your boss. But you want to be careful about getting *too* close to your hiring authority, however much you like him or her. It is a political reality that, more than any other local official, in many locales the chief is seen as closely connected to the appointing authority, whether that authority is a mayor, police commissioner or city administrator. As a consequence, when that appointing official leaves there is sometimes a tendency to shove out the police chief, as well. The idea is that the new boss will want to appoint his own person as chief law enforcer. This practice is almost a tradition in some locales. Even there, however, exceptions to the practice can arise when the chief is seen as doing an excellent job, independent of his boss. That is the kind of reputation *you* want to have in the community. It also may mean that you stay when your boss departs.

The best and most ethical solution for you is to serve your boss with loyalty and professionalism while you maintain your own identity and independence to the extent feasible. You want your reputation to be built on what *you* have done and what *you* stand for. If the local leadership changes you stand a better chance of remaining in place in order to finish what you started.

None of this is to say that you cannot have a beer with your boss or flip burgers in his backyard. How close you want to be to your supervisor is a decision you will have to make for yourself based upon your knowledge of the local political scene and how well your boss is regarded there, in addition to how highly you think of him or her.

There is nothing in your ethical core that says you must slavishly bind yourself to a poor leader who is making consistently bad decisions for the organization and the community. There is nothing that says you must go down with a bad leader who is mean-spirited, unethical or just plain crooked. Here, distancing yourself from a malevolent superior is the right thing to do, both from an ethical and career survival standpoint.

Be fair to your boss, just as you expect him to be fair to you. Give him your honest advice and your best efforts. Tell him the truth and do not seek to undermine his decisions or authority. But do not lash yourself to the mast of his ship when it is going down due to his own malpractice.

DON'T COMPROMISE YOUR IDEALS FOR ACCEPTANCE

You have said it before and you meant it: My integrity, my ideals are not for sale at any price. The crooks on the street should know that. Your employees know it, too, or should. The players on the local political scene need to know it, as well.

The best way to let everyone know what you are all about is through what you say and do every day. The model behavior you display in the community for all to see will fill a book about what you will and will not condone regarding ethical actions by yourself and your people. Telling people what you are all about is good. Showing them via your own actions is a lot better.

Modeling your ideas for everyone to see is really not rocket science. Some of it may come from seemingly little things, but it all adds up, for better or worse. The examples of "worse" are practically without end. If you drive fast and are frequently stopped with impunity by your own officers, you hardly should be surprised when a local politico asks you to "fix" a speeding ticket he has received. Word gets around. If you accept expensive gifts from local businesses at Christmastime, you should not be shocked when one of the gift-givers demands special privileges from your officers. If you are carrying on a well-publicized extra-marital affair (and most of them do get publicized, sooner or later), you should not be indignant when a local official asks you to do something unethical or unlawful. After all, by your own actions you have signaled to the world that you are willing to lie, cheat and hurt others. Why wouldn't you help a pal do the same? Make sure the examples you set are always good ones.

The trap for you is to think that you will be admitted to the inside corridors of power and given the "secret handshake," so to speak, if you cheat for an unethical player on the political scene. You may be helped to survive career-wise by some sort of political *détente,* or so the faulty logic goes. You are smart enough to realize that nothing could be more distant from the truth. You have no desire to be granted acceptance by someone for whom you have no respect. With some luck, you may make it through an entire career without ever confronting such a challenge to go over to the dark side. But if the confrontation ever does occur, you'll know what to do.

By acting in an unethical fashion you set yourself up for political blackmail by people who know you must protect your image as an ethical, upstanding leader in the community. By compromising your ideals in the hope of gaining approval and acceptance you will have started down a slippery slope that likely will end in an irreparably damaged or terminated career.

Don't forsake your ideals for anybody or anything. They are the essence of who and what you are. Anyone you encounter who cannot grant you approval or acceptance because of the ideals you represent is not someone you want to count as a friend.

BE WILLING TO TRUST WHEN TRUST IS EARNED

A grizzled veteran was giving advice to a rookie cop. "For the first six months on the job, don't trust anybody," he said. "After that, don't trust hardly anybody."

That is rarely good advice for encouraging a healthy mental attitude towards one's new employer. As chief, you can ill afford to harbor an equally untrusting attitude towards those within and without your organization. Experience doubtlessly has taught you there may be persons in local politics whom you would be unwise to trust completely. They have earned that distinction not by your bias but through their actions that have displayed their shortcomings in ethical behavior. Having seen their failings demonstrated, you have wisely decided to be very cautious in your interactions with them. You can be cooperative, you can be courteous. But you also will be careful.

Knowing who the questionable characters are is part of your survival package as a police leader. To the extent possible you will avoid them. When necessity requires you to interact with them you will do so while watching your back–and your own actions. You know them for what they are and will observe them accordingly. That is simply a good survival practice.

Even as you keep an eye on the bad or questionable characters your good mental health requires that you must be willing to trust those who have proven themselves trustworthy. That is obviously an absolute must when dealing with people inside your own police organization. It is no less true with the officials and others who inhabit the political world beyond the walls of your agency.

You cannot get your job done if you mistrust *everyone*. Beyond that fact, that brand of paranoia surely will have very detrimental effects on your mental and emotional health. As you know from your officer safety training, it just isn't healthy to see a bad guy hiding behind every tree. The same holds true for those you work with on the political scene.

You will find it difficult if not impossible to do your job as an exceptional leader if you elect to trust no one. By granting your complete trust to a select few who have by their demonstrated character and tangible, honorable actions earned it, you will be an emotionally healthier and clearly more effective leader. You cannot do it all by yourself. Granting trust where it is deserved will aid you immeasurably in accomplishing your multiple leadership tasks.

NEVER BREAK THE RULES FOR ANYONE

There may be few professions that have as many rules as does law enforcement. Most exist for good reason. When a field of work contains within it the right to take away freedom and even life itself under a certain set of circumstances, the practitioners of that work had best be carefully controlled in their own actions.

Law enforcement employees face good rules, bad rules and rules that are seldom, if ever, enforced. There are rules for virtually everything, from how one's uniform is to be worn to sexual matters (no sexual relations on duty, please.) There are sanctions–some of them severe ones–for breaking the rules.

As a law enforcement leader you are practiced in both following and enforcing the rules. If you are smart, you serve every day as an example of how your employees should behave under the guidelines that govern cops' behavior. Rules are a big deal to you.

You also serve as a good role model in obeying the rules that exist outside of your department. The guidelines you follow cover the spectrum from the traffic codes to the income tax statutes.

You have lived long enough and been around policing for sufficient time to realize that not everyone takes the rules and following them as seriously as you do. That's one of the reasons that you and your people have jobs as rule enforcers. The reality is that some people look at rules as intended for someone else, not them. Rules are to be bent, broken or ignored.

Unless your experience is an incredibly exceptional one, over a career you will work with at least one or two appointed or elected officials as well a few other community "notables" who are willing to wink at the rules, at least insofar as their personal obligations are concerned. These are probably the same folks who feel that they cannot get a ticket, or that you will "take care of it" if they do. They may expect that their teen gets warned rather than busted when he's caught stealing. They may expect free, extra services for themselves and their friends that they know your department cannot provide to "regular" citizens. In sum, they expect you to break your rules for them and won't like it if you don't.

You probably want to be liked. That's normal. You probably don't want noise and outright opposition from those in the community who have an easily-accessible bully pulpit for expounding their negative views about you and your department. You frankly do not want or need extra trouble from a Big Shot on the local scene.

In spite of what you don't want and don't need, as an ethical leader you have no choice other than to follow the rules and expect others to do the same. It may help to explain courteously to the rule-breaker that what he wants you to do is contrary to the law or other guidelines that you must function within. All the while trying hard to sound nonjudgmental, you can stress that you want to keep the both of you out of trouble. If he has any class at all, he will get the message and back off. Regardless of his response, you still have to do the right thing. That means that you follow the rules and expect others to do the same. You don't have to stick your nose in the air and talk down to the "sinners." It doesn't mean that you have to flaunt a "holier than thou" attitude. It *does* mean that you don't break the rules. Not for anyone. The potential consequences are too great to do anything less.

HAVE A MENTOR TO POSE YOUR DILEMMAS TO

Everyone needs someone to talk to about his or her fears, frustrations and problems. You may have preached that reality to youngsters new to your law enforcement organization. You likely have stressed it to them as a mental component to officer survival. At the same time, you may have told them of the value of having access to the sage advice of one who has travelled the road before, like a senior officer, for instance.

You should apply the same, sound advice to your own life as leader of the organization. You, too, could use someone to talk to on occasion. You need someone who will listen patiently to your concerns and perhaps help you find an experience-based solution. You, too, need counsel on occasion. You need a mentor.

You may feel that the term *mentor* is overused today. It probably is. But you also can see the value of drawing upon the experiences of someone who has previously faced the trials that you are facing now. Why, then, wouldn't a sane person want to spare himself the grief that someone else has already endured and survived?

Not every wrinkly green thing out there qualifies as a Yoda. There are way more frogs than genuine Jedi masters. You will need to be very cautious about who you look to for advice and who you decide to emulate. Bad advice and poor role models will leave you worse off than you were before.

Rely on known reputations and your own powers of observation to tell you who you want to approach for advice. He doesn't have to be literally the chief next door, as modern communications have moved practically everybody right into your office. What is his track record in the business and how is he regarded by others? Reach out to your fellow chiefs for some ideas. Your potential mentor could be a senior police chief, but he also might be a veteran manager/leader from some other line of work. After all, professionals beyond policing experience many of the same problems that a law enforcement CEO faces. Pick carefully, then make contact. Don't be too shy to ask for help.

Most professionals will be honored that you have asked for their assistance. Most will be willing to give that help, assuming that they have the time to do so. Spend some time with your chosen mentor and see if your personalities and philosophies mesh well. If one or both of you are not comfortable with the relationship, express your thanks and move on. The next person may be a much better fit.

There is nothing that says you can only have one mentor. You can learn something useful from many people. Ask good questions and really listen to the responses. You'll almost certainly end up smarter for the effort.

One more thing: You should be willing to return the favor. As you grow in experience and knowledge, be open to sharing what you have learned with less-experienced law enforcement leaders. Be ready to serve as a mentor yourself. As a leader, it is your job to help law enforcement get better. Good mentors do that.

DON'T CONFUSE APATHY WITH SUPPORT

Sometimes it's just easier to tolerate something rather than make a big fuss over it. Until, that is, the grievance becomes too big or painful or destructive to continue to endure. An unpleasant event sometimes follows. That holds true for marital relationships. It can prove equally valid for police leadership.

Discontent within either the department or the community can fester quietly for some time before it erupts to the surface, frequently with noisy and disruptive consequences. The fact that things appear quiet at the moment does not necessarily mean that everyone is in love with you or your way of doing things. It is seldom that any chief gets that kind of affection and support. Cops are not like that. Neither are most communities.

You can help prevent some nasty surprises that can quickly become political liabilities by staying in touch as best you can with all of the groups that exist both inside and outside the department. Surprises will always happen, but you can minimize them if you listen to as many voices as possible. Mix with your employees and mix with diverse members of the community. Converse with the professional pols, but listen to the guy who runs the corner market and the mom who is worried sick about gangs, too. Find out what people are angry about, frustrated by, frightened of. Be especially attuned to what your department is doing that people think is making things better–or worse. Learning that can tell you what changes you need to make in your way of doing business.

The idea is to find out what is on peoples' minds before they become so concerned about it that it surfaces in multiple, angry letters to the editor or calls to elected officials. When that happens, you have reached the point where apparent apathy has been replaced by a perceived crisis requiring action. You want to deal with the issue proactively before it is transformed into a public event, whenever possible. That means keeping a sensitive finger on the pulse of *all* the communities that make up your political environment.

Never stop paying attention to what is going on around you. New chiefs generally pay a lot of attention. They worry about everything. Sometimes, as they become more experienced, they also become more comfortable. There's a good and a bad side to that. You don't want to worry yourself sick. But you also may be tempted to relax your vigilance of your political surroundings. And that's not such a good idea. It can result in unpleasant surprises.

Practice leadership by walking around your agency and your jurisdiction. Look and listen carefully. The people you encounter are probably not truly apathetic. You can never afford to be.

REMEMBER THAT YOU ARE EVERYONE'S CHIEF

A Texas sheriff was fond of saying that he made a point of ignoring a particular minority group in his jurisdiction, as he knew its members would never vote for him anyway. He just didn't care what they thought about anything, he said.

You cannot afford to share that lawman's shortsighted view of his job's responsibilities. The point is that you were selected to be *everyone's* chief, with no exceptions. Being human, you will like some individuals and groups more than others. But you are ethically bound to serve each with equal devotion. That is your job as a leader.

You have a lot to do inside your organization. In addition, you have much to attend to each day that requires you to spend time listening to a lot of different people from outside your agency. You also have writing and speaking assignments to handle and projects you must take care of for your boss. In other words, you have plenty to occupy your available time. When you are that busy, you might be tempted to shrug off the views of the small voices. Those voices might be emanating from ethnic minority groups, fringe political organizations or groups and individuals occupying the outermost orbits of the community's solar system. The temptation may be there, but it is a temptation you must resist.

There are both ethical and practical reasons why you cannot ignore any part of your constituency. First, it would not be the right thing to do. You were appointed to be the entire community's chief of police, not just the chief law enforcer for a particular political party, ethnic group or neighborhood. You are everybody's chief of police.

Unlike the Texas sheriff, the ethics you hold fast will not permit you to ignore a group of people simply because you do not like or agree with them. They still are members of your community and you are duty-bound to protect and serve them. You have to address their interests and concerns just as earnestly as you do anyone else's. You meet with them when they want to talk to you. You listen to their worries, whether you agree that they are legitimate or not. They, too, are your customers. They may not always be right, but they are nonetheless your customers. They merit some of your attention and effort.

Being a politically-savvy and pragmatic individual, you also must pay attention to even the quietest voices in your community because you don't want to be surprised by something you could have seen coming. Sometimes unpredicted events can turn up the volume of the formerly soft voices. If you were not listening previously, you will be forced to listen now. An example may be found in the soft voices complaining of racial profiling that overnight turn into shouts when a minority teen is shot by one of your officers. If you're smart, you'll pay attention to those voices when they are still barely whispers. That doesn't mean you have to do what they tell you. But you should give the speakers a hearing. You may learn something you really need to know.

Virtually every community has a very few voices that are so far out in left field, so nearly deranged that you will be wasting your time if you spend much time listening to them. You should be able to figure out pretty quickly who these voices belong to. The guy who wants to give you weekly warnings about the impending end of the world is one of them. Count on your support staff to screen these people away from you whenever possible. Very little good will come from entertaining them. But those over-the-edge voices should be very few. All of the others you should pay attention to.

You are everybody's chief. Always act like you are.

LISTEN TO THE "OUT" GROUPS, TOO

Some will tell you that local government–the government that you are a part of–is nonpartisan, grassroots government where political affiliations and rhetoric are not important. Perhaps there really are communities where that is true. It's doubtful that yours is one of them. Politics play too much of a role in American culture. People are too wrapped up in whether they (or you) happen to be Democrat, Republican, Libertarian, Conservative, Liberal or whatever.

In politics, there is virtually always a group that is in control and one or more others that are out of power, at least at the moment. Often, that "out" group is concentrating on returning to power as soon as possible. All of that may not affect you directly. But affect you it may, one way or another, sooner or later. That is yet another reality of the political environment you live in.

You likely already have learned that there is little that is nonpartisan in local nonpartisan politics, at least in many communities. Political competition in one form or another is virtually always there, whether you are dealing with a town board or a city council. For every person who wins an office there's someone who lost one, and perhaps wants it back someday. Political fortunes can change quickly on the local level just as they can on the national scene. Today's "out" party or individual may be tomorrow's winner. The fact that the public safety faction controls the town board today doesn't mean that the economic development coalition won't take over tomorrow. Political control can be a fluid thing.

As a politically astute police leader you will work at maintaining good relations with the local, chronic candidates almost as hard as you labor at staying in touch with the current office holders. Any one of these folks may be sitting on your governing board next year or the year after that. It simply doesn't make sense to make them enemies if you don't have to. True, some of them may not have treated you or your department well in the past. But undoubtedly they have at least some friends and supporters or they would not be regarded as political players in the first place. It makes little sense to go out of your way to alienate them. Cops are not the only ones that can hold grudges.

Perhaps the last election turned out of office some local politicos you never did have much use for. Perhaps they had said bad things about you or your department. Maybe they had consistently voted against the things you needed to do your job well. The temptation to gloat now that they have come to their political Waterloo (at least temporarily) may be almost overwhelming. But don't do it.

First of all, you are a bigger person than that. You travel the high road, so stay on it. Second, sometimes today's sidelined players are back on the field tomorrow. They could once again be among your bosses.

It makes no sense to deliberately tick off officials you may have to work with again. One chief burned his bridges to cinders by lashing out verbally at his former boss when he resigned his post to take a chief's job in a nearby city. Two years later his new city manager retired. Guess who became his new boss in his new town?

You might be a lot wiser to follow the lead of the veteran chief who sent "thank you" cards to departing members of his city council each time the members of the board changed. He scribbled personal notes and found *something* nice to say even to councilors he did not particularly like. He did his best to cement at least a tolerable relationship with these people for the cost of a few postage stamps. He was looking out for his future and that of his organization. You should, too.

SUMMARY

As a police chief you will work with politicians without becoming a professional politician yourself. You will work in a political environment and be affected by the decisions that politicians make. You must navigate your way across a political landscape without losing either your way or your ethical standards.

To stay in the know and protect both your organization and yourself, you will have to talk and listen to a host of people and yet believe what you hear selectively. You will have to guard against becoming too close to any political official, including the one who appointed you to your position. You must not compromise your morals and ideals for anyone, but you should be willing to grant trust to those who have earned it. Trust or no, you can never break the rules for anyone.

In working with many others, it will be worth your while to seek out a mentor, a "senior advisor" who already has traveled the route you want to go. A veteran chief may fill that role very well. As an ethical non-politician who must live and work in a highly political environment, you will meet a lot of different people with some very diverse views. It is important to remember that you are everyone's chief, and that includes the unpopular or "out" groups, too. They all deserve your attention. Leaving anyone out can mean trouble for you, so don't do it. Meanwhile, keep your eyes and ears open for political maneuvering by any and all who inhabit the political landscape.

As the leader of your law enforcement organization you must understand how politics work without becoming a politician yourself. You must move easily in a political environment without allowing anyone in it to dictate your decision-making. By protecting your independence you also guard your integrity.

Like it or not, you are a part of the political scene even though you resist being a politico yourself. You must stay aware of the ever-changing political landscape for the benefit of your organization. You can do it, just as you competently carry out the many other difficult tasks of the police chief's position. That can give you a greater sense of personal satisfaction than winning any political race!

POINTS TO REMEMBER

- Although you are not a politician, you must be politically savvy.
- Talk with and listen to as many people as possible, but don't believe everything you are told.
- Do not form too close a political alliance with anyone.
- Don't compromise your ethics to gain acceptance by a politician (or anyone else.)
- Be willing to trust those who have earned that trust.
- Never break the rules for anyone.
- Don't overlook the value of having a mentor.
- Know that an absence of noisy criticism does not necessarily mean unqualified support for you and your policies.
- Don't show favoritism to any political or special interest group.
- Do not ignore the views of "out" groups and minority organizations.
- Never forget that you are a professional.

Chapter 14

SURVIVING THE JOB

Police chiefs have died doing the job they loved, the job that was almost totally consuming. Very rarely they have perished at the hands of a despicable criminal. More often they have died as the result of the cumulative stress brought about by being under public scrutiny, organizational pressure and political game-playing 365 days a year. Still others have not died in office but have seen their health ruined and their lives shortened due to the relentless pressures of the job. *You do not want to be the next victim.*

You teach your young cops that theirs is a potentially dangerous line of work but that there are things they can do to increase the chances that they will survive to enjoy a long and happy retirement. You refer to that training as officer survival. At your level of the organization, there is something called career survival. It deals with getting through a long and rewarding tour as a law enforcement leader without getting fired (too often!) or dying of stress-related maladies. This is the sort of survival that you most frequently will deal with as your organization's CEO. You won't have to face too many bullets from bad guys. What you will face on a regular basis are the slings and arrows of politicos, local gadflies and various, self-appointed police experts. You must prepare yourself to survive these threats just as thoroughly as you prepare yourself to defeat the dangers of the street.

For you, surviving the job means taking care of yourself physically and emotionally. Yes, you *could* face some of the same hazards to survival that your cops can encounter at any time. More likely, however, the threats and frustrations you will face are organizational and political ones. Just as your body armor helps to protect you on the street, the lifestyle and attitudinal armor that you don will serve you well in surviving *off* the street, too. This chapter will assist you in assembling that "other" armor that will help you remain physically and emotionally fit as the chief of police. It will aid you immensely in surviving the job.

FAMILY COMES FIRST

It is unlikely that anyone approaching the end of his life has ever wished that he had spent more time at work and less with family. It is all too easy to become engrossed in the challenges and, sometimes, the rewards of your job as police chief. The rewards come when you see that you are actually helping make for a better department and a better community. When things are going well or just the opposite, it is all too easy to permit your job to become all-consuming. Nevertheless, you must resist the temptation.

There are feelings and needs besides your own to consider in your life as a law enforcement agency CEO. They belong to your loved ones. More than a few of your peers have proffered that they are what they are today because of the patience, support and love of their closest family members, with their spouse holding first place on the support team. Many long-time law enforcement people readily will confess that their career and their marriage have only survived because of the strength of their partner. Consequently, that is the first person you need to look to in taking care of your loved ones throughout a long leadership career. That same person is continuing to lend you support in the face of your almost overwhelming load of work and job-related stress. You owe your spouse a lot.

In your job as chief you literally can find something to attend every day and night, weekends included. If you run out of things to attend, you always can put in personal appearances on the late shift and ride along with your officers. Since you want to be seen throughout your organization and the community beyond, all of these activities are good for you to engage in–but do not spend *all* of your free time in this way.

You do not owe your organization and your employer all of your life to the effective exclusion of your own family. What you are seeking instead is a healthy life-work balance in which you reserve plenty of time for those closest to you. Make sure that you don't work late *every* night. Don't go in early *every* day. Don't find something you must attend after-hours on *every* night of the week. Practicing good time management skills can help keep you from falling into those traps.

Always have time for family. That is a cardinal rule. It'll keep you healthier even as it benefits the emotional well-being of all your loved ones.

SAVE TIME FOR YOU

Family is vital. You must spend as much time as possible with your loved ones. You already have learned that your busy work schedule will claim a lot of your time. That cannot be helped. What you *can* help, however, is how much time you reserve for your own pleasures and pursuits.

To remain physically, emotionally and mentally well, you absolutely must have time for *you.* Particularly as a new chief, you will feel the need to get a lot done in as short a time as possible. That will result in plenty of early starts and late stops to your day. The temptation will be great to put aside until later things that you might want and need to do for yourself. Giving in to that temptation is a bad idea.

You owe your employer your best. You probably have that inscribed somewhere as one of your personal, ethical commandments. But you cannot give your employer your best unless you first take care of yourself. That requires leaving time for the things you don't *have* to do but *want* to do.

Permit yourself time for the diversions that make you feel better when you otherwise would feel angry, stressed out or just generally unhappy. It does not really matter if what interests you is physical exercise (always good), reading, model making or bird watching. The point is to do *something* that you can throw your mind and body into that will distract you fully from the concerns of the work world.

It is acknowledged that your diversions often will have to make concessions to the demands of your job. You probably won't have as much time for your distractions as you would like. You may have to fit in a few minutes when you can and then do it again at the next opportunity. The point is to do it and not totally swear off the things that you want to do until later. Otherwise, later may never come.

You may have to get creative in your scheduling to get it all done. One chief who enjoyed writing short stories for publication got up an hour early almost every morning so he could get creative before the cares of the day intruded. Another let his boss know early on that every couple of months he would need to take a few days off to pursue his hobby as a successful wildlife photographer, thereby also nurturing his mental health. His boss was wholly supportive and displayed some of the chief's color prints in his own office. This city manager realized that an emotionally healthy chief is a reliable and productive one.

Save time for you. In the process you will help yourself stay sharper on the job. You just might save on some money for doctors and medications, as well.

EXERCISE REGULARLY

It is possible to look at your busy schedule and determine that there is not time for anything but work and events closely connected to work. It is true that there certainly will be days like that. But not every day has to be unless you let it.

As in the other things that you do to take your mind off of your work, you may have to be clever about when you find the time to exercise your body while you give your mind a time out. For some chiefs that means hitting the gym before heading to the desk in the morning. For others it mandates forsaking a big lunch in order to jog or get in an intense workout over the noon hour. For yet other law enforcement CEOs regular exercise requires them to fit in a 20 or 30-minute session at whatever time it becomes feasible during a long day.

Once more you may have to get creative about how you find the time to do something to help stay healthy on a job that will steal your health if you let it. Ideally you might prefer to exercise for an intense half-hour at the same time each day, five days a week. Your work schedule likely varies, however, and in reality you may not be able to count on a workout that is that regular in its scheduling. You instead may have to acknowledge that the best you can do is three days a week with an extra session thrown in on the weekend. The time at which you do it may have to vary from one day to the next. The point is that you will do *something* in the way of exercise for 20–30 minutes a minimum of three days a week, with more thrown in as often as possible. You will be mentally and physically healthier for the effort.

If you are considerably overweight or have not done any real exercise for a while you will naturally want to get a physician's advice before you start an exercise program. That's a part of taking care of business, too. You don't want to kill yourself getting healthy.

Different people prefer different ways of exercising. Some prefer doing it solo, as they enjoy the peaceful moments in which they can think and reflect sans other human beings. Others feel that their drive to exercise is strengthened when they have an exercise partner or partners pushing them while sharing some social discourse. Whatever works for you is fine. What matters is that you do *something* on a regular basis to preserve your good health.

WATCH THE DIET AND THE BOOZE

One experienced police chief commented that he had never met a law enforcement CEO who had not put on at least ten pounds during his first year in the chief's office. It looked to him that the combination of calorie-filled, "official" breakfasts combined with lunch and dinner "eat and meets" were just too much for the average chief's willpower to overcome.

This isn't a book about diets or greasy, rubber chicken dinners. You will need to call upon your own powers of restraint and common sense to avoid porking-up as your tenure as chief grows. It may mean that you sometimes have to order a plain English muffin when everybody else wolfs down ham and eggs. It may mean soup and salad instead of a full meal at a working lunch. It may occasionally require you to skip dessert when everyone else is having one. Or it might mean exercising harder later so you can have a treat now. Whatever the case, the same strength of purpose you call on to face the rest of your job's challenges can help you eat with a little restraint in order to stay healthy. Never seek solace in food and see your doctor if you even suspect that you have fallen victim to an eating disorder. You owe that self-care to yourself and those who love you. It's one more means for managing your job rather than allowing it to manage you.

You also will be asked to affairs where you will be invited to have an adult beverage–or two or three. You realize already that it is important that the chief never be seen to lose control of himself and his senses, even on his own time. Some chiefs have chosen not to drink alcohol at all, for just that reason. Others simply do not like the taste or effects of the stuff and consequently don't imbibe. Probably still more smart police bosses elect to drink alcohol in *very* careful moderation.

There is nothing that says you cannot have a drink with friends in an off-duty, social environment. (Drinking on-duty must be out for you. Here, too, you should model the behavior you expect from your people.) The key is that you always exercise very good judgment with *any* alcohol consumption. You must never drink to the point of intoxication or to the extent that your judgment is impaired. You do not drive after drinking. Police chiefs still lose their jobs with depressing regularity for driving under the influence. You do not hang out with people you know to overconsume and act stupidly. In other words, in your drinking or non-drinking pursuits you must never forget that you are a highly-visible role model in the community. You may find that community very unforgiving where it comes to perceived misbehavior by their chief law enforcer. Sadly, there are a few people out there who *want* you to screw up and act like a fool. Act like the responsible leader you are. Never give a venomous individual the satisfaction of seeing you act irresponsibly.

The stress of the job and a predisposition to abuse alcohol have contributed to police chiefs becoming addicted to alcohol. This shouldn't be surprising, as the law enforcement profession is merely a microcosm of society as a whole. There are alcoholic doctors and lawyers and pastors. There are also alcoholic police chiefs.

Once you have gotten past the denial that is all too common for alcohol abusers, only you know for sure if you have a problem with alcohol. If you do have a problem, there is no amount of consumption short of none at all that will work for you. That's what being an alcoholic means. If you suspect that you have a drinking problem, seek help from a professional counselor, physician or Alcoholics Anonymous. Your life and your loved ones are too important to surrender to alcohol. Get the assistance you need and preserve your career as an effective leader and loving family member.

CURB YOUR EGO; ADMIT IT WHEN YOU'RE WRONG

Violence ranging from bar fights to international wars has occurred because people were unable to control their egos. Marriages and friendships have ended because one or both parties found it impossible to say "I'm sorry." Government leaders, including police chiefs, have lost their jobs when they were unable to bring themselves to apologize for a boneheaded decision or act.

The position you hold in your community is an important one. At least for the moment, no one else can claim to be the police chief. Your actions and opinions are important to people both inside and outside your organization. You are a significant local leader.

But you are not so important that the rules don't apply to you. You are not so vital that you are special, meriting special treatment. You can be replaced, and one day you will be. The next guy or gal will get the same attention you did. He or she will be just as important.

The point is that an effective chief keeps his ego under control. He does not allow his self-confidence to swell into arrogance. He works with others without letting his ego get in the way of an effective, respectful relationship. He is courteous to others who are not so "important" as he is. He keeps his ego under control, and so must you if you are to be regarded as a modest, down-to-earth and effective leader as opposed to a self-important jerk.

Think what you are about to say before you say it. If it occurs to you that it will come across as a put-down to your listener, don't say it. Come up with a better way–a more polite way–to say essentially the same thing. You are going to occasionally hurt someone's feelings without intending it. Do not cause damage where you do not have to do so.

No matter how sharp and how careful you are, you are going to make mistakes from time to time. That is a part of being human. Sometimes your error will affect others. Less frequently it may appear to others that you have intentionally caused them inconvenience or discomfort. Whether what happened is what you intended or not, be sensitive to the feelings of others. If an error of yours has caused pain to someone else, do not be hesitant to express your regrets. Apologies, where merited, make you look strong, not weak. There is no shame in admitting when you are wrong. It's the right thing to do. You only compound the damage by refusing to acknowledge it.

There may be other times when you know that the other party to a dispute is at least as culpable for the disagreement as you are, perhaps more so.

It takes a big person to express regrets first, especially when he feels he is not the cause of the problem. But you should not be hesitant to take the first step. Hopefully, the other person will acknowledge his or her part in the flap. If not, you still have done the right thing, the mature thing. You have taken the high road, which is the path where chiefs belong.

Do not apologize when you know an apology is not required. Doing the right thing does not require that you apologize for doing it, even if someone is unhappy about what you did. But other times a sincere apology is the right thing. A big person is willing to admit that he is not perfect. You *are* a big person with big abilities. Never be afraid to do that right thing.

WATCH OUT FOR THE BADGE BUNNIES

It might at first appear a waste of ink or even an insult to your intelligence to include sexual misbehavior in a discussion about leadership. The truth remains, however, that too many law enforcement careers have been cut short by sexual adventures and misadventures, often ones of an extra-marital nature. Sad experience has shown that it is not just the hormone-besotted young cops who have gotten themselves into trouble, either. Veteran law enforcement leaders, police chiefs among them, have seen their careers damaged or ended due to their sexual escapades.

Of course, cops didn't invent sexual behavior–or misbehavior. Creatures that looked a lot like humans were being attracted to powerful leaders of the pack long before man learned to walk erect. Too many powerful (and powerless) people to count have gotten themselves into sexual difficulties ever since. Powerful politicians have done it. So have many other "celebrities" and public figures. Innumerable murders and countless wars have been committed in the wake of sexual indiscretions.

So, what does all of this have to do with you, you might reasonably ask? Just this: In your own barnyard you, too, are a powerful figure, a minor celebrity of sorts. On occasion you just might attract the attention of someone who may want to have some of your perceived power and celebrity status rub off on him or her. These are the so-called badge bunnies and police groupies–mostly of the opposite gender–that your young cops find fascinating. The problem is that sometimes even mature law enforcement officers who ought to know better find themselves equally fascinated as well as flattered by the attention. You cannot afford to be one of these "mature law enforcement officers."

The fact that these people exist should neither shock nor unduly alarm you. You've known for a long time that they are out there. The challenge comes in how you handle their focus on *you* should it ever develop.

You are probably a lot more mature and have much better judgment than you did the day you entered police work and discovered that other people actually could be sexually attracted to your shiny new badge with its attendant authority and image. Now you are smarter than that. You are only too aware that anything perceived as immoral or reckless behavior on your part could result in serious damage–perhaps terminal damage–to your career as chief.

It won't do any good to lament the hypocrisy with which some of your fellow Americans view matters sexual. The banker and the baker may engage in their own illicit sexual liaisons, but they are likely to throw a self-righteous fit if their police chief does the same. It doesn't really matter if their way of looking at things is valid or not, that's the way it is. You knew or should have known when you took the chief's job that you would face some "interesting" expectations. This is one of them.

Your personal high standards and expectations of yourself have kept you out of other bad situations that would have damaged your reputation for integrity and cast doubt on your ability to serve as a positive role model. This is another of those situations. Responsibility and self-control are what you are all about. It is not too much to ask of yourself that you continue to be an exceptional role model in this very sensitive but not so private part of your life.

DON'T BE WHERE COMMON SENSE SAYS YOU SHOULDN'T BE

A young police chief was spending his off-duty evening in a bar packed with noisy revelers. At some point during the night's festivities he became embroiled in a loud argument with a drunken female bar patron. One thing led to another and eventually an altercation ensued. The chief ended up charged with assault, an allegation he finally beat in court. But before his legal innocence was established he and his department had suffered a couple of black eyes from the local newspaper and radio talk shows.

The chief was particularly lucky. He somehow managed to retain the confidence of his boss, his employees and the majority of the community. He was allowed to keep his job. He was, in other words, the very fortunate recipient of a near-miracle. Strangely enough, he was never asked to explain publicly what he was doing in a bar at a late hour arguing with a barfly.

Should you find yourself in similar straits one day, you should not count on experiencing such good fortune. It is far better that you conduct yourself in such a way that you do not have to depend upon divine intervention or a particularly understanding boss to keep your job. One of the best ways of accomplishing that is to stay out of the places that could get you into trouble in the first place. Every jurisdiction in America has some of those places. You should know where they are in yours.

Situations can get you into trouble as easily as bad locations. A "situation" may arise when you are invited to somebody's bachelor drinking party. Or it could develop when you are invited to an event that your common sense should tell you will involve some heavy drinking and, just maybe, some recreational drug use. That isn't a "situation" for a police chief to get himself involved with, either. Don't go. If you're already there and your senses tell you things are apt to go badly, get out immediately. The chief does not need to be part of a "situation."

Doing the right thing does not require that you be either a monk or a teetotaler. You are allowed a life away from your job. You are permitted to go to places where alcohol is served and people sometimes act silly. But you also should remember the requirement for some dignity that properly accompanies the office of chief of police. That demand for a reasonable amount of decorum mandates that you are smart enough to know where not to go and who not to go with.

The unfortunate chief described here learned the hard way that it was unwise to loiter in a bar known to have a rowdy reputation. He learned that he should have left when things started to go downhill. He also learned that one never wins a debate with a drunk in a bar. And he (hopefully) figured out that the whole thing could have been avoided if he hadn't made a poor decision to go where he did in the first place.

Sometimes being smart means knowing when to leave. Police employee parties and union blowouts are well-known for the things that get said and events that unfold as the alcohol-fueled evening goes on. When you accept invitations to these events (and you should), it is important to know when to leave. When the meal is over and/or the serious celebrating begins, it is your cue to express your appreciation and depart. That way you do not later experience the consequences of something you said or did or something that was said or done to you. There is always the chance, too, that you'll later have to sit in disciplinary judgment concerning an incident that occurred at the event. You hardly can do so with impartiality if you were a player in the drama.

No one is expecting you to live your life in seclusion. But it is not too much to expect that you conduct yourself in a fashion so that you never have to be ashamed. You minimize your chances of having to explain yourself later if you stay away from situations and locations that your common sense tells you could blow up. That, too, is what a responsible leader does.

AVOID BECOMING A WORKAHOLIC

So, if you can't hang out in bars, does that mean that in order to be "safe" you should spend every waking moment at your desk? Nothing could be more distant from the truth.

You have known people who spent virtually all of their time at work. You probably doubted their sanity and wondered what other things in their lives they were dodging by occupying all of their time with work. You probably vowed that such a thing would never happen to you. That was a wise promise. Now you need to keep it.

Of course, now that you are laboring in the chief's position with its seemingly endless list of things to do you may be finding it a bit harder to keep your promise. There is, it seems, always something to do as the responsible CEO in charge of an always-important and sometimes-challenging organization. You are almost never, it seems, really off-duty, as your electronic umbilical can jerk you back to work even when you are asleep or miles distant on vacation. You are never fully "off the clock," or so it may feel.

Time away from the job is important to your continued physical and mental health. Rest and play are both necessary to your emotional well-being. You know that. Getting away from your work for a while is vital. How long and how often you can do it will vary depending on whatever else is going on at the moment. But *some* time away from work on a regular–not constantly postponed–basis is absolutely necessary.

Good time management skills can help you save time for yourself by maximizing your productivity at work. By eliminating the time wasters (gossiping, surfing the 'Net, engaging in protracted telephone conversations, calling or attending unnecessary meetings) to the extent possible you can regain workday minutes that would otherwise be lost forever. Getting more done at work means taking less stuff home for the evening or weekend.

Virtually everyone's day includes some time wasters. Track what you do at work. Keep a log for a time, if you have to. You almost certainly will discover some non-productive time that could be better utilized. Then, try to eliminate the distractions in order to get more done and free up some truly "downtime" for later. But remember to use your newly-found minutes for something you really want to do, not to accomplish more work!

If you are consistently laboring at your job nights, weekends and holidays, you may be at risk of becoming a workaholic. Or you already are one. If you truly would rather handle a project than spend time with your loved ones, that's not a good sign, either. It is probably time for re-prioritizing what is really important to you.

What you are doing on your job is important. By serving as an effective leader you are doing some good things that will help others. That is admirable and praiseworthy. You are a good person. But if you don't also take care of yourself and your personal relationships just how long you can continue to stay healthy enough to do a good job at work may be in question.

Get away from the rigors of your position on regular occasions. If you have done a good job as a leader, the place will run just fine for a while without you. Try really hard to leave the worries and responsibilities behind. They will be waiting for you when you return, refreshed and reinvigorated to face them down.

HAVE FRIENDS AWAY FROM POLICE WORK

Cops have been accused of practicing something called "professional incest." It basically means that they are often guilty of talking to and associating with other cops to the exclusion of just about everybody else. Police chiefs do it, too.

Law enforcement practitioners are not the only ones guilty of talking shop. Doctors and lawyers and plumbers do it, as well. A gathering of attorneys almost certainly will lead to a discussion of writs and torts and retainer fees before the evening has ended. The practice is no healthier for them than it is for you, the police executive.

It's fun to talk with those with whom you have something in common. Other law enforcement people can understand and empathize with some of the struggles of your difficult job. You can gather some emotional support by visiting with them. To that extent conversing with your fellow law enforcement CEOs can be helpful to you as a police boss. Your peers can be good for you.

On the other hand, to remain well-balanced in an increasingly complex society you need to talk about something besides the issues of the police chief's world. You need friends and conversation partners who have little or nothing to do with law enforcement.

You can learn a lot from people who are not in policing. The CEO who runs the local hospital or school system or grocery store probably knows something about leadership, too. His personnel issues (and isn't it always about the personnel?) may not be all that different from yours. People are pretty much alike across the spectrum. Some of his problem solutions may be applicable to the problems you face, but you will never know if you don't make his acquaintance.

But nothing says that your every social interaction must be productive. You are allowed to enjoy yourself, too. You will find it enjoyable to talk about something besides felons and cops. There really *are* other topics for conversation, and many of them are more enjoyable than your work menu of discussion topics. Variety can be a good thing.

The nature of your job has probably encouraged you to be a ham, and it is good that you like to talk about what you do for a living. But having non-cop friends willing to talk about something else is important, too. It is emotionally healthy to test your mind with something besides job-related scenarios. It doesn't really matter if you talk dogs or soccer, talking about *something* besides your day job is emotionally healthy.

Having non-cop friends is important. It can help you reaffirm that there are relatively normal people in the world. That in itself should be your motivator for experiencing life beyond policing.

KEEP READING AND LEARNING

Today there is a virtual glut of information readily available on just about every topic imaginable. Law enforcement leadership has its own library of periodicals, books and web sites full of advice and opinion.

You cannot stay up to date in your ever-changing field without keeping track of what's going on elsewhere in your business. But it is clearly impossible to read everything that comes across your desk either electronically or on paper unless you neglect the many other responsibilities of your job.

Your challenge is thus to be selective in what you read. Most of the sales material you can pass along to others in your agency. The remaining collection will require you to be highly discriminating. The executive's practice of article skimming will be your friend. By catching the title and the first few lines of a given piece you quickly can determine if your further time and interest is warranted. If not, you safely can move on to the next one.

Many chiefs try to keep up with current events by monitoring a daily paper and a weekly news magazine, printed or electronic. That's a good practice for you to emulate. You also will want to keep track of one of the article clipping services on the Internet which focuses on governmental or criminal justice system happenings on a national level. Many elected officials and city managers do the same. Keeping up with the news could bring you some new ideas or even keep you from being embarrassed one day from a lack of knowledge concerning a "hot" topic.

Job-related stories and articles should not be all that is on your reading list. You also should read for your own enjoyment, whether that means looking at fiction or fact. Some chiefs indulge themselves with military history while others enjoy science fantasy. Whatever works to take you far away from the job is fine. The important thing is to read sometimes for entertainment first, and knowledge second. The two really can go together.

Life-long learning of the formal variety also can enrich your life immeasurably. Courses and seminars that keep you current in your profession are important for maintaining your effectiveness as a leader and subject matter expert. Equally important, however, are courses you may take on-line or in-person that have nothing to do with being a police chief. Here the emphasis for you should be on personal growth and the pure enjoyment of learning something new. A leader who is enjoying his own life is often a better role model and CEO.

There is a growing body of evidence indicating that a brain kept active is a brain that stays healthy and alert longer. That should provide you with additional motivation for life-long intellectual endeavor. Woody Allen once said that his brain was his second-favorite organ. It should rate at least as high on your list of important things.

IT'S VITAL TO HAVE A CONFIDANT, OR SEVERAL

What you have preached to your novice police officers can provide good advice for the chief, as well. In instructing your young cops about the physical and emotional stresses of their job, you may have informed them of the need to share their deepest concerns with *someone.* You have talked to them about the career-ending damage that can be inflicted by keeping it all bottled-up inside themselves. You have discussed the unintended consequences and hurt to loved ones that can flow from a troubled individual who won't talk about what is bothering him.

The same things that you told your troops on the subject of officer survival can prove equally helpful to their boss in the realm of career survival. You cannot keep all of your fears, frustrations and worries penned up inside, either. Not unless you want to damage both your physical and emotional health. Not unless you want an ulcer or persistently high blood pressure. Not unless one day you want to have "The Big One" while seated at your desk.

Like your officers, you will need access to a good listener, an individual who can refrain from either judging you or jumping straight to antidotes you should apply to your problems. You need someone willing to listen more than talk, empathize more than criticize. You need a saint, but someone else will have to do.

For many law enforcement leaders an understanding and loving spouse serves as the invisible "administrative assistant" who listens to their mate's observations and concerns. If you are fortunate enough to have such a partner consider yourself blessed indeed. Take advantage of his or her strength at every opportunity. Don't forget to express your gratitude for it, either. Fortunately, there are other help options, too. And you do not have to limit yourself to just one confidante if you are lucky enough to have several patient listeners available.

Whether you consider him a mentor or not, a fellow chief of police can be an especially valuable listener for your thoughts and worries. He probably has a good idea of what you are going through and may have been there himself. He also appreciates the need for confidentiality concerning your discussion. Nevertheless, for your protection and his it is a good idea to tell him if what you are relating must go no further.

Again, don't overlook the value of talking with trusted individuals outside of your own profession. Life experience can prove more valuable than job experience. Do not cheat yourself of some valuable insight.

You will have to be the judge of your particular situation, but oftentimes members of your own department, including those on your command staff, are not the best choices to hear your innermost concerns. There may be things that you simply do not want them to know. If you put the burden of confidentiality on them and that trust is violated, your relationship with your subordinates may be forever changed.

Choose carefully who you talk with, but do choose one or more people you can talk to about virtually anything. Provide that priceless service to them in return. You will be much better off for the experience.

KNOW THAT THERE WILL BE DISAPPOINTMENTS

Life isn't perfect and you don't always get what you want or deserve. You learned that at Christmastime a long time ago. But you lived through that long-gone childhood experience and have survived many subsequent disappointments. You'll likely make it through some more.

The honeymoon period that you might have enjoyed as the new police chief may not have lasted as long as you hoped it would. Eventually your new boss said "no" to something you really wanted to do. Such is life. But you survived the experience and may have arrived at your goal another way, perhaps even eventually getting what you needed.

Any chief who has held his or her position for a time knows that things do not always work out as intended. Good ideas will sometimes fail to acquire the support needed to become reality. Personnel hired with great hopes occasionally will implode with great fanfare. Thoughtful promotional decisions made after careful deliberation on rare occasions will culminate in unmitigated disasters. Perhaps worst of all, friendships made based upon trust will prove false. All of these are disappointments that you as the chief have faced, or will in the future.

As traumatic as they are, both professional and personal disappointments are parts of life. They are going to happen, and eventually some big ones are going to come your way. They happen to your peers, too.

One veteran chief known for his high ethics and impeccable integrity imported from out of state an experienced leader he had known for a long time and made him part of his command staff. The man almost immediately engaged in dishonest behavior and the chief had to terminate him. The chief suffered considerable professional as well as personal embarrassment as a result of his failed appointment and retired not long afterwards. He had suffered a supreme disappointment and never fully recovered from its effects.

Things are going to go wrong from time to time. Some of the disasters may even be your fault. That does not mean that you are a poor leader or a bad chief. Sometimes "stuff" just happens. Your boss and your people likely know that you are human and will make mistakes on occasion. You will survive.

Disappointments will come your way periodically, no matter how good you are at what you do, no matter how exceptional your organization happens to be. Accept that and do not lose faith in either yourself or your employees. A leader is measured in how he handles the bad times even more than in how he handles the good. Don't disappoint the people who are counting on you. Hang in there for the better days that are coming.

REALIZE THAT MOST CRISES HAVE A SHELF LIFE

A long-time chief of police was recounting the number of incidents that he thought at the time they happened would mean the end of his leadership career. He stopped counting after he named over a dozen. At the time he was doing the counting he had recently retired with honors after a long and much-decorated tenure.

In your high-profile business there will be crises and outright disasters. On occasion, your employees will make serious mistakes and do dumb things. In rare instances they will do bad things, even criminal things. And on even more rare occasions, you probably will make highly-visible mistakes of your own. That comes with the territory when you are a CEO in a fishbowl in a world that is quick to find fault and place blame.

Many of your peers have found from experience that very often things considered major crises one day are forgotten the next. The same holds true for the news media's focus on a happening that from your point of view is bad news. The reporters are relatively quickly off to chase the next scandal or shooting and your "negative" situation becomes yesterday's news.

None of that is to say you should not be concerned about mistakes or improper behavior in your department. Obviously it is your job to fix any real problems and fix them quickly. The memory of actual misconduct may fade, but your obligation to deal with it effectively won't. You still have a job to do.

Bad news does not resonate forever. Initial, intense interest will fade. The danger for you is that you will regard the declining interest as a sign that you do not have to address an actual problem. You do, of course. Whether it is personnel or procedures, real or perceived, problems in your organization must always be dealt with so that they are less likely to recur. It is never acceptable to turn your back on a situation that led to a crisis because you think and hope it will not happen again.

Once you honestly have addressed a problem, be willing to let it go. Your people will not appreciate your endlessly berating them over a bad happening that is addressed and over. Be willing to release it, for your own emotional health and that of your organization.

SUMMARY

Being a police chief is a job that literally could kill you. But only if you let it. Fortunately, there are a lot of things you can do to keep yourself alive and healthy.

Maintaining a healthy balance between your job and your time away from work is vital. Your loved ones must always take precedence over the demands of work. You also must leave time for your own healthy pleasures and pursuits.

Enjoying yourself must not involve drinking or eating to excess. Your physical health is as important as your emotional well-being. Exercise whenever you can and don't engage in diversions that will cause you embarrassment from irresponsible behavior. In a very few words, don't act stupidly.

In saving time for youself, also save time for friends from outside law enforcement. Find someone, preferably several people, that you can talk to about whatever is troubling you. Offer that same service to others.

As important as your job is to you, never let it become all-consuming. Pledge never to become a workaholic. Do things for yourself that feel good. Read. Exercise. Play. Accept that life will include disappointments and be willing to forgive yourself and others when things go wrong.

Living to transition from a contributing career to a rewarding retirement should be your ultimate goal. It is an objective that is well within your reach.

POINTS TO REMEMBER

- You cannot take care of your job unless you first take care of yourself.
- Family and loved ones must come before work.
- Part of taking care of yourself means exercising regularly.
- Watch your diet and your alcohol intake to avoid trouble.
- Show some class–admit it when you are wrong and apologize.
- Attend to your personal morals in addition to your physical health.
- Be smart enough to know where and with whom you should not hang out.
- Becoming a workaholic will ruin your physical and mental health.
- Maintain friendships that have nothing to do with your job.
- Never stop learning.
- Always have someone you can talk to about anything and everything.
- Realize that there will be disasters and disappointments but that you can overcome them.
- Know that at the end no one will ask you how much time you put in at work.
- Never let your work run or ruin your life.

Chapter 15

HOW TO KNOW WHEN IT'S TIME TO GO

You've had a lot of fun being the chief of police. Most of the time, anyway. But it can't last forever, nor should it. You eventually deserve a break, and somebody else deserves a shot at doing the job as well as you have. (He or she won't, of course, but merits the chance to try, anyhow!)

In spite of the doom and gloom you have heard, most law enforcement CEOs are not eventually run out of town just ahead of a lynch mob. Most of them do not find themselves locked out of their own building with their "stuff" piled outside, although such things have occurred. Most chiefs do, as a matter of fact, leave at least mostly on their own terms and at least largely on their own schedule. Your goal should be to be to increase the odds that you leave fully on your own terms and schedule as opposed to someone else's.

It is inevitable that a time will come when you should leave the chief's job, whether it's for a new and better one, to change careers or to go sit by the fire. You naturally want to be the one to select which it is for you. Fortunately, there are some common sense things you can do to improve the chances that you will control your own destiny when it comes time to leave your present position. Those things are examined in this chapter.

On the other hand, the politics of the world you inhabit may dictate when you must leave. Events beyond your control may determine that you exit before you would like. It could happen because of a radical change in your community's political leadership. It might occur due to the fallout of events occurring within the community or department over which you had absolutely no control but had perceived responsibility. It could happen because of a major mistake–or a series of them–that you made. Or it could occur for some other and perhaps bizarre reason. Regardless, it has become increasingly clear that you are headed for unemployment in the near future. There are things you can do to take some of the sting of that always-uncomfortable scenario. Those things also will be discussed here.

Knowing when it is time to depart and how to go out the door for the last time with your head held high is just as vital as many of the other things you have done during a rewarding and contributing career. Here is some help for getting it accomplished.

THE SIGNS THAT IT'S OVER

A rattlesnake doesn't always rattle before it strikes. But if you stay alert, you should see it coiled beside your path before it can surprise you. The same holds true for the work paths you must tread every day. If you stay on your toes and keep your eyes and ears open you may be able to detect trouble lying in wait before you become its victim.

There is not a universal set of hazard flags that always signals danger ahead. The warning symptoms can vary from one situation to the next and one locale to another. But you should be able to identify some trouble indicators common to a situation where the CEO may find his future in doubt. Some of them may turn out in the end to mean nothing at all; some may be the result of coincidence or accident. But others might offer the kind of warning rattle you would be unwise to ignore. Some may tell you that it's time to act before you become a victim. Some of these "pay attention" warning shots may include the following:

- Your troops and your staff are clearly treating you differently. You have determined that it isn't your imagination. They may be avoiding you or simply acting more reserved when they are in your presence, but clearly the atmosphere has changed and it is not a one-day occurrence.
- People are not returning your calls or e-mail messages. Those inside and outside the organization are declining your invitations to lunch or coffee. Individuals who normally contact you on a regular basis stop doing so.
- You encounter overt hostility from individuals who have never acted that way towards you before. Your directions are ignored or evaded. Your own people appear to have little fear of the consequences of openly disrespecting you.
- Your boss is evasive. If he or she is among those avoiding you, that is yet another warning sign that all is not well. A boss who is normally accessible to you who suddenly becomes distant is not a good thing. He may be putting off giving you the bad news.
- You actually get a warning that serious trouble is ahead. A friend or colleague, inside or outside the department, advises you that plans are being formulated to remove you from your position. Ask for as much detail as you can get. It may let you know whether or not hope remains to save your situation.

- You receive a steady drumbeat of inquiries about your welfare. This is obviously the opposite of being ignored and avoided. Instead, you receive a spate of calls from your colleagues inquiring if you are "alright." Some will be calls of support from genuine well-wishers who care about you. Others may be probes for "inside" gossip on what is going on and your future plans. One or two of these people may have their sights set on your position.
- You discover a bloody horse's head in your bed. Just kidding. However, for you the equivalent of being invited to sleep with the fishes could be a "no confidence" vote by your employees. This is an indication that more than a handful of people may want to remove you. More about that later.

The more of these indicators you detect, the more at risk your employment situation may be. Even so, your position is not by any means hopeless. You still have options. You still have cards to play. What you need now is yet more information.

If you are in doubt about your employment future, accessing the best possible source of that information should be your next move. That source is your boss.

IT'S OK TO ASK HOW YOU STAND

You know that it is essential to keep your senses attuned for any indication that things are amiss on the job security scene. You absolutely must do that. By remaining accessible to your employees and your staff, the public and the local political leadership, you may be able to pick up on some warning signs in time to address real or perceived issues and avoid a terminal encounter. Staying in close touch with the leadership of your local employees' association or police union also can help you avoid nasty surprises.

But for getting to the heart of problems real or perceived there is no substitute for going straight to the source. That requires going to your boss. It requires asking some direct questions of your direct supervisor.

There is no benefit to be gained from worrying yourself sick about what your boss may or may not be thinking about your future. You owe it to yourself (and to anyone who has to live with you) to find out the answer so you can either relax a little or start planning for your next job or retirement.

You probably have always believed that the best way to approach a need for information is head-on. When the information you need is about *you* the formula remains the same: ask. It is perfectly alright to tell your boss that you have heard something that has made you uneasy and you'd like to be sure things are clear. You can then tell him what you've heard and get his response to it. His visible reaction to what you have just said may tell you almost as much as what he says in response. It likely will be as uncomfortable for him as it is for you, but it's a conversation that needs to take place.

Hopefully you will have a good enough read on your supervisor from your previous association with him to recognize if he is being straight with you. If he tells you that things are OK and you believe him, that pretty much ends the conversation. You can now change the subject. Pursuing him further with "Is it *really* OK?" kinds of questions will make you look and sound like someone lacking in self-confidence. Don't do it. Naturally, you do not want to have this conversation with your boss very often throughout your career. Coming to him on a regular basis for reassurance will signal that you are an insecure and weak leader. That is an image you certainly do not want.

If your boss responds to your pointed inquiry by telling you that there *is* a problem, you must be ready to respond with confidence, assuming that your intent is to remain employed where you are. If you were already aware of the issue, now is the time to tell him your side of the story. Afterwards you may find that your boss's perspective has changed. You may even have turned him into an ally. On the other hand, if what he tells you is all new information, you should assure him that you will waste no time looking into it, including talking to others, in order to determine if something you are doing needs changed. Then, keep your promise by investigating and, if need be, acting. Keep your boss advised as to what you are doing and provide him with progress reports on your accomplishments.

Signs that you are in troubled waters do not mean that you are going to drown. If you seek and obtain adequate warning you stand a good chance of addressing the issue successfully and remaining in your position. Bosses really don't like the fuss, cost and bother of finding a new chief very often. On the other hand, through your very straightforward approach to your boss you may find that an irrevocable decision to fire you has already been made. If that's the case and the decision really isn't subject to change at least you know the score and can begin making plans to cut your losses and get out with the best deal possible.

None of this will you know if you don't ask. You cannot fight phantoms. You must be able to see and feel what you are facing. Asking your boss some direct questions will enable you to do that.

DON'T MAKE BIG DECISIONS WHEN YOU ARE EMOTIONAL

You have heard the advice before: Avoid making important decisions when you are upset. It's good advice for a leader. It's equally advisable for your approach to life in general. Most assuredly it applies to you when you are thinking about a major career decision in the wake of threats to your continued tenure as chief.

More than a few law enforcement chief executives have returned to their office after receiving a chewing out from their boss and swore to stick the job where the sun never shines. One law enforcement boss routinely followed such sessions by going on the Internet to look at police chief openings elsewhere. On each occasion it took his Chief Advisor–his spouse–to tell him to knock it off and get back to business.

Cops are generally egotistical, proud people. They don't take too kindly to being put through the wringer by anybody. You are probably the same. You may tend to respond quickly and forcefully to what you see as an affront to your integrity, dignity or character. You may be tempted to expand the conflict through a counterattack of your own. Particularly if your boss is the subject of your diatribe, it probably won't help your case much if you are literally in a fight for your professional survival.

A few words of time-proven advice: Think about it–a lot–before you make a dramatic statement or take some dramatic action (like quitting, for instance) immediately upon hearing something from your boss or the elected officials above you that upsets you. Bite your tongue before you sound off. Take the issue back to your office and mull it over before you draw a line in the sand and blurt out something you cannot take back. Think before you speak or act.

You'll probably want more time for thought than you can secure by simply retreating to your office and stewing about things for a few minutes. You might be well-advised to take it home with you and discuss the situation and your planned response with a patient, trusted person. You may want to call a colleague or two and get their read on your predicament. If you are fortunate enough to have a mentor, get in touch with him right away. He may have been through a situation similar to the one you are facing now. He may have some valuable advice for you. (There's a very good chance he'll tell you to slow down and calm down.)

It is much easier said than done, but try really hard not to get mad. Restraining your first impulse to say or do something hurtful in retaliation could be easier to accomplish when you stop to realize that your future and that of your family may be at stake.

Think before you act. Then, think and consider some more. Sleep on it overnight, or several nights. Decide with a calm mind what you want to say and do. Then go ahead and act on your best judgment once you have reined in your emotions. The delayed decision will be a better one.

LEAVING ON YOUR OWN TERMS

Assume for a moment that you have made the decision to leave your job, or that the decision for you to leave has been made for you. You are going, the only question remaining to be answered is *how*.

Cops don't particularly like having terms dictated to them. Most police chiefs like it even less than the average street cop. You will want to reserve to yourself much of the decision-making about exactly how you will leave your post, once the decision has been made that it is going to happen. How successful you are in participating in that decision-making may depend upon your people skills as well as your negotiating abilities. If you are to succeed, you absolutely must retain a courteous, professional demeanor throughout the process, even if the emotions you are feeling would lead you to a far different response.

Simply put, you want to get as much as you can out of a difficult, unpleasant situation. How much leverage you will have will depend on a number of things, not the least of which is the circumstances that resulted in your pending departure. If you are guilty of a serious act of malfeasance you are unlikely to have much bargaining power concerning how you leave. Another important factor to be considered is your boss and his attitude towards you as well as his willingness to take your wishes into account. Finally, the amount of publicity your job situation has received will impact how much leeway your boss and elected officials will have in negotiating your termination. If the local news media take a strong stand for or against you your supervisor's decision-making options will be more limited than if the discussion is taking place in a public vacuum. Obviously, this can work for or against you. Likewise, a strong stance in either direction by your friends and enemies in the community will have an effect on your boss's choices in seeing you out the door. (That's one more reason for making lots of friends and contacts in your community!)

Ask for what you think you must have in order to continue your life beyond your present position. Be realistic. Don't short-change yourself, but don't get greedy, either. At the same time, if you don't ask you probably won't get. Don't be bashful. Even if you do not have a contract that specifies you are eligible for a specific amount of severance pay, ask for a reasonable amount, anyway. Three months of severance pay is not unreasonable. Your boss may not want a highly-visible fight over three months of salary. Maybe your boss is not willing (or not allowed by his bosses) to offer severance but will look favorably on continuing to pay for your family's health benefits for a certain time period beyond termination. You may need to get creative in taking some of the sting out of your termination.

The fact that you have a contract specifying what happens when you leave does not preclude you from asking for more. If the contract specifies severance pay, you may be able to secure health benefits for a while, as well, if you approach the discussion candidly and in good faith.

Some departing chiefs have secured the assistance of an attorney for dealing with their employer at termination time. You will have to be the best judge as to whether or not you want or need one. The presence of an attorney may result in additional protections for you. But bringing a lawyer into the discussions likely will result in your employer calling one in, too. Now something being handled relatively informally has taken on a whole new air as legal formalities come to the forefront. A relatively peaceful process may become adversarial. Beyond the legal costs you will have to decide if an attorney will strengthen your position or result in additional distractions.

Get what you can, settle where you must. It is your future and that of your loved ones that is under discussion, so don't be shy. There is a fine line to be walked here. If you come across as arrogant or threatening to your boss, it's a safe bet that the negotiations are over. Be firm but be courteous and respectful, as well. Both of you want to get an unpleasant situation behind you. Reason and diplomacy on your part may end up being emulated on the other side of the desk.

KEEP YOUR RESUME CURRENT

Even when things are going swimmingly you should have an up-to-date resume readily at hand. There are uses for it besides serving as an aid to searching out a new job. A reporter may want it while doing a story about you. So might a firm that is seeking to use you as a consultant or expert witness.

Keeping your resume current means you won't have to rush to get one ready when there is a sudden need. Keeping it up to date also means that you won't have to ship out an incorrect or incomplete version if the document is needed right away. You just never know who might want to know all about you, and quickly.

In keeping your personal material up to date for future employment possibilities you should accompany it with references who know your side of whatever controversy or disagreement led to your leaving. Be sure you brief your references fully before you put their names down. They need to have the ammunition to defend you against rumors or biased information floating around out there.

Your reference list will raise red flags to a future hiring authority if your current boss is not included. Assuming that your relationship with him remains a tolerable one (because you have worked hard to keep it that way!)

speak with him about including his name. After talking with him attempt to gauge what he is likely to say about you. If in the end you elect to leave him off the list, be prepared to explain to the hiring authority why you have done so. That, of course, will require an answer to why you left in the first place. Tell the truth. Hopefully you will be able to provide an explanation without seriously damaging your cause. You will need to be sure that your references know the whole story so they can back you up, if need be.

In preparing your updated resume be sure to include the accomplishments that highlight your recent leadership successes. You are seeking to offset any negative influence from whatever situation caused you to leave your current employment. Again, this is not the time to be falsely modest about the good things you have done. List them and emphasize the importance they had in making your organization better. The more recent they are, the better. It's good that you were an effective first-line supervisor 15 years ago; it's much more relevant that you turned around an ailing department starting 24 months ago. List your leadership accomplishments honestly and be prepared to flesh them out in detail.

REALIZE WHEN IT'S NOT FUN ANYMORE

Admit it, a lot of the time it's fun being the police chief. You get to work with some great people who are striving in an important cause. You truly feel you are making a difference in your community and the law enforcement profession. (You are!) People stop you in restaurants or on the street to make requests and complaints or ask your opinion on things. What you have to say *matters,* at least to some. You're smart enough to realize that once you no longer wear the chief's badge many of those folks will no longer care *what* you think or do. Yes, it can be a pretty good deal being the boss of an important public safety organization.

If you are anything like most police CEOs, there are many days you actually enjoy going to work. Even with the sometimes-uncomfortable decisions you have to make, there is a big sense of accomplishment in what you do each day. You will miss it when it's over.

One day it will be, all the same. If you are fortunate, you will get to choose when that day is approaching. If not, the decision will be made for you. Your goal is to pick the time on your own terms. If you continue to operate in an ethical and intelligent fashion, you greatly increase your chances of doing just that.

Much has been made of the story that chiefs have a short tenure as their jurisdiction's head law enforcement officer. Some do. But "bad news" tales always draw more attention than favorable scenarios. The short-tenure stories overlook one reality. The fact is that law enforcement is also full of examples of chiefs who have served 15, 20 or more years as their agency's CEO and then retired with great fanfare. In other words, the accurate picture is by no means all doom and gloom. Don't assume that you *have* to end your career by being thrown out with the garbage.

Your best guideline for successfully bringing your career at your current agency to a close is honestly deciding when the job is *consistently* no longer enjoyable. Everyone has bad days, but when the bad ones outnumber the good, it is time to make an important career decision. Regardless of the reason, regardless of how unfair it may be, regardless of the fact that you had nothing to do with bringing the current situation about, *it's time to go.*

You may have given the advice to one or more of your employees: when the job is no longer fun, it's time to do something else. Life is too short to be miserable most of the time. That is good, possibly life-saving advice that you should take to heart yourself.

AVOIDING THE ROLE OF LAME DUCK CHIEF

A lame duck is a bird that has become disabled and can no longer accomplish many of the things that it used to do. The term has been applied to leaders who have had their wings clipped, usually because they are leaving their organization soon. They are regarded as less relevant than before.

You may have seen this uncomfortable scenario played out at some time during your own law enforcement career. The boss is leaving, of his own volition or otherwise. But it's not happening right away. He is going to be around awhile, possibly for months. Everybody knows he's going, and he *knows* that everybody knows he's going. People, especially his own employees, now treat him differently, and not necessarily *better.*

If the chief is liked and respected by most, his treatment will be gentler but still different. He may find his employees lowering their eyes when encountering him in the hallways. Some will avoid him entirely. Members of the community who used to call will stop doing so as they wait to see who the baton of authority will pass to next. Both inside and outside the organization people will begin theorizing about who the next chief will be, or if his identity is already known what he will be doing that may affect them. If he has not been selected yet, the maneuvering will begin among those hoping to become the new boss. All of this will be distracting and uncomfortable for the outgoing chief.

If the lame duck chief is not all that well-liked within and/or without the department he may find the atmosphere even less pleasant. He still may be ignored and avoided by many. But he also may find himself fair game for unkind remarks by those who feel they have a score to settle with their old boss. One lame duck chief arrived at work one morning to find a stack of empty moving boxes piled outside his office door. The gesture wasn't intended to be helpful or kind. Another found his nameplate missing from his door. People can be cruel when they want to be.

You do not want to serve for an extended period as the lame duck chief. Once you know you are leaving, your goal should be to make the break a clean one and make it as quickly as possible. Take some accrued time off while still receiving a salary if that is an option, but get out of there with dispatch, even if you are being treated well. Your hanging around is uncomfortable for everybody, *you* perhaps the most of all.

You almost certainly will find your authority weakened as your employees prepare for life after you. Your staff may join the jockeying for favorable positions once you are gone. In the meantime what *you* want likely will become a lot less important to them. And that's only true if they *like* you. If real animosities exist between you and your leadership staff, things could be much more unpleasant.

If the agreement you reach with your boss requires you to stay on duty for a time in order to get paid, your hands may be tied as to how long you stay. Chances are, however, neither of you wants that situation to exist for any greater length of time than absolutely necessary. Remember to try and negotiate an arrangement where you can collect pay and benefits for a time without actually being in the office. That arrangement could prevent some unpleasant moments for a number of people, you and your boss included.

When the decision has been made to leave, get it over with as quickly as possible. Get on with the next stage of your life. There should be a lot of it remaining!

THE MEANING OF A "NO CONFIDENCE" VOTE

Whether it takes place at a high school or a hospital or in a law enforcement organization, a vote of "no confidence" in the boss taken by an employee group is the "nuclear option" for telling the CEO and *his* boss that the majority of the employees is very unhappy. It may arise from a single, high-profile issue such as the firing of a popular employee or from a series of events and unpopular decisions by the boss that can date back months or even years.

At one time, a majority vote of "no confidence" in the CEO and his policies clearly meant that most employees wanted him to leave. Today, sometimes they still do. But other times they are simply trying to get attention paid to the fact that from the group's perspective things are going badly and immediate action needs taken. They may be feeling ignored. In that situation the vote can be seen as a warning shot, albeit one fired very close to the target's head. If the shot was taken at you, it will be up to you to determine through some immediate probing of your own whether your people truly want you gone or just to change your ways to better suit them, or better suit a very influential part of "them."

There is a good chance, of course, that you can prevent a "no confidence" vote from occurring in the first place if you stay alert to what's going on in your organization and which issues appear to have a significant number of people upset. Visiting with your association or union officers on a regular basis and remaining accessible to them can help prevent trouble by letting you know what is bothering employees and what you might be able to do to turn down the heat. If staying in touch tells you that the "no confidence" label is coming no matter what you do, you will at least have time to prepare your agency's supervisors and your own boss so that no one gets surprised. The advance knowledge also will give you a chance to let family and colleagues know what is in the wind. You do not want them to be ambushed, either. You will need their support.

If you are able to sidetrack a "no confidence" vote by a legitimate effort to solve the perceived problem, so much the better. But assuming the vote has now occurred, you must carry out several tasks in response. First, look at the text of what was voted. What, exactly, are your people complaining about? Is it something you can address? Second, note who backed the vote. Was it an overwhelming number of your employees? Were command staff and supervisors in support of it? Brief your boss about the vote and what you think it means. Let him know your plans to address it. He may want you to fill in his elected board, as well. You also should expect the local media to have the story, so be ready with a calm reply for them. You should acknowledge that you are aware of the vote and will be talking with its organizers to address the situation. Never indicate that you are angry, insulted or planning to bail out.

Having received a "no confidence" vote, you have a limited number of responses to it, including:

- Quit
- Wait to be fired
- Fight it.

The first two options are pretty cut-and-dried as to your required action. If you decide to stay and fight, there are more things you need to accomplish.

Try to determine what brought about the vote. Was it decisions you made, unpopular changes you made in the department, alleged misconduct on your part or something else? Does it look like your people really want you to leave, or do they just want you to do something very differently in the future?

Talk to the people supporting the vote, and remember this is not the time to be combative or confrontational. Be direct but remain professional. Find out if there is something you can do that is ethically and morally acceptable to you that would satisfy them. Is it something you are *willing* to do without sacrificing your principles? Meanwhile, do not publicly display anger, fear or frustration. Don't attack the opposition–professionals don't do that. Show via your behavior that you are still in control and will persevere. Emphasize that you and your people have gotten through tough spots before and will master this challenge, too. Don't be arrogant. Demonstrate that you are self-confident and calm.

Brief your friends, fellow department heads and the other important contacts you have nurtured within the community. Ask for their continued support while you work through the latest challenge. If you have a Chief's Advisory Committee, bring the members in, brief them and ask for their backing. This is not the time to let pride overwhelm your need to ask for assistance. You are fighting to keep your job here, so be prepared to pull out all the stops.

If you have maintained the good working relationship with the news media that you should have, you will be able to rely on them to let you tell your side of events. (Be sure you don't surprise your boss with this.) Tell your story without criticizing the employees who apparently have engineered the coup attempt. Never do or say anything improper or unethical, but fight hard for your survival. You have come too far to give in to adversity now. You have a job to finish.

Do not hide; mingle with the community and remain accessible. Talk to people, and do not be afraid to include the "no confidence" vote in your conversations. People *want* to ask you about it. By telling them what is really going on you may be able to generate additional support for your position.

Any time you tell your side of the story, do so in a calm, professional manner. Avoid blaming and labeling your own employees. If you do, your words eventually will get back to them and they will be more determined than ever to do you in. Fight hard, but fight fair.

Stay in close touch with your boss and ask him to aid in your defense. He can help you by relaying your side of events to his elected bosses who are probably getting nervous over the commotion. Do the same with people in your organization whom you know still support you. Tell them what they can do to help you. They may be able to help turn the tide of negativity, especially if you can demonstrate that you are taking concrete steps to address your people's grievances.

You may not be able to overcome the ill effects of a "no confidence" vote.

Life is not at an end if you fail. But plenty of chiefs have survived them before. It's clear that you definitely won't win if you don't fight. Only you can decide if it is worth the battle. If you are like most good leaders, you'll decide that it most assuredly is.

WHAT ARE YOU WILLING TO DO TO SAVE YOURSELF?

The young police chief had been hired to clean-up and professionalize a poorly performing department. He did that. Then, the local political leadership changed. Two of the disgraced officers the chief had dismissed from the department were elected to the small town council. The chief's future–or lack of same–was clear to him. It was time to go and he did so before the ax fell. He was not willing to go through the abuse of being dismissed by the new administration. He was certainly not willing to do whatever it would take to be found "acceptable" to his new bosses. Sadly, with the chief's departure the department quickly returned to its previous, substandard state.

Hopefully, you will never walk into a situation as fouled up as this chief encountered. But you could. Regardless of the challenge to your continued tenure you may one day face, you will be required to decide if overcoming the threat to your continued employment is worth what it will require of you. You will have to decide what is nonnegotiable when it comes to your beliefs, principles and ethics. Because of the kind of professional you are, you will be unwilling to give up something ethically important just to keep your job. That's the way it should be.

Whether the complaints against you are via a "no confidence" vote or something a bit less dramatic, you now must determine how much you are willing to give in order retain your job, assuming that your position is still salvageable. Clearly, some concessions must be off-limits. It's doubtful that you will want to re-hire a crooked or brutal cop you have discharged just to make his buddies happy. It's not likely that you will agree to allow your officers to participate in dangerous or unethical practices just to get them to back off from wanting your head. And you obviously will be unwilling to turn your back on unlawful behavior by your boss or the local elected or appointed officials just to remain employed. Indeed, there are plenty of things you will never do to save your job. But what *will* you do? Be careful of stepping onto a slippery slope that can only draw you downwards.

Everyone likes job security. Everyone likes to know when his next paycheck is coming and where it's coming from. Because of the kind of person you are, you know that you could never live with yourself if you abandoned your core beliefs and bent your personal, ethical guidelines in order to remain employed. You probably will be unable to shake one nagging thought, as well: Why would you *want* to remain employed at a place that would expect you to break your own rules to keep your job?

If you can revisit a decision, policy or procedure without giving up something important to you and still satisfy your critics enough to keep your job, so be it. That is your decision to make. Before you do that, take a good, hard look at what you have agreed to do. Have you in actuality given away something you should have considered to be nonnegotiable? Be honest with yourself. You will have to live with your decision for a very long time.

It really gets down to this: Do the right thing, even if it hurts at the moment. You will like yourself much more later on.

THERE IS LIFE AFTER BEING CHIEF

Leaving the chief's job doesn't mean that you have agreed to pose in front of a firing squad. It doesn't mean you're required to surrender your first-born or slice off any of your body parts. It doesn't mean that life is over.

The good news for you is that you really can walk away from the job with your head up and know that life will still be good the next day, and the next. Granted, once you walk away you may want to take advantage of a little downtime to relax and reflect before you launch in a new direction. But once you have taken it easy for a while you will be ready to go forward again. There is plenty of life yet to be lived.

You can take comfort from what a lot of other good law enforcement bosses have done before you. Some have gone on to be highly successful leaders at other police agencies. That is perhaps the first decision you have to make. Do you want to return to the chase and resume your role as an outstanding police boss on a different stage? Your self-imposed "cool down" period may have helped you decide if that career move is in the cards for you. Go for it if you want. There is no doubt that you still have a lot to offer your profession. Certainly your experiences at your last position have prepared you for whatever challenges a new department might throw at you. You can do it if you choose.

But maybe you don't choose to do it. Then you can be reassured by the fact that many ex-CEOs not greatly unlike you have realized a great deal of enjoyment from doing things having nothing to do with leading a law enforcement agency, or *any* agency, for that matter. In other words, it is perfectly alright for you to do something you *want* to do rather than *have* to do. You have permission to enjoy yourself. You have earned it.

Of course, your future plans may still be tied closely to your financial picture. You might need to receive a paycheck for a while. Plenty of chiefs who have left ahead of you have taken on second or third careers as college instructors, consultants and advisors to public and private security concerns. Others have made complete career changes and gone into everything from running a dude ranch to working in an organic food store. They have discovered what you will soon learn for yourself: There are plenty of honorable endeavors in the world that don't involve carrying a badge and gun.

You are alive and (hopefully) healthy in both mind and body. You have a lot of life ahead of you. It's time to start living it well.

SUMMARY

Being the chief of police is like nothing else in the world. It can be a real kick. It also can take you from the heights of exhilaration to the depths of despair overnight, and back again practically the next day. Your job is interesting in the extreme, but one day it will end. The important thing is to have it end on your terms to the extent possible.

You can help that happen by staying alert to what is going on around you. If you cannot figure out your standing with your boss, *ask*. Realize that there will be times when your supervisor has really ticked you off or the job just isn't fun. Don't make big decisions (like quitting, for instance) when you are upset about your treatment. Give it some time.

When it really is time to go, try to make the break as quickly as feasible. Once people know you are leaving, for better or worse they will not treat you the same as before. Being a lame duck chief can have disadvantages, so avoid the role to the extent that you can. If you hang around too long you may be tempted to allow the department to run itself. This is never a good idea, as the organization likely will indeed run itself–right into the ground. You owe your employees and your citizens better than that. Stay engaged and involved until you are actually out the door. Make your exit a graceful one (never burn bridges!) and get on with the next phase of your life.

The best news of all is that there is a terrific life still ahead when you are not the chief any more. You likely will worry less and sleep better. You'll also find that you still have great friendships from both inside and outside policing. Enjoy them as you make new friends in your new life, whether that life involves law enforcement or not. Good things remain to be discovered and enjoyed.

POINTS TO REMEMBER

- If it's really not fun anymore, strive to leave on your own terms to the extent possible.

- Learn to recognize the signs that the end is near.
- It's alright to ask your boss how you stand.
- Don't make life-changing decisions when you are emotional.
- Determine the actual meaning of a "no confidence" vote by your employees.
- Carefully consider what you will and won't do to keep your job.
- Don't ever abandon your employees or adopt the attitude of a "short-timer."
- When the end is in sight, resist the temptation to let the department run itself–it won't do it very well.
- Keep your resume up to date.
- Try to avoid the role of a "lame duck" chief.
- Know that there is still a great life ahead when you are not the chief.

Appendix

Advice From the Chiefs

A group of experienced chiefs of police was asked for brief, succinct advice for the aspiring, new or veteran law enforcement CEO. Excerpts from the chiefs' suggestions are provided below. While the advice is wide-ranging, it is possible to see hints of the same themes appearing time and again.

- Always do the right thing. Your officers are watching you.
- Surprises are for Christmas. Keep your boss informed and do not let him or her be caught unfamiliar with the issue.
- Life is short. Get out when it's not fun anymore.
- You are the consummate independent candidate and you run for reelection every day. Your term extends only to today, and you may not be reelected to serve tomorrow. You are a campaign committee of one and your campaign platform is your performance, your conduct and your command presence.
- Take some time off every 90 days.
- The police chief owes loyalty to the appointed official or elected body who direct the entity for which he works. Caveat: There is no compromising one's professional integrity and the chief should never weigh loyalty against honesty and ethics.
- Playing politics, taking sides, backroom deal brokering and political power plays will, sooner or later, cause you immense grief and may cost you your job. If a political deal has to be kept secret, it would be prudent not to be involved. Also, be mindful of political hot buttons and heed the advice about not discussing religion and politics.
- You will be replaced some day.
- Use humor often and anger seldom.
- If you choose to show anger, do it wisely.
- If you don't know the answer, tell them so.
- If you make a mistake, admit it.

- Don't jump to conclusions.
- Always say "Hi!"
- Never compromise yourself because someone is always watching.
- Always be able to say at the end of the day that you made a positive difference in someone's life.
- Strengthen your lower jaw muscle so that your lower jaw isn't always hanging down in surprise.
- Your greatest enemy as police chief is time. If you're not adept in controlling the time demands made on you by others, you will soon find yourself with more problems than you can effectively handle. If you cannot control your time, you cannot control your job. Getting organized is the best way.
- Draw a line in the sand early. Let people know that no one gets any breaks. I'd rather be fired for doing my job than for not doing it.
- Tackle difficult issues head-on. Do not allow time for false interpretation by others. Be clear, concise and consistent.
- Be yourself. Over a period of time people will accept you for who you are. If you are doing the right thing for the organization as a whole, some people will like you and some will not. However, the majority of people will respect you.
- Know as much about the decision-makers in the municipality as you possibly can. Know their career path, education, religion, family, goals and what they want their legacy to be. If you do not know take them to lunch and ask them. The reason you do this is to better understand their critical thinking capabilities and what they believe in. You also will know very quickly on what issues they will be adversarial.
- Be very intentionally consistent in thought and deed.
- Communicate, communicate, communicate at all levels within your department.
- Remember, your every move will be watched, dissected, regurgitated, evaluated and discussed.
- Working in __________? I think I could write my own book. I would be happy to share some personal stories, but readers might find it unbelievable.
- When your staff has ideas, don't ask "Why should we?" Instead, ask "Why shouldn't we?"
- Do not micromanage. You stifle your creative people and set yourself up to bottleneck decisions and ultimately fail.
- Remain connected and visible. You cannot overestimate the value of your appearance in roll calls, team meetings and in the lunch room and hallways. It may seem like a little thing, but it means a great deal to the

employees.

- My experience with the budget before I became chief was extremely beneficial in my new role as chief.
- Never forget that you are a police officer first and the chief second.
- Be proud of your department and say so in the community.
- Know what's going on. Comment on recent arrests, investigations and incidents. Congratulate employees on milestones like anniversaries, births, graduations, etc.
- Your job will have highs and lows. If the lows ever outnumber the highs, get out.
- As a chief I think we feel compelled to handle things as they occur and to move on to the next thing. We think that others will see us as weak or indecisive if we don't respond right away. Especially in areas of discipline I think it is important to be patient when handling employees. Don't use a hammer if it isn't necessary. If they are a bad employee, they will do something again that will allow you to get rid of them. If you respond too harshly because you know they should go, you will be perceived by the officers as unfair. People's natures don't change. If they are a problem they will build the case for you to get rid of them and if they aren't they won't make the mistake a second time. Time is a terrific tool most people don't understand how to use.
- Sometimes people, politicians included, don't expect you to fix something but just want you to listen. You should listen.
- Be confident in who you are. In order to be confident in who you are, you need to know who you are. This is not an arrogant or boastful pride but a true understanding of your principles and character. This is a confidence that is based on those principles that help us know that our motives, actions, thoughts and deeds are always striving toward what is right.
- Be grateful for where you are. This does not mean we are complacent. No, we should always be striving toward our goals and vision. However, we need to have a true understanding that we are not successful because of ourselves. I have found that if it were not for the people that work for us, the people we work for, our friends and our family we would not be where we are regardless of our abilities. Always be grateful for the people that actually do the work that makes you look good, be grateful for the support of your superiors that give you their trust, be grateful for your true friends that hold you accountable with the truth, and be especially grateful for the sacrifices of your family that allow you to work in this noble profession.

INDEX

D

E